Racism at Work

The Danger of Indifference

Binna Kandola

Pearn Kandola Publishing

Published by:
Pearn Kandola Publishing
Latimer House
Langford Locks
Kidlington
Oxford OX5 1GG

First published in Great Britain in 2018 by Pearn Kandola Publishing.

ISBN: 978-0-9562318-8-8

British Library Cataloguing in Publication Data
A catalogue record for this book is available from the British Library

Typeset in: 9.5pt Formata

Cover design and typesetting by MCC

Illustrations for 'Race at the Rovers' by Des Campbell

Printed in Great Britain by Ashford Colour Press Ltd

Dedication

This book is dedicated to Jas, Sunny and Grace.

Acknowledgements

Even though I wrote this book on my own, I seem to have an awful lot of people to thank.

Of course a project like this, which has taken several years to complete, requires a lot of support – emotional as well as practical – from a great many people.

Helping me to gather the vital information for three case studies were Kully Bains, Neha Isaac, Josh Linden, Eleri Mason, Harry Verner and Laura Williams.

The look for the 'Race at the Rovers', 'The Count' and the 'Wanted' poster, as well as the cover design, is due to the creativity of James Craig.

The fact that the book has a screenplay – 'Oscar', featuring the likes of Will Smith, Leonardo di Caprio and Freida Pinto – is the product of working with BAFTA-award-winning Abigail Burdess.

Paul May was, as always, a constant advisor and inspiration. Since we decided to create our own publishing arm (because, it may be hard to believe now, no one wanted to publish a management book about bias), Paul has played the vital role of editor, advisor and critic. Did I ever buy you that pint to thank you for the last book, Paul?

Big thanks go to Jane Hammett for her patient and diligent copy-editing.

Then there's a bunch of people to thank at Pearn Kandola – not so much a team as a well-oiled machine, headed by Laura Hollitzer and including Mike Idziaszczyk.

Ruth Hunt and Lesley Saxton have been constant companions: creating space in my diary, keeping the world at bay, and turning my handwritten scrawl into the text you are reading now.

Thank you to my partners at Pearn Kandola – Kathryn Palmer, Stuart Duff and Nic Hammarling – for allowing me time to work on the book, and for always having faith in me, even though I had nothing tangible to show for such a long time.

There are always quite a few moments when I am writing a book during which I will doubt myself. Writing this book, the self-doubt came very early. I will be forever grateful to Uzma Hamid-Dizier at Slaughter and May, and Nadia Younes at the International Monetary Fund (IMF) for their encouragement and their conviction that I had to write this book. Thanks also to Martin Reeves, who read an early draft and whose perceptive comments were very helpful.

Finally, to Jo, my wife, who has helped carry out some of the research, particularly on the sections on race and gender, and who – annoyingly – has made some excellent suggestions about the content and structure of the book.

At times, writing books like this takes all my attention. The people most affected by this are my wife and our daughter Grace. Thank you for your absolute support, patience and understanding.

"This book sets new heights in thought leadership focusing on the harsh realities of racism in the workplace. An essential for read for everyone working in the field of culture, diversity and inclusion."

Arun Batra, Ernst & Young LLP

"Binna Kandola's deeply insightful book, shows that racism is unfortunately still very much alive today, It's time that racism be openly examined and discussed. Let's get going… read this book, reflect, share with others, and join forces to lessen racial biases."

Lisa Kepinski, Inclusion Institute

"A radical and invaluable read for anyone working in this field."

Rob Neil, Interim Chair of the Civil Service Race Forum, Ministry of Justice

"This evidence based approach makes it essential reading for policy makers, CEOs and HR professionals. But more importantly Kandola's practical list of actions reminds us that we all have a part to play in building a just and equal society"

Barbara Roche, Former Minister for Women and Equalities

"Binna Kandola's book is a clarion call to become more informed, understanding, compassionate self and organizationally aware. If we take the opportunity to learn from him, our lives and workplaces will be richer for it."

Karen Murphy, Facing History and Ourselves

"This is an important insight to behaviours and one which should be read not just by those tasked in HR roles but by all those involved in recruitment processes."

John O'Brien MBE, The ONE HUNDRED agency, Omnicom

"A thought provoking account of the complexities of racism at work and the impact bias behaviour has either at a conscious and unconscious level. A must read for all organisations and individuals who are involved or curious about diversity in the workplace."

Tola Ayoola, Cabinet Office

"A timely and well evidenced book that challenges us to rethink how we perceive racism in the 21st century. A must read for all senior leaders and anyone that has influence over other people's careers."

Uzma Hamid-Dizier, Slaughter and May

"This book provides a practical, yet nuanced approach to an urgent topic."

Claudia Hammond, Presenter 'All in the Mind'

Contents

Preface

'What are you working on?'

It's an innocuous enough question – and a guaranteed ice-breaker. But I hesitated to answer. My ideas were at an early stage, forming and reforming, and I didn't know if I was ready to share them. On the other hand, if I did tell her, I might get some useful input and suggestions. My friend was involved in diversity work at a senior level and had taken a keen interest in my recent books on unconscious bias and gender bias. She'd worked hard to increase the number of women in leadership positions in her organisation and I respected her opinions. She'd understand my project immediately. So, for the first time outside my own head, I heard myself saying: 'I'm writing a book about race bias in organisations.'

She frowned into her glass, then gave me a puzzled look. 'So,' she said, 'what's it about?'

Maybe she'd misheard. I repeated what I'd said, a little less confidently. And she told me that racism was a thing of the past.

In fact, she said, the Women's Movement could learn a lot from the Civil Rights Movement and its success in achieving racial equality. Sure, there were pockets of racism in society and there always would be … But thankfully, in her organisation, as in all modern, right-thinking organisations, racism was a historical curiosity – an unsavoury and regrettable aberration of less enlightened times, but no longer an active force.

The encounter knocked me off balance. Here was a respected person, active in the diversity and inclusion field, telling me that racism was a non-issue. It was gauche of me to bring it up. My book's imagined audience evaporated.

And yet … the project wouldn't leave me alone. It gnawed at me, demanded attention. I couldn't give up this easily. I began telling other people about my venture, and their reactions varied. Most were enthusiastic, but there were also some sceptics.

Then it hit me. Those who understood my project and responded to it were a diverse group. Those who didn't get it were, without exception, white.

I didn't want to discover this unsettling fact. I didn't want it to be true. I had to test the observation – and talking about the book became a mini-project in its own right. Over many weeks and months, and in many different situations, the results were consistent. Without exception, minority friends and clients immediately understood what the book was about, and could see the need for it. One friend, a black British woman, simply sighed, 'At last'. Many white friends and clients grasped the point of the book as well and encouraged me to pursue it. But every single naysayer was white.

The sceptics included people responsible for ensuring equality in their organisations as well as consultants advising clients on equality issues. If experienced and engaged practitioners could see no need to discuss race bias in organisations, it would be impossible to gain senior-level commitment to take action on the issue. After all, if there's no problem, there's no need for a solution, is there? This was going to be a tougher assignment than I had first thought.

I didn't take on this project lightly. To begin a discussion about race, whether in a real-world setting or in the pages of a book, is to invite anxiety. There are so many aspects to the debate – the inglorious history, the entrenched antagonisms and, not least, the strong emotions prompted by race – that no one can approach the subject without great wariness. The ground we are about to tread together is treacherous.

Yet, it is these very difficulties that make race such an appealing topic for settings in which controversy is welcomed – such as radio talk shows. The emotional charge of race is amplified by the belief that discussion of it is being suppressed. The fact that there are already at least two sides to any story makes it legitimate to use reports of apparent racism as triggers for debate: 'Do you think the Oscars are racist? Call now – we want to know what you think.' There's rarely a shortage of callers eager to participate, representing a wide spectrum of opinion. But while the switchboard may light up, little light is shone on the topic itself. When the main aim is entertainment, rather than enlightenment, facts and contexts are less important than reactions and opinions.

Debates on race are fractious, challenging and confrontational. This is why most of us choose to avoid the topic altogether, looking the other way – until, perhaps, a case arises that we simply can't ignore. Even then, we may have no better response than to wring our hands and wait for other news to push whatever has made us uncomfortable out of the headlines.

These personal reactions are understandable. But we can't use them as excuses for ignoring the toxic effects of racism on the organisations we serve and use. Our organisations are designed and managed entities: we get to say what they are like and how they behave.

Racism has not been eradicated, despite the enormous strides taken over the past fifty years. It has mutated into new and subtler forms and has found new ways to survive. The racism in organisations today is not characterised by hostile abuse and threatening behaviour. It is not overt nor is it obvious. Today racism is subtle and nuanced, detected mostly by the people on the receiving end, but ignored and possibly not even seen by perpetrators and bystanders. Racism today may be more refined, but it harms people's careers and lives in hugely significant ways. Racism in organisations continues to exist due to our complacency and indifference.

This book describes the origins and evolution of the race bias that distorts our organisations. It explores the effects of race bias. And it confronts the actions that we need to take to make organisations truly equal.

Racism is not a thing of the past – yet. But we can make it so.

Chapter 1

The race zombie

Race – a short word that casts a long shadow. We all belong to the human race, yet race divides us. And race is a topic most of us would rather not speak about, and we certainly do not feel comfortable discussing it in the workplace.

The belief, the so-called 'science of race', that some categories of human beings are superior – intellectually, physically, emotionally and even aesthetically – is no longer widely accepted, but terms like 'race' and 'racial group' persist in the vocabulary, and the derivative terms 'racism' and 'racial prejudice' are very widely used. Pseudo-scientific theories of racial distinctiveness may have been unmasked and consigned to history, but our everyday language shows that the concept of race continues to figure prominently in our thinking. We can't avoid using the term 'race' and its cognates, despite the discomfort its use creates.

The concept of race is still very much alive – and kicking. We might want to believe the old idea of defined, separate and immutable human groupings has been discredited – at least in scientific terms. However, we still talk about race, even as we talk about not talking about it. It's a slippery subject. Catching hold of the issue of race and understanding its impact on our organisations and communities is fraught with intellectual, psychological and political difficulties.

Racial theory may be dead, but racism lives on. Like the zombie, the notion of race doesn't know it's dead.

The explicit meaning of the term 'race' has shifted over time. While it is no longer overtly used to denote the superiority of some groups and the inferiority of others, race does relate to physical features and physical distinctiveness. Colour is one of the key ways in which we differentiate one person from another. There are many ways in which we could distinguish people, but colour has become one of the most significant. It seems natural, unavoidable, but as we will see, this was not always the case.

So while researchers from a wide range of disciplines, including genetics, anthropology and evolutionary psychology, find no value in the idea of distinct races, the concept has become so ingrained in our daily lives that it is difficult to disentangle it. Physical characteristics, including elements other than skin colour, such as hair texture and eye shape, are used to put people into clearly defined groups. We may consciously believe that race plays no part in our actions, but the legacy of racist ideas, actions and imagery lives on publicly in stereotypes – and privately in our unconscious minds. The belief that we, as individuals, could not be racist, and by extension that our organisations can't be either, is one of the most serious obstacles that exists in making racial equality a reality. Be in no doubt: indifference is now the principal way in which racism is perpetuated in organisations today.

Race throws up a number of fascinating issues, which I believe we need to discuss briefly. The first seems quite basic but is at the heart of the discussion about race: how do we label and describe different groups? Second is the issue of how we describe ourselves. Third, just how natural is it to use colour as a means of distinguishing and differentiating between people?

Labelling race

All attempts to create discrete, objective and distinctive racial classifications have failed. Consequently the categories that each society has created will have meaning to people from that society but may not mean much to people from another society.

Every society has its minorities. Members of minority groups often look indistinguishable from the majority but, having been characterised as the 'other', they are often also seen as inferior in some way. In these cases it's not physical characteristics that distinguish between people, but culture. This is the broad distinction between race and ethnicity: racial groups are indicated by heritable characteristics and ethnic groups by their way of life – food, dress, religion, and so on.

Despite this apparently sharp distinction in terms, race and ethnicity do overlap and the words are often used interchangeably. This is particularly clear in anti-discrimination legislation, where the terms are taken to be synonymous.

The word 'race' may be problematic but there are added problems in how different groups are described and how the people in those groups describe themselves. To understand the complexities, one only has to look at the racial data some countries collect in their censuses to examine and understand their citizens.

In many ways, the desire to collect the data is one indication of that society's desire to quantify, analyse and then tackle the bias experienced by some groups. The categories that are produced are nearly always imperfect and culturally specific. The UK 2011 census had five broad groups: White; Mixed/multiple ethnic groups; Asian/Asian British; Black/African/Caribbean/Black British; Other ethnic group. Within each broad group there were a number of more specific categories: for example, Asian/Asian British was subdivided into Indian, Pakistani, Bangladeshi and Chinese. The 2010 US Census[1] also has the category 'Asian people', which comprised Chinese, Japanese, Filipino, Korean, Asian-Indian, Vietnamese and – the catch-all – other Asian. The way the group 'Asian' is defined therefore varies. The categories are based on geography, colour, nationality and older racial classifications – all in themselves somewhat vague and contestable terms.

For both countries, nevertheless, these categories do not describe something with absolute precision. And it has always been this way. Alexander the Great had a classification to identify different peoples based primarily on colour.[2] He was not suggesting inferiority but simply registering differences in appearance. It was imprecise but it worked for him. In Tudor England the word 'Moor' was commonly used, but it was a somewhat loose term describing a wide variety of people, including anyone who was Muslim.[3] Imprecise, yes, but it was understood by the people using it, if not the people being labelled.

In addition to the official classifications, many academics have their own ways of classifying people. However, the imprecision of race and ethnicity as categories means that membership of a minority varies between contexts. In 1988 I attended a psychology conference in Atlanta, Georgia. At that time there was an ongoing debate in the UK as to whether the term 'black' should be used to describe all visible minorities. At the conference I met two African American psychologists who informed me that people from India, or – like me – of Indian origin, due to their economic success, were considered to be 'white'. On learning this, I had the curious realisation that having left the UK 'black', I had arrived in the USA 'white'.

One effect of increasing migration – and perhaps of its reporting – is the growing experience of cultural relativism, as people find their self-images challenged or devalued by moving to a new place, or by finding new people moving into their communities. Race categories are vague, not due to lack of effort but because the idea of 'race' is deeply flawed. Every society has its own racial classifications, and they are all different. The categories are socially constructed.

Concomitant with the racial categories are racial hierarchies. These exist in every society and in some parts of the world, such as the United Arab Emirates (UAE), they are explicit and openly acted upon. Other societies may deny their presence but, like it or not, they exist and are influential. Racial hierarchies benefit the groups at the top and disadvantage all other groups to a greater or lesser degree. It does not matter how we label the groups: the impact of racial hierarchies is much the same in the countries which actively research the subject and those which do not. Some countries actively investigate, uncover and seek to understand the way racism operates in their society. Ironically, this research is often a source of comfort to those in countries where there is little data: this is not their problem. Racism, I have been told on many occasions in my career, is an 'Anglo-Saxon' problem. Ignorance enables people to remain in a state of denial.

The impact of racial hierarchies is something that will be referred to on many occasions in this book, not least relating to their existence in today's supposedly meritocratic, colour-blind organisations. In this book I shall make reference to visible minorities – people who are a different colour from the majority in that society. It's not perfect or precise – but then, nothing is when it comes to discussing race.

Self-description

Governments need to identify discrete groups in order to understand, statistically at least, the experiences of their citizens. But as individuals we may have a different view – after all, we all know how complex our identities are, so why can't we be allowed to describe ourselves?

Tiger Woods created a stir when he referred to himself as 'Cablinasian' – a designation he coined himself. His mother is of Thai, Chinese and Dutch descent; his father is of African American, Chinese and Native American descent. Woods was criticised for not identifying more with African Americans, instead opting to define his own category. The argument reveals the complexity of identity. As the philosopher Kwame Anthony Appiah[4] points out:

> The reasonable middle view is that constructing an identity is a good thing (if self-authorship is a good thing) but that the identity must make some kind of sense. And for it to make sense, it must be an identity constructed in response to facts outside oneself, things that are beyond one's own choices.

Or, to put it another way, as Michael A. Fletcher argues in The Undefeated,[5] 'Tiger Woods says he's "Cablinasian," but the police only saw black.' It seems Tiger Woods is not at liberty to define his own identity without the cooperation of the rest of society.

Fletcher makes a powerful point. Status doesn't necessarily protect people from being labelled and viewed with suspicion. You could be a celebrated Harvard professor entering your *own* home in Cambridge, Massachusetts, USA (Henry Louis Gates, Jr. arrested for breaking and entering), a Premiership footballer out shopping in Cheshire, UK (Everton's Victor Anichebe arrested outside a friend's jeweller's shop when police thought he was a jewel thief), or a celebrated novelist and politician in Paris, France (Azouz Begag stopped by police for – if you will pardon my French – *conduire tout en étant noir*, otherwise known as Driving While Black).

Identity is partially self-created and partially constructed in response to how others perceive us. And control over our identity can be dispersed even more widely when the law steps in to define us. In 1982 Susie Guillory Phipps applied for a passport. Her application was marked down due to a discrepancy on her form. She said she was 'white' but her birth certificate said she was 'coloured'. Phipps thought of herself as white, and was shocked to discover she was not. According to *Ebony* magazine:[6] 'I was sick … I couldn't believe it.' She went home crying. Phipps had unwittingly fallen foul of a law known as 'the One Drop rule'. Anyone who was '1/32 Negro blood' was deemed 'coloured'. In the state of Louisiana, colour went so deep that it didn't even need to be visible.

Phipps unsuccessfully sued the state to have her racial classification changed. A white professor brought in to testify as an expert witness said that most of Louisiana's population were at least 1/20 'negro' by ancestry.[7]

The notion of racial purity has long been dismissed as vanishingly improbable, given humans' propensity to resettle. As long ago as 1867, no less august an authority than *The Times* declared:

> *There is hardly such a thing as a pure Englishman in this island. In place of the rather vulgarised and very inaccurate phrase 'Anglo-Saxon', our national denomination, to be strictly correct, would be a composite of a dozen national titles.*[8]

The apparently timeless category of 'British' – a designation that carries a high political charge today – was formally created just 300 years ago with the Act of Union in 1707. This identity took hold only thanks to the unity created by finding a common enemy in the French.[9] At the time of writing, it's beginning to fall apart.

How we are perceived by others is critical to their evaluation of us. In organisational settings this perception affects who is selected, how their performance is appraised, the amount they are paid, and the development they are given – all issues that are explored in this book.

Minorities in organisations are aware of how others perceive them and the racial group they are seen to belong to. This in turn affects the way the minorities themselves respond and their perception of their abilities and potential.

Doing what comes naturally

It is easy to believe that racial prejudice is both inevitable and unchangeable: that we are born with a disposition to dislike and disparage people of a different colour, and that being wary of people of a different colour is a natural reaction. I've heard this many times, and there is something comforting and reassuring about it: I can use this neat explanation to account for any negative feelings I have about other groups; I can tell myself I'm having an instinctive response – one that has enabled the human species to survive and thrive. There's just one problem with this train of thought: it's wrong.

Our views of people of a different colour and appearance are not fixed at all. They have changed throughout history.

The psychologist Richard Crisp,[10] having reviewed recent evidence, concluded that the human race has become so successful because of our ability to relate to people who on the surface appear to be very different. It is 'natural' for us to get along with one another – to appreciate difference, to be intrigued and fascinated by it, not to be appalled.

Too often, we are blind to the evidence of how much progress we still have to make in tackling racism and its effects. Nevertheless, the fact that the success of our species is due to our appreciation of others is a cause for optimism and hope.

The aim of this book

The aim of this book is to examine race, via its observable effects and facets, focusing on the workplace. Today, race defies the more traditional frontal assaults of analysis, so we must understand it through the traces it leaves in frustrated ambitions and compounded inequities, and in the ways it distorts both our thinking and our institutions.

I propose a three-stage model for the evolution of race and racism:

- **Stage 1:** Obvious differences, such as skin colour, are noticed but no inferences about other people are drawn from them.

- **Stage 2:** The differences, particularly in skin colour, become associated with intellectual and psychological attributes. A hierarchy of humans is created, with different groups occupying different levels of power, virtue and freedom.

- **Stage 3:** The hierarchy is deemed to have flattened out and racial prejudice is believed to be receding into the past. Racial prejudice, some would like to believe, remains a problem among older, working-class, and less well qualified groups. The educated and polite claim to be colour-blind and deny they are prejudiced in any way.

We inhabit a Stage 3 society, characterised by denial, complacency and indifference. Our rejection of race's continuing influence over our thoughts and actions is also becoming a central aspect of the problem of dealing with it in organisations.

Structure of the book

This book is in three parts. Part 1 looks at the way race has evolved, and the ways it has changed are described in the early chapters. As a species we moved from not having colour prejudice to creating hierarchies of races, with some people being asked whether they were human at all. The racist ideologies, supported by bogus race science, were denounced and led to our current stage of thinking: racism is a thing of the past and in these post-racial times we lead colour-blind lives.

Part 2 examines the research about racism today and shows how, like a virus, it has mutated. The metamorphosis has been so successful that people in the majority even question whether it is an issue any more. I will explore the current manifestation of racism, known as modern racism. While we are all on the lookout for overt, obvious hostile actions, modern racism is subtle, covert and indirect. Modern racism is so insidious that we may not be aware that we are behaving in racist ways ourselves.

Part 3 takes current research on racism and explores in depth how it is manifested in organisations. Finally, there is a section outlining a range of actions that research tells us is effective in reducing racial bias – if we can be bothered to do them.

There are also three very different case studies examining race in football, race in accountancy, and race in Hollywood. Usually, case studies are provided in a book to illustrate the main ideas and themes of the book. They are designed to add colour and highlight messages, and I hope the case studies here act in the same way. These cases, however, were also the inspiration for the book, as I saw how similar the race issues were in these very different sectors.

Human beings tend to prioritise the visual over our other senses. But even if we accept that our leading categorical decisions will most likely be visually cued, there's no inherent reason why we would choose to pick skin colour as the most important marker of difference. Race is not a natural phenomenon, but a socially constructed concept. Its origins are more recent than you might imagine – and more fascinating.

Racism has transformed itself so successfully that some of us find it hard to believe it still exists in our organisations. But as Roger 'Verbal' Kint says in *The Usual Suspects*: 'The greatest trick the Devil ever pulled was convincing the world he didn't exist.'

1. Prewitt, K. *What Is Your Race? The Census and Our Flawed Efforts to Classify Americans* (Princeton University Press, 2013).

2. Snowden, F.M. *Before Color Prejudice: The Ancient View of Blacks* (Harvard University Press, 1983).

3. Onyeka. *Blackamoores: Africans in Tudor England, their Presence, Status and Origins* (Narrative Eye Ltd, 2013).

4. Appiah, K.A. *The Ethics of Identity* (Princeton University Press, 2007).

5. Fletcher, M.A. Tiger Woods says he's 'Cablinasian,' but the police only saw black. *The Undefeated* (2017). Available at: https://www.google.co.uk/amp/s/theundefeated.com/features/tiger-woods-dui-arrest-police-only-saw-black/amp/.

6. What makes you Black? *Ebony Magazine* 115–118 (1983).

7. Omi, M. & Winart, H. *Racial Formation in the United States: From the 1960s to the 1990s* (Routledge, 1994).

8. Mason, D. Changing ethnic disadvantage: an overview In *Explaining Ethnic Differences: Changing Patterns of Disadvantage in Britain* (ed. D. Mason) (Policy Press, 2003).

9. See ref 8. Mason, D.

10. Crisp, R. *The Social Brain: How Diversity Made the Modern Mind* (Robinson, 2015).

Part 1
Racism: The Early Years

Chapter 2

How a world without colour invented black and white

As Alessandro de' Medici, the Duke of Florence and head of the powerful Medici family, rode into Rome one day in 1535, he couldn't help noticing fresh, welcoming graffiti scrawled on the walls of the city. The messages said: 'Hail Alessandro of Colle Vecchio.'[1] Alessandro was due to meet Charles V, the Holy Roman Emperor, to answer charges made against him by exiled Florentines. We might think the locals were expressing their support for Alessandro by greeting him in this way, but the graffiti was an insult. Colle Vecchio was the village where his mother had been born – and Alessandro's mother was a freed slave. The reference taunted the Medici duke with his humble origins and let him know that not everyone accepted his authority.

The fact that Alessandro was black wasn't mentioned.

If the Romans had thought to mention Alessandro's colour, it would not have been seen as an insult, but as an irrelevant detail. It was his social status, not his physical appearance, which people noted, judged and used as a weapon.

It is difficult to identify precisely when the change in views about people of a different colour took place, but we do know a change occurred around the time of the slave trade. In the early sixteenth century, skin colour was not seen as an indicator of someone's personality, qualities or intellect. By the nineteenth century this had changed dramatically and the ideas of the so-called science of race – the idea that some humans were superior to others – now permeated everyday life. At this time there was believed to be a strong relationship between a person's physical features and attributes such as intelligence.

The English writer, Thomas Adolphus Trollope, a pillar of the British community in nineteenth-century Italy, saw in a portrait of Duke Alessandro not a leader but a

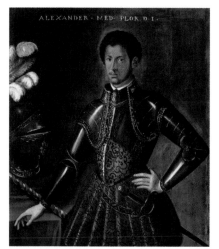

ALEXANDER · MED· FLOR. D. I.

Portrait of Alessandro de Medici, first Duke of Florence 16th century, Galleria Degli Uffizi (© De Agostini Picture Library Getty images)

'wretched youth'. He continued: 'The small contracted features, the low forehead and mean expression are altogether unlike any of the Medici race, in whom, whoever else they might be, there was always the manifestation of intellectual power.'[1] (p309)

Based on appearance alone, Trollope deems Alessandro atypical of the powerful, wealthy and intelligent Medici clan. Instead, Trollope found him to exhibit 'lowness of the type'. (p309) Fascists in the twentieth century would seek to deny that Alessandro's mother could ever have been African.[1]

In the years between the Roman public's assessment of the duke's person and Trollope's damning classification of his portrait, the basis of judgement changed radically. By any measure, this was a remarkably rapid as well as a fundamental transformation. Once an irrelevance, colour gained the power to tell us everything we needed to know about a person's intellect and character.

Surface differences: the classical world

For much of human history, people did not stereotype others based on the colour of their skin. Racial or colour prejudice as we know it today did not exist during the Egyptian, Greek and Roman empires. Racial prejudice is therefore not an inherent human function. We created races – and, in so doing, we created racial prejudice. Frank Snowden, the Harvard history professor, describes this in his book *Before Color Prejudice*.[2] The provocation in the title comes in the word 'Before'. To our modern sensibilities it does not quite make sense: since colour prejudice is something that we have had to battle with, it is difficult to conceive of a time when it genuinely did not exist.

The ancient Greeks and Romans noted that people came in a variety of hues, which gave an indication of where they came from. But they inferred nothing more than this. It was perfectly obvious that people from Africa were darker than those from Rome and Greece. The Greeks knew Africans as people from *aithiopia*, a word derived from *aitho* ('I burn') and *ops* ('face'). Ethiopians were therefore 'burned-faced people'. Marcus Manilius wrote a poem in the first century AD in which he describes the colour of people from different parts of the world, remarking that Ethiopians were the darkest, Indians were less sunburned, Egyptians were mildly dark and Mauri (or Moors) were lighter black. As a taxonomy, Manilius's scheme is no worse than contemporary attempts to describe people by the colour of their skin.[2]

Alexander the Great also noted the similarities between people from different regions: for example, although many Indians were similar in colour to Egyptians, others in the south were the same shade as Ethiopians. The distinctions went even further: Ethiopians could be dark (*fuscii*) to very black (*nigerrimi*).[2]

Even in these early accounts, it is the 'other' people who have a colour. The observers did not think too much about their own skins – a point noted by the Arab historian Ibn Khaldun. Whites were not described by their skin colour because 'whiteness was something usual and common (to them) and they did not see anything significantly remarkable in it to cause them to use it as a specific term'.[2 (p7)]

For ancient Egyptians, Greeks and Romans, slavery did not depend on a racial ideology. Nor were slaves exclusively black – in fact, most slaves were not.[3] Slaves could, and did, come from anywhere, and Slavic slaves were fair-skinned and blond.[4] The key dividing lines between people were religion and language, not appearance.

Egyptians had long had contact with black people from the Kush (now Sudan and South Sudan). They had traded, worked and fought alongside one another. The Egyptians did not consider the Kushites' skin colour significant or unusual. When people from other parts of the Mediterranean encountered Kushites, they were taken aback by the strangers' appearance, but the indications are that this initial surprise was quickly overcome. The Romans readily deployed black soldiers across their Empire, including its northern extremity at the fort of Aballava on Hadrian's Wall (modern Burgh by Sands, near Carlisle in England).[2]

These equable views about black people did not change from Egyptian times to the Roman era, a period of several thousand years, during which time intermarriage and inter-mating were not frowned upon. The Bible's references to black people are similarly positive. While some people may know that Moses married a Kushite, they may not realise that she must have been black. When Aaron and Miriam, his brother and sister, are annoyed with Moses' choice of wife, it is Miriam who is punished.[2] Ebed-Melech is another Kushite referred to positively in the Bible. Elsewhere, the Old Testament writers refer to other people who were black, such as the Nubians, but their colour has no particular significance.

We should not assume that people were colour-blind, because they were not. Black people can be seen in Egyptian artwork and some surviving expressions also reveal that skin colour was noticed: for example, the Greeks and Romans used the saying 'to wash an Ethiopian white' to describe a futile activity. The Bible says something similar: 'Can the Ethiopian change his skin or the leopard his spots?' (Jeremiah 13:23).[2] Beyond acknowledging these obvious visual differences, it seems that colour was of little interest to God, Moses or people more generally.

A child growing up during these times would not have acquired the associations about black people that we have today, because such views were not prevalent in those societies. Historically, referring to someone as 'black' carried no pejorative associations in the way it would today. In fact, some historians believe the identification would elicit positive, favourable associations.[4]

The ancient Romans and Greeks had a very positive view of Africans. Nubians were praised by Pliny and Solinus for their wisdom, piety, courage and justice. When Romans and Greeks encountered more hostile groups further south, they did not stereotype all Africans; they did not consider them all to be the same. The people from the continent of Africa were recognised as being as varied as those from Europe.[2]

Skin colour was not used as a shorthand to infer the qualities of another person. This can be witnessed in the work of the poet Menander (c.342–292 BCE), who wrote that it makes no difference whether someone is physically different from a Greek, such as an Ethiopian or a Scythian (a nomadic people occupying the central Eurasian steppes) – it is merit that counts. Although Egyptians looked down on outsiders, anyone who learned the language and adopted Egyptian dress was accepted as one of 'the people'. According to Luxorius, a sixth-century Roman poet living in Carthage during the reign of the Vandals, excellence was a quality that could be found in all people, wherever they came from.[2]

As a consequence of these attitudes, black people operated successfully in a range of professions. They could be found in the military, working with horses, acting as diplomats and ambassadors, and engaging in commerce and trade. Skin colour was no bar to working in these occupations, nor to being involved in science, philosophy and religion.

The dark-skinned Muslim, or Moorish, forces led by Tariq ibn Ziyad who entered the Iberian peninsula in 711 were widely regarded as powerful and noble.[5]

In the Middle Ages there were notable black bishops, including St Augustine, and priests such as Juan Latino, the sixteenth-century writer of the epic poem *Austrias Carmen*.[6]

The status of black people in Tudor England was not dependent on their colour. Black people were not just tolerated in majority-white societies; they could expect to acquire positions of power, wealth and influence on the basis of their talents and achievements.

Examples from this period in England include:

- black tradesmen and artisans (in the thirteenth-century book the *Domesday Abbreviato*)

- the representation of black people in artwork in Westminster Abbey

- a well-known black trumpeter referred to as John Blanke is shown in an image in the 1511 Westminster Tournament Roll, commissioned by Henry VIII

- the African ladies-in-waiting Catherine of Aragon brought with her when she arrived in England in October 1501

- the black woman chosen for the crest on the coat of arms for The Worshipful Company of Brewers. She was a 'dark-skinned, flaxen-haired demi morien' chosen in honour of their patron saint, Thomas Becket, whose stepmother, some wrongly believed, was Moorish.[5]

There were xenophobic attitudes but in England, for example, these were directed towards the French and, later, towards Catholics. This is shown in John Stubbs's *The Gaping Gulf* of 1529, in which the targets of his anger are the French and Catholics. In contrast, the Moors are praised.[5]

The virtues of civilisation

Up until the seventeenth century, cultures were compared, contrasted and evaluated in terms of how civilised they were, not by the colour of their peoples' skins.

Civilised societies were defined as having both a private and a public sphere. The private sphere was common to all people: food, security and procreation. The public sphere was key to distinguishing between societies, and involved debate about how people should live their lives. Any society could be civilised as long as it had developed a functioning public sphere, which required a level of education and a willingness for the rulers and the ruled to make decisions jointly.

It was integral to a civilised society to live life in accordance with civil, military and religious virtues. The civil virtues were justice, prudence, temperance, magnanimity, fortitude and peace. There were then the military virtues: power and courage. For Christian societies, the religious virtues were faith, hope and charity. 'Virtuous' people were those who, regardless of their background, honoured and practised the virtues of their society.

Anyone who possessed the virtues would be considered with esteem, whatever their colour. On this basis, Machiavelli highlighted several African leaders who epitomised these virtues: for example, Masinissa, Jugurtha and Hannibal. In

Machiavelli's eyes these men were considered not as exemplars of 'the other', but as universal role models.[1]

Mediterranean communities were introduced to each other by trade, conflict, and the accident of proximity. But when people from distant Britain came into contact with Africans, they were far less familiar with them. Nevertheless, even when white adventurers came into conflict with Africans, they did not categorise their opponents as 'savages', but saw them as people defending their own land.[2] In effect, the difference in skin colour had no neutralising effect on the incomers' empathy. These white people instinctively felt that Africans saw the world in the same way as they did.

The conquest of race

As far as we know, there have always been slaves and people prepared to exploit others.[7]

Until the fifteenth century, being dark-skinned did not necessarily mean a person was of lower standing, or a slave. The shift in attitudes can be seen in changes in policies and in language and, once it had occurred, those with darker skin were seen as property rather than people, and as inferior rather than equals.

Slavery was common in Islamic Spain, with most slaves coming from sub-Saharan Africa. In the fifteenth century, except in the areas now known as Granada, Málaga and Almería, Spain had been conquered by Christians. In 1505, the defeated Moors, who were referred to as Moriscos, were forced to convert to Christianity.[8] Although a person's status was higher if they were Christian, those who had converted were still seen as different. The process of de-legitimisation was institutionalised when Charles V introduced the *sangre azul* – literally, 'blue blood' – inheritance law to prevent those with Moorish lineage from inheriting land or wealth. This was built on with the idea of *limpieza de sangre*,[5] or purity of blood, which was taking hold on the Iberian peninsula, and was a precursor of the 'One Drop rule'.

While racism began to emerge alongside the slave trade, the term 'race' was both rare and neutral in the sixteenth century, with none of the baggage it has today. While Shylock refers to 'tribes' in *The Merchant of Venice* and Othello is described as black, the notion of 'race' as such is presented in neither play. Nor is there any reference to race in the King James Bible, which was written in the same period.[9]

Sixteenth-century Italians used the word *razza* to refer to types, breeds or stocks, but more as an observational term than an ascription of value.[1] The word recognised that people had different origins and heritage, but it did not mean they had fixed abilities or intellectual capacities.

By way of contrast, the *Oxford English Dictionary* records the first use of the word 'white' to describe a person's skin colour as taking place in the early seventeenth century. It's noticeable that, although 'the other' is described from the point of view of the default dominant group, the defining group sees no need to define itself in the same terms.[9]

Africans living in Tudor England were referred to variously as blackamoors, blacks, Moors, negroes and Ethiopians. 'Moor' was a somewhat loose term to describe a wide variety of people, including Muslims. Some of these terms were derived from Greek and Roman writers, and 'Moor' may have been picked up from descriptions in Continental Europe and West Africa.[5]

During the same period, however, the word 'negro' could describe someone with black skin, a black person who was a slave, or a person of low status and standing. As with 'Moor', the term itself was used with little consistency and a wide range of people were described as negro. Far from indicating a homogeneous group, people described as negro could hardly be more different geographically, theologically and culturally. Members included:

- sub-Saharan people from different regions, speaking different languages and observing different religions (Muslims, Christians and animists)
- North African Muslims
- people born in Spain, baptised and Castilian-speaking but with sub-Saharan ancestry
- Moriscos
- people from the Canary Islands
- Hindus and Tamils brought to the Iberian peninsula by Portuguese slave merchants
- African Americans brought to Spain by their colonialist Spanish owners.[8]

The denigration of people with dark skin began to gain momentum with the growing trade in humans. While subtle distinctions were sometimes made about a person's actual colour (for example, 'clear black', 'almost black', 'dark black', 'very dark black'), the term 'negro' was clearly now being used to make a statement about status.[8]

Indications of changing perceptions towards 'the other' arrive almost casually in the historical record. An offhand, gossipy comment by Olivares to Philip III of Spain refers to Pope Sixtus V's conduct towards one Cardinal William Alton in 1588, saying that 'he treated him like a black man'.[10] [(p9)]

Similar shifts in language can be seen occurring in lands colonised by Spain. 'Latino' meant someone who was educated and fluent in Latin. People from the conquered lands of South America, however, were referred to as Ladinos and were seen as sly and deceitful. The subtle shift from Latino to Ladino marks a change in attitude: difference was becoming equated with inferiority via the mechanism of enslavement.[6]

So, what changed? How did someone's skin colour come to define them, and to invalidate their virtues? The reason attitudes changed and colour came to be judged more harshly is due to a combination of factors, the first of which was the dawning realisation that there was good money to be made in the transatlantic slave trade.[5]

With race starting to have an impact on the way people thought and acted, commerce, science, philosophy and religion all played a part in changing how colour was viewed and, as a result, how human beings regarded and treated one another.

Commerce: the trade in people

Let's imagine that the slide towards modern notions of race and racism can be crystallised into a tipping point: a day in history when these socially constructed concepts are completed and launched. I will choose 8 August 1444, when the first large European slave market was held in a meadow on the outskirts of Lagos, on Portugal's Algarve coast.[11] A fleet blessed by Prince Henry the Navigator – who donated his one-fifth share of the auction proceeds to the church – returned from Mauritania with a cargo of 235 black Africans. The expedition was mounted in the name of the Order of Christ – and executed with terrible efficiency:

> *Our men looked towards the settlement and saw that the Moors, with their women and children were already coming out of their dwellings, because they had caught sight of their enemies. But they, shouting out, 'St James', 'St. George', 'Portugal', at once attacked them, killing and taking all they could. Then might you see mothers forsaking their children, and husbands their wives, each striving to escape as best he could. Some drowned themselves in the water; others thought to escape by hiding under their huts; others stowed their children among the seaweed, where our men found them afterwards, hoping they would thus escape notice.[12]*

At the slave auction, the captives were graded by colour: white, black and mulatto (mixed race). The lighter the skin colour, the higher the price. The commander of the expedition was knighted for his achievements. The slave trade was therefore inaugurated as a godly, profitable and admirable exercise. The initial hunting trips also benefited from their presentation as part of Europe's continuing conflict with Islam.[11]

The transatlantic slave trade thrived until the mid-nineteenth century, by which time much of the world had been colonised by European nations. Today, the industry is an embarrassing reminder of less enlightened times, and we celebrate those people who worked to bring about its abolition. But although the slave ships no longer ply the oceans, the trade's cultural legacy lives on. The attitudes and prejudices which developed during that period, and which enabled it to continue for so long, are not so easily eradicated or consigned to the history books. The stereotypes attached by commercial interests to different groups of people remain with us today and while we work hard to eradicate them at a conscious level, it is much more difficult to remove them from our unconscious thoughts and beliefs. We must recognise the enduring power of this legacy if we are to tackle racial prejudice in organisations today.

The slave trade was not the only phenomenon that contributed to the formation of racism as we know it today. Other powerful systems of ideas embraced and sustained the view that human beings could be placed on a hierarchy from superior to inferior. The most prominent of these was the institution of Christianity.

Religion: belief and bias

In the vigorous slaving nations of Spain and Portugal, a series of treaties and papal bulls issued in the late fifteenth century gave slavery a legal basis – and a religious one.

Pope Nicholas V's *Dum Diversas* papal bull of 1452 formally authorised Afonso V of Portugal to conquer Saracens and pagans and consign them to 'perpetual servitude'. The papal bull *Romanus Pontifex* continued the theme. In 1493 Pope Alexander VI blessed slave trading in the New World controlled by the Iberian powers.[5]

The transatlantic slave trade could be justified by the simple belief that some people were inferior to others. Anything that could be used to bolster this belief was used, whether bogus science or obscure passages in the Bible. In particular, a section of the biblical account of the flood was used to perpetuate the new racist ideology:[13] the world having been devastated by a wrathful God, Noah's sons must lead the regeneration and repopulation of the planet. Shem fathers the Semitic or Asian people, Japheth the European or Japhethic people, and Ham the African or Hamitic people. One night Ham sees his drunken father sleeping naked. On waking, Noah realises what has happened and puts a curse on Canaan, his grandson: 'And he said, "Cursed be Canaan! A servant of servants shall he be unto his brethren"' (Genesis 9:25).[13]

Even learned theologians find the denouement of this tale difficult to understand. A more logical curser would have targeted Ham rather than Ham's son. More pertinently, neither the hungover Noah nor the story's writer make any reference to colour. As a biblical justification for the notion of racial differences, this passage is extremely slight. Nevertheless, the ringing phrase 'a servant of servants' was all that some people required to add moral weight to a lucrative trade. The specific singling-out of the Canaanites was conveniently generalised to apply to all Hamitic – that is, African – peoples.

The transatlantic slave trade began in 1619 when a British pirate ship landed in Jamestown, Virginia, and traded 20 African slaves for tobacco.[13] The people who bought the slaves regarded themselves as decent Christians, and there seemed to be some moral unease on the part of the buyers. Thankfully, Noah's muddled curse came to their rescue.

The curse of Canaan, contorted and disputed as it is, provided apparent scriptural support for the enslavement of black people, and has even been used to explain the claim that Jews are racist - a pseudo-fact that can, in turn, be used to bolster anti-Semitism.[4] The curse was such a pervasive influence that Robert Byrd, a Democratic senator from West Virginia, quoted it as part of his 14-hour filibuster to prevent the Civil Rights Act from being passed in 1964.[13]

Science: race as fact

In Renaissance Europe, a time of growing colonialism and the development of the slave trade, there was an intellectual desire to classify the world in order to understand it better. Cultural and philosophical ideas also contributed to the view that people could be ranked in a hierarchy. One system used an Aristotelian typology to divide the world into people who were civilised and those who were barbarian. A number of criteria were established in late medieval Europe to determine this assessment:

• the existence of civil society, with a key factor being the existence of cities

• written laws

• rules relating to inheritance

• the institution of marriage

• correct commercial relations

• the use of clothes to determine status.[10]

These criteria were used to evaluate and categorise cultures. Conveniently, the Europeans making these evaluations found they could describe themselves as 'civilised' and Africans as 'barbarians' – even though, according to the strict application of the approach, some African cultures, such as the Congolese, should have been placed in the 'civilised' category.

Of course, the great irony of this approach is that classical civilisations like Rome contained mechanisms for people to change their status from 'barbarian' to 'civilised': if people accepted Roman law and spoke Latin, then they were accorded the full rights of citizens.[2]

In the sixteenth and seventeenth centuries, rather than passively accepting the views of the church and of ancient philosophers, people began trying to understand the world for themselves by their own observations, measurements and conclusions. As a result, typologies were created in all sorts of disciplines, the periodic table of elements being a particularly powerful example of such a rational approach. The table is not merely descriptive, but is predictive too. If nature could be understood by identifying separate, internally consistent and discrete categories, then it's a seemingly small and logical step to assume the same method must be applicable to the understanding of human beings.

In fact, during the same period, attempts were made to classify human beings. Initially, the groupings, based principally on colour and geography, were haphazard and inconsistent. Physical characteristics quickly became the culturally legitimate means of identifying and separating human beings from one another.

Carl Linnaeus was a remarkable eighteenth-century Swedish botanist. The advice he gave his students to maintain a healthy body are still recommended today: exercise, eat more fruit, drink plenty of water, avoid alcohol and sugar – and eat chocolate for its beneficial effects.[14] Linnaeus developed a classification system designed to accommodate all living things – flora, fauna and human beings. For centuries students have learned that 'King Philip Came Over For Good Spaghetti', the mnemonic for Kingdom, Phylum, Class, Order, Family, Genus, Species. His description of animal, mineral and vegetable kingdoms has been turned into popular games and quizzes. Any member of the system can be described within it: everything has its proper place. For example, Hominidae are a family, Primates an order, Mammals a class, and Chordata the phylum.[13]

He identified five sub-species of *homo sapiens*: American, European, Asian, African and Monstrous. He linked geographical location to physical characteristics and, straying from his strictly scientific method, added personality traits: 'Americans were considered to be reddish, stubborn, merry, and angered easily; Africans were black, relaxed, crafty, and negligent; Asians were sallow, avaricious, and easily distracted; and Europeans were white, gentle, and inventive'.[13] The Hottentots were an example of the Monstrous because it was thought the males had only one testicle.[15]

A hierarchy had been created, with Africans at the bottom and Asians not much higher. In Linnaeus's hierarchy, the Americans were at the top. Some people believe Linnaeus's taxonomies were racist and that his work laid the foundation for much of the racist thinking that followed. His supporters say this is unfair and that Linnaeus did not suggest that the traits he identified were fixed and unchangeable. Education was key to his ethos: he believed that if people were educated, then they could become more cultured. His supporters describe him as Eurocentric, rather than racist – which may not seem much of an exoneration, although it does suggest his thinking was more a product of his environment than the result of a patent ideology. Although his work was later used for racist purposes, Linnaeus cannot reasonably be held responsible for its subsequent misinterpretation and misappropriation.[15]

As we have seen, people had long noticed differences in skin colour, but no assumptions were made about the significance of such differences other than their origin in variations in climate. Now, as scientific method began to dominate over intellectual fashions, the idea that differences went more than skin deep started to take hold. In 1736, the German scientist Johann Friedrich Blumenbach wrote *On the Natural Variety of Mankind*, placing the Linnaean categories in a hierarchy with Caucasian at the top, followed by Mongolian, Malay, American Indian and Ethiopian – or, as this order has been handily simplified, White, Yellow, Brown, Red and Black.[13]

By 1764 there were, according to *The Gentleman's Magazine*, 20,000 black people in London. While most of them were poor and obscure, some also became well known – including Francis Barber (born Quashey), the Jamaican manservant of Samuel Johnson, and Olaudah Equiano, a freed slave who campaigned to end the slave trade.[17] In 1788 *The Gentleman's Magazine* featured an article in which 'the Negro' was described as:

> … *possessed by passions not only strong but ungovernable, a mind dauntless, warlike and unmerciful; a temper extremely irascible, a disposition indulgent, selfish and deceitful; fond of joyous sociability, riotous mirth and extravagant shew … Furious in love as in hate; at best a terrible husband, a harsh father and a precarious friend.*[16 (p135)]

As if this isn't damning enough, the writer concludes: 'as to all other finer feelings of the soul, the Negro, as far as I have been able to perceive, is nearly deprived of them'.

Thomas Jefferson believed someone's colour was important: it told us a lot about a person's character. Skin colour was not just an indication of a person's emotional state, but also of their beauty. Jefferson saw the 'eternal monotony' of the black skin as an 'immovable veil' that covers all emotion. He claimed that not only were Africans less beautiful than white people, but also that they sweated more, smelled worse and were better suited to working in hotter climates. And although black people were as brave and adventurous as white people, their courage was actually based on stupidity, as they were less capable of identifying real danger.[18]

Jefferson also agreed with *The Gentleman's Magazine* that higher intellectual functions were not to be found in black people. Appreciation of education was beyond their intellect and imagination. In other words, black people were designed to be slaves. Jefferson also knew that slaves in ancient times were not black, and he addressed this fact. He argued that the white slaves 'were often the rarest artists. They excelled too, in science, in so much as to be usually employed as teachers to their masters' children'.[18] (p154) It seems th at, even though black people were expressly designed to be slaves, white people just couldn't help being better at that too!

Jefferson summed up his beliefs thus: 'I advance it therefore as assumption only, that the blacks, whether originally a distinct race, or made distinct by time and circumstances, are inferior to the whites in the endowments of both body and mind.' Of North American slaves, he said: 'In general, their existence appears to participate more of sensation than reflection... [I]n memory they are equal to whites, in reason much inferior, as I think one could scarcely be found capable of tracing and comprehending the investigations of Euclid; and that in imagination they are dull, tasteless and anomalous.'[18] (P150/151)

Jefferson called on science to test if his observations were true – and science answered with alacrity. Dr Samuel George Morton amassed an impressive collection of over 800 skulls which he measured, assuming there must be a relationship between the size of the cranium and the intelligence of their owners. He discovered that negroes had the smallest skulls, along with Indian and Chinese people. The largest skulls – and therefore the biggest and most powerful brains – belonged to the English. The Germans and Americans came a poor second. It was later discovered that Morton had not measured his skulls at all accurately, and had published incorrect results which – conveniently – supported his theory.[19]

There is no evidence that traits such as intolerance or greed vary according to a person's colour, hair texture or nose shape. Even within a specific geographic region, there will be variations between people's physical appearance. Biologists refer to this as *cline* – the gradual changes in appearance that occur as one moves from one location to another. For example, the people living at the source of the Nile are noticeably darker than those living at the delta. The changes along this stretch of water are gradual – there is no sudden demarcation point.[13]

Racist ideologies were commonplace and accepted by some of the greatest philosophers of the time, including Kant, Hume, Hegel and Locke. According to Voltaire:

> *The negro race is a species of men as different from us as a breed of spaniels is from that of greyhounds. … If their understanding is not of a different nature from ours … it is at least greatly inferior. They are not capable of any great application or association of ideas and seem formed neither for the advantages nor the abuses of philosophy.*[19 (P63)]

In the nineteenth century the French aristocrat, Joseph Arthur, Comte de Gobineau, presented his four-volume work *An Essay on the Inequality of the Human Races* to the world – and bequeathed us the myth of the Aryan master race.[19] He endorsed the scientific racism of the time and declared that mixing the races was to the detriment of those of superior stock. He maintained there were three races – black, yellow and white. Black people were physically strong but intellectually inferior. Yellow or Asian people, while they were intellectually and physically inferior to whites, enjoyed a materialistic orientation and motivation which helped them to overcome some of their biological differences. Whites were superior intellectually, aesthetically and culturally. The white race was further subdivided, with Aryan being the most superior.

With the conceptualisation and compartmentalisation of race established, the possibility of subversion emerged: once you've created dividing lines, there are lines to be crossed. White entertainers 'blacking up' is a knowing categorical error that carries a titillating charge. We can see an early example of this in the troupe known as the Ethiopian Serenaders, who entertained audiences by singing, dancing and behaving in line with stereotypes about black people. But the posters advertising their shows made it clear that the performers were in fact white and did not behave in this way normally.[16] Over time, even this parody of black people changed for the worse, from good-natured clownish buffoonery to a cruder portrayal. Meanwhile, popular books and comics of the late nineteenth century, such as H. Rider Haggard's *King*

Sheet music cover image of the song 'songs of the Virginia Serenaders Yaller Gals A Southern Refrain', (Photo by Sheridan Libraries/Levy/Gado/Getty Images)

Solomon's Mines (1885) and Edgar Rice Burroughs' *The Son of Tarzan* (1917), showed the lone or outnumbered white man pitting his wits against tribes of hostile and backward natives.[20] The belief that black people were born to be slaves was so strongly held that the psychiatric condition drapetomania was created to account for black people who wanted to be free. Freedom for black people was officially an abnormality.[20]

In Britain, Darwin's cousin Francis Galton developed views on eugenics which were taken up enthusiastically in Europe and America.[19] Social Darwinists, who had no actual connection with Darwin, came under consistent attack during the early to mid-twentieth century for their view that some races were superior to others.[19] Edward Burnett Tylor, the founder of social anthropology, maintained there was more that made people similar than made them different:

> We may draw a picture where there shall be scarce a hand's-breadth difference between an English ploughman and a negro of Central Africa … For the present purposes, it appears both possible and desirable to eliminate the consideration of hereditary varieties or races of men and to treat mankind as homogeneous in nature, though placed in different grades of civilisation.[21] (p7)

Tylor introduced the useful concept of survivals:

> These are processes, customs and so forth which have been carried on by force of habit different from that in which they had their original home, and they thus remain as proofs and examples of an older condition of culture out of which a newer has been evolved.[21] (p10)

These echoes of ancient beliefs affect us today. Survivals masquerade as facts and provide containers for prejudice.

The race-based society

Religion, philosophy and science were all used to support the idea of a hierarchy of bias and, with it, support for slavery. Fortunes – both metaphorical and monetary – hinged on the belief that some groups, and Africans in particular, were subhuman. In the nineteenth century, this proposition was debated seriously, with some people even arguing that Africans were created separately from the rest of humanity.[22]

The race-based society has been usefully described by Smedley and Smedley:

- Racial groups are seen as discrete and separate from one another in a biological sense. Physical characteristics become the principal method by which groups are distinguished, and include skin colour, eye shape and hair texture.

- The races are not equal, and therefore hierarchies can be created. Broadly speaking, white people or those of European descent are at the top of the hierarchy, black people or those of African descent are at the bottom, and other races occupy places in between.

- It is not only physical characteristics which are inherited; so are personality traits, behaviours, attitudes and intelligence.

- The differences are unalterable, so it makes sense for groups to live separately from one another and for intimate relationships between people from different groups to be prohibited.

- Finally, the beliefs about race become enshrined in a legal system that upholds and supports them.[22]

Colour was – and remains – a key differentiator. In the mid-nineteenth century, Irish people, southern Europeans and Eastern Europeans were seen as physically and culturally different from other Europeans, and were ranked lower on the social hierarchy. But their whiteness and Christianity enabled them, over time, to be accepted into the 'white' category.[19] Where once virtue was valued and colour was of superficial interest, colour now reigned supreme as the basic determinant of someone's value.

Asians in the UK: a history of retained otherness

So far, this chapter has looked at a rather formal account of history by tracing the changing attitudes of those in power and how this affected behaviour towards Africans. Black skin was now associated with low status and hierarchy. We have seen how models and narratives were created to account for differences between groups – and to ensure that hierarchical restrictions were observed. A brief history of the Asian experience in the UK can act as an exemplar of how stereotypes and prejudices are constructed around 'the other', and how people who are neither at the top nor the bottom are viewed and treated. Much of what follows is drawn from the exhaustive research of the distinguished historian Rozina Visram in her book *Asians in Britain: 400 Years of History.*[23]

On 22 December 1616 an Indian youth was baptised at St Dionis Backchurch in the City of London. This is the first recorded baptism of an Indian person in England. The young man, who was baptised as Peter, had come to England two years previously. Among those witnessing the event were King James I, the Privy Council and the governors of the East India Company – a trading enterprise set up by Queen Elizabeth I.

People from India came to the UK for a variety of reasons. At one end of the spectrum were ayahs (nannies) and lascars (sailors). Other Indian visitors welcomed to the shores of the UK included writers, philosophers and princes. The Indians, or Asians as they are described today, were seen in many different ways – from being inferior to being equals.

Lascars and ayahs were seen as expendable labour. Employed to bring cargo to England or to look after the children of returning English families, they were regularly abandoned with no means of supporting themselves and no way of returning to India. An advertisement from 1775 was written by a 'slave girl', abandoned by her mistress when they had arrived in Britain, who declared herself willing to serve a lady on a trip back to India. In return the advertiser would 'serve her for three months after the arrival here without wages, provided the lady engages at the expiration of her term to her freedom'. (p13)

Lascars and ayahs being dumped on arrival in the UK was seen as a national scandal. Philanthropists established charitable schemes to help them. The lascars' skills as sailors were highly regarded, although they were never seen as people who could captain a ship. One writer lumped lascars together with Chinese and Greek people as 'filthy dirty people'.

The British in India became used to employing large establishments of servants – many more than they could possibly have afforded in the UK. Many brought their servants with them when they returned to the UK. They were employed as valets, footmen, cooks, maids and nursery maids, as well as running household accounts and finances. One English captain returning to England brought back his steward, cook, valet, groom, groom's assistant, barber, washerman and 'other officers', in addition to 15 'coolies' to carry his bags.

But there is also evidence of a growing Indian professional class. In 1914 Gandhi wrote a letter supporting the Empire in the war that had just broken out. The letter was signed by 53 Asian professionals from Edinburgh to London. The fact that people from India were able to find employment in established fields in the UK suggests a degree of acceptance which was not the case in other countries, such as France.

Indians coming to the UK often found the attitudes of the British at home more hospitable, humble and curious than those of the British in India, who were seen as arrogant and superior. That is not to say the Indians' experience was necessarily free from racism. Although the native British had a continuing interest in Indian art and culture, there was also a noticeable strain of contempt. Fanny Burney wrote in a letter of 1789 of the 'negro servants' of families returning from India. She considered their voices 'inhuman' and their conversation 'barbarous'.

When in 1913 Rabindranath Tagore was awarded the Nobel Prize for literature, D.H. Lawrence, in a letter to Lady Ottoline Morrell, was appalled at the esteem in which Tagore and other writers from 'the East' were held:

> I become more and more surprised to see how far higher, in reality, our European civilisation stands, than the East, Indian and Persian, ever dreamed of. And one is glad to realise how these Hindoos are horribly decadent and reverting to all forms of barbarism in all sorts of ugly ways. We feel surer on our feet, then. But this fraud of looking up to them – this wretched worship-of-Tagore attitude – is disgusting. (p49)

Not everyone of influence shared Lawrence's disgust or paranoia, however. Indeed, Queen Victoria had promoted her attendant Abdul Karim to the role of 'Munshi' – a clerk or secretary. Understandably, perhaps, people in the royal household and others in prominent positions took the opportunity to criticise the appointment when they could. But the queen was adamant that the reason behind these criticisms was 'race prejudice'. She expanded on this theme in a letter she wrote in 1898 to the future Viceroy. She advised him to come to his own understanding of the people of India 'and not be guided by the snobbish and vulgar and overbearing and offensive behaviour of many of our civil and political agents'.

Victoria's views, and her emphatic expression of them, certainly ran against the countervailing attitudes of the time – what we might call, ironically, 'Victorian values'. For example, British women in relationships with Indian men were disapproved of and even seen as 'depraved'. (p68) In 1910 a committee found that 'there is unfortunately a prejudice in the labour market against the coloured British subject'. However, the recommended solution for ending the discrimination was repatriation.

Nevertheless, businesses were being set up in the UK by people from India. Tata Industries opened a London branch in York House in Twickenham. (Today Tata owns, among many other concerns, the last surviving chunk of the British motor industry, Jaguar Land Rover, and the remains of the UK steel industry.) Professional businesses such as accountancy firms were established by Indian people, as well as restaurants, tobacconists and cigar manufacturers.

In a 1933 survey of London businesses, 48 were identified as Indian-owned. These included accountants, book-keepers, guest houses and restaurants. Indian food had long been appreciated by British people, and the 1747 cookery book *The Art of Cookery Made Plain and Easy* contains a recipe for 'how to make a curry the Indian way' and another for 'Pellow' (pilau) rice. By 1938, 26% of the labour force in British shipping was Indian.

Indians were also working to become doctors (1,000 of them in 1945, 200 in London), journalists, barristers, writers, editors, poets, musicians, and religious and political thinkers. Further along the social scale, many Asian people worked as pedlars – licences were easy to obtain and their customers were the working-class. W.B. McCarter, owner of Fruit of the Loom, was selling his goods to a successful Indian retailer, Charlie Verma. Dublin wholesalers were so unhappy that McCarter was doing business with Verma that they threatened to boycott Fruit of the Loom products. McCarter refused to be intimidated by the wholesalers and continued to deal with Verma.

As can be seen, British views of Asian people were ambiguous and contradictory. There was admiration and respect at one level, disgust and superiority at another. This situation has been described as 'exotica – fanatica'[24 (p348)] and it continues today.

The stereotypes associated with 'Asian' are a mix of positive and negative. I regularly ask people in organisations about the characteristics they typically associate with Asians (as well as other groups), and find that they include positive terms (educated, mathematical, hard-working) and negative ones (stick together, religious fanatics, sneaky).

My findings are not unlike the following list of typical group characteristics which was issued as a factual analysis in 1878 by the Professor of Sanskrit at Oxford University:[16]

Hindustani	Spirited	Tamils
Sikh	Martial	Pariah
Marathi	Ambitious	Active
Rajout	Proud	Patient
Garkha	Hardy	Telegu
Bengali	Calculating	Busy

Distinguished visitors to the UK from India were treated very well. Dwarkanath Tagore, the grandfather of Rabindranath, was a successful businessman and entrepreneur. On arriving in the UK he was introduced to a parade of notables, including Queen Victoria, Charles Dickens, William Thackeray and Henry Mayhew, and granted the freedom of the city of Edinburgh.

On the other hand, Indians were not seen as leaders, and obstacles were put in their way to prevent them occupying leadership roles. Entry to the Indian Civil Service was by competitive exam – which sounds progressive and egalitarian. However, the exams were held in London, ensuring that only the wealthiest Indians could sit them. Even so, many of these select candidates still failed, despite their excellent academic qualifications. In the first 15 years of open competition, only one Indian candidate passed. And after 40 years, 1,000 people had been chosen for the highest ranks of the Service, just 20 of whom were Indian.

The purpose of describing Asians in the UK is to demonstrate how their experiences and perceptions are both similar to, and different from, those of black Africans. The similarities relate to the sense that they are inferior to the native white groups. They are different in that the stereotypes also carry some positive associations, which leads to different expectations and opportunities.

1. Brackett, J.K. Race and Rulership: Alessandro de' Medici, first Medici duke of Florence, 1529–1537 in *Black Africans in Renaissance Europe* (eds. T.F. Earle & K.J.P. Lowe) (Cambridge University Press, 2005).

2. Snowden, F.M. *Before Color Prejudice: The Ancient View of Blacks*. (Harvard University Press, 1983).

3. Grint, K. *The Sociology of Work*. (Polity Press, 2005).

4. Shavit, Y. *History in Black: African-Americans in Search of an Ancient Past*. (Routledge, 2013).

5. Onyeka. *Blackamoores: Africans in Tudor England, their Presence, Status and Origins*. (Narrative Eye Ltd, 2013).

6. Fra-Molinero, B. Juan Latino and His Racial Difference in *Black Africans in Renaissance Europe* (eds. T.F. Earle & K.J.P. Lowe) (Cambridge University Press, 2005).

7. Donkin, R. *Blood, Sweat And Tears: The Evolution Of Work*. (Texere Publlishing, 2002).

8. Casares, A.M. Free and Freed Black Africans in Granada in the Time of the Spanish Renaissance in *Black Africans in Renaissance Europe* (eds. T.F. Earle & K.J.P. Lowe) (Cambridge University Press, 2005).

9. Foley, J. Multiculturalism and the Media in *Multi-America: Essays on Cultural Wars and Cultural Peace* (ed. I. Reed) (Penguin Books, 1998).

10. Lowe, K. Introduction: The Black African Presence In Renaissance Europe in *Black Africans in Renaissance Europe* (eds. T. Earle & K. Lowe) (Cambridge University Press, 2005).

11. Wolf, K.B. 'The Moors' Of West Africa And The Beginnings Of The Portuguese Slave Trade. *J. Mediev. Renaiss*. Stud. **24**, 449–469 (1994).

12. Chronica do Descobrimento e Conquista da Guiné, by Gomes Eanes de Zurara, Paris, 1841; English version The Chronicle of the Discovery and Conquest of Guinea translated by Edgar Prestage, London, 1896-1899, volume 1, page 65-66.

13. Prewitt, K. *What Is Your Race?: The Census and Our Flawed Efforts to Classify Americans*. (Princeton University Press, 2013).

14. Berglund, K. The Keen Eye: Linnaeus: The Man Who Saw Everything in *The Linnaean Legacy: Three Centuries After His Birth* (eds. M.J. Morris & L. Berwick) (Wiley Blackwell, 2008).

15. Skuncke, M.-C. Linnaeus: An 18th Century Background. in *The Linnaean Legacy: Three Centuries After His Birth* (eds. M.J. Morris & L. Berwick) (Wiley Blackwell, 2008).

16. Jackson, P. *Maps of Meaning: An Introduction to Cultural Geography*. (Routledge, 1989).

17. Walvin, J. *Passage to Britain: immigration in British History and Politics*. (Penguin in association with Belitha Press, 1984).

18. Jefferson, T. *Notes on the State of Virginia*. (J. W. Randolph, 1853).

19. Omi, M. & Winant, H. *Racial Formation in the United States: From the 1960s to the 1990s*. (Routledge, 1994).

20. Sue, D.W. *Microaggressions in Everyday Life: Race, Gender and Sexual Orientation*. (Wiley, 2010).

21. Tylor, E.B. *Primitive Culture*. (Harper & Row (Original work published 1871), 1958).

22. Smedley, A. & Smedley, B.D. Race as biology is fiction, racism as a social problem is real: Anthropological and historical perspectives on the social construction of race. *Am. Psychol*. **60**, 16–26 (2005).

23. Visram, R. *Asians in Britain: 400 Years of History*. (Pluto Press, 2002).

24. Hutnyk, J. The dialectic of here and there: Anthropology 'at home' and British Asian communism. *Soc. Identities* **11**, 345–361 (2005).

Part 2
Racism Today

Chapter 3

Our heart of hearts: How racism mutated

Prejudice in general, and racism in particular, are not static; they evolve. Racism has been likened to a virus that mutates, taking on different forms as it adapts to a changing environment.[1] Its mutation is made harder to observe by its being deeply embedded, not only in our traditions and institutions, but also in our unconscious lives.

Behaviours can be separated into those which are under our conscious control and those which are not. These two types of behaviour are not necessarily related to each another[2] and this is a focus of this chapter.

It could be argued that conscious behaviours – the ones we find easier to recognise and control – represent the real person, and the others are bogus. Nevertheless, people with whom we interact pick up on and identify our unconscious behaviours.

Our public attitudes to race have changed, and surveys have measured this evolution over many decades. Today, people in the majority group make far fewer overt hostile actions towards minorities. When racist acts occur, they are widely condemned rather than being condoned as they were in the past. The positive changes are due to a widespread disapproval of racist activities in society: it is no longer socially acceptable to express racism directly. Explicit attitudes towards race have been measured consistently over many decades, so it is possible to track how they have changed. For example, in 1942, 44% of people in the USA were willing to accept integrated transport. By 1970, the figure was 88%.[3] Changes in attitude, in all age groups and religions, have also occurred in relation to issues such as education and intermarriage.[2]

Even in the 1970s, however, a note of caution was sounded by attitude researchers, who said that answers to their survey questions 'may well indicate not what the American really feels in his heart of hearts, but what he thinks he ought to say'.[3] They went on to say that while changes in attitude are not necessarily indicative of changes in behaviour, changes in general opinion do create a context in which changes in behaviour are more likely to occur.

The lack of tolerance for racist behaviour makes navigating one's way through daily life, for visible minorities, less hazardous than it once was.

Unfortunately, the store of negative images and stereotypes we have inherited from the past is less easy to eradicate. A lack of tolerance of hostile behaviours is not necessarily the same as genuine equality of opportunity. A reduction of racist acts does not automatically mean black people will feel they are being fairly treated in the workplace.

The forms of prejudice we live with today have different names, one being modern racism. Modern racists neither express nor endorse racist views and stereotypes. They believe in greater integration between people. However, modern racists also believe racial equality has been achieved and that we need no further policies to promote equality. If racism has been neutralised, then it's reasonable to maintain the status quo. For people who think in this way, racism is over and there's nothing left to discuss. Modern racism reveals itself at opportune moments, is oblique rather than confrontational, and often leads to a conflict in our own personal values.

In other words, racial prejudice has not disappeared; it has mutated. This chapter looks at how racism manifests itself today:

- Avoiding minorities and minimising contact
- Finding the 'right time' to discriminate: context and opportunity
- Finding ways of expressing negative attitudes indirectly (by criticising a policy, for example)
- It is about differences in 'values', not abilities.

Finally, I look at the conflict that can arise within us when we sense that our conscious beliefs are not matched by our feelings.

Avoiding and minimising contact

Few of us believe we are racist. This means we have no obvious reason to turn the spotlight on ourselves and examine our own attitudes and motivations, which can be complex and contradictory. We can believe strongly in equality and yet at the same time hold negative views about some minorities, creating conflict within ourselves. This tension is resolved in some instances by avoiding contact with those groups. In doing this, such individuals will recognise that racial discrimination is bad, and yet, because they have little or no contact with minorities, will not recognise that they are themselves racist.[1]

In his book *The Blind Side* (about the footballer Michael Oher and the family who adopted him), Michael Lewis says: 'The effort the locals put into avoiding obvious racism rendered the near-total lack of interaction between black people and white people in Oxford, Mississippi, almost as invisible as it was in the rest of the country'.[4]

Measures like the Bogardus social distance scale indicate the extent to which people would object to marriage between black and white people, or to having a black friend round to dinner. Today, around nine out of ten people respond positively to such questions. However, only 10% of white people in the USA have black friends and 68% have never had a black person to dinner.[5] Although people agree with the *idea* of people of different colours mixing socially, they don't do much of it themselves.

While someone who explains that they have minority friends may seem on the surface to have little problem with diversity, it all boils down to what we mean by 'friends'. Genuine friendships are based on a high degree of interaction and closeness. Close friends are like family – and are sometimes better than family. The connections of friendship are strong, enduring and meaningful. At school, where there may be great diversity, people will interact with one another: they are obliged to. But these connections are not necessarily deep and do not often extend much beyond the playground. Indeed, the friendships rarely continue once people have left school.[5]

These relationships matter. Not knowing people from other racial groups, and having limited experience of contact with them, makes people more likely to stereotype others. Group isolation also fits into a pattern of people denying the possibility of their being prejudiced while avoiding contact with other groups. This is one of the key ways in which racial discrimination differs from sex discrimination. Men and women are in constant contact with one another, but it is possible for people to avoid meaningful contact with other racial groups.

This process has been described as self-segregation. Minorities such as immigrant communities may self-segregate because issues of language, culture and discrimination encourage them to stay within communities where they are most comfortable.[6] However, dominant groups can also self-segregate, even though they may not recognise they are doing so, and may wish to blame minorities for the resulting distancing effect.[7]

Finding the 'right time' to discriminate: context and opportunity

On 13 March 1964 Kitty Genovese, a bar manager, was murdered in her home city of New York. The media reported that she was stabbed to death in the sight of 38 witnesses who did not intervene or call the police. The story has been much revisited since – the number of witnesses has not been substantiated, and it seems neighbours did try to intervene and summon help. Nevertheless, the attack and its context clearly spoke to a society concerned about its own lack of concern. Inspired by the Genovese case, researchers Latane and Darley[8] published a study in 1968 to investigate people's reactions to witnessing a crime. They found that if a person is on their own when they witness a serious incident, they will take action. But if other people are present, the responsibility for action is diffused and individuals are less likely to act. This becomes even more interesting when the colour of the victim is taken into account, because context is king when it comes to behaviour towards minorities.

If a lone bystander was asked for help, there was virtually no difference in the response given to a white or black victim. But if other people were present, colour became a factor. In this situation, the white victim was helped twice as often as the black victim (75% versus 38%). The researchers also found that participants denied, often vigorously, that race had in any way affected their decision to offer support or not.

Here, a certain degree of un-self-awareness quickly makes itself felt. Individuals often tell me that they, and the organisations they represent, are not, and *cannot* be, racist. I'll hear something like this: 'I grew up in a multicultural city and went to a school with a great diversity of people. I don't treat minorities any differently than I do the majority.' This is a very positive attitude and a sincerely held belief. But research shows that, despite such positive statements, our behaviour at the non-verbal level can betray our best statements.[9]

The rationalisation of our behaviour in this way means we often fail to consider whether race has any part to play in our actions and decisions.

Research shows that modern racists will make more racially discriminatory decisions if the conditions are right. In one study, participants were given ten candidates to evaluate. Five candidates were clearly unsuitable for the role, leaving five qualified people, three of whom were black. Since three people were to be selected, at least one black person had to be chosen. The panel could, of course, have chosen all three black candidates. In the control group, the participants could choose freely. However, the test group was given a message from the CEO saying that since the hiring company had few black customers, it would be preferable to choose a white person.

The Modern Racism scale was created to detect the more subtle ways in which our beliefs about other groups are expressed. No difference was found between high and low scorers on the Modern Racism scale in the control group: both chose equal numbers of black and white candidates on average. In the test group, the low modern racists selected slightly fewer than half the black candidates on average, whereas the high modern racists selected fewer than one black person on average. In other words, if you give modern racists a reason for discriminating, they are likely to take it. The environment in which we work can therefore have a significant impact in terms of whether modern racists will make unfair decisions.[10]

The prevailing social norms clearly affect whether people are prepared to express negative attitudes towards minorities. This idea was further explored by *Dovidio et al.,* who found that where the social norms were not obvious people were more likely to behave in discriminatory ways that were both more apparent (for example, offering less help to minorities) but also more subtle (for example, the display of spontaneous non-verbal behaviours).[9] Organisational cultures and the attitudes of leaders play an important part in the expression of modern racism.

Individuals may consistently support policies that promote diversity, yet stereotypes about minority cultures persist and have an impact on their decision-making and behaviour. In situations where behavioural norms are quite clear, people will behave in line with them. Where the code of conduct is less clear and more ambiguous, residual feelings will rise to the surface and lead to more discriminatory behaviour.

Increased competition
It is not just about opportunity to discriminate; the culture also matters. One sure-fire way of increasing bias and prejudice between groups is to increase competition by suggesting that the subordinate group, in this case the minority, is limiting the opportunities of the dominant majority.

The imagined damage does not have to stem from competition for jobs or housing, though these may be the most obvious points of sensitivity. The dominant group may perceive an increased level of competition through fears about its own shrinking relative size. Participants in one study[11] were shown data on either the current or the projected increased number of minorities. Pro-white, anti-minority bias was higher in the latter condition. The data presented to these subjects generated a belief that the majority would lose some of its dominance in the future.

A classic example, and one which has been accepted into corporate life, is the so-called 'War for Talent'.[12] Written by McKinsey consultants, it was a panicked publication showing that, as the workforce became ever more diverse, the importance of making the most of the pool of 'talent' would increase. Except, of course, the proportion of people with 'talent' was never going to go down; it was just going to change. What *was* going to decrease was the proportion of white men in the category labelled as 'talent', and the 'war' was for those who wanted to maintain the numbers of this particular group.

Finding ways of expressing negative attitudes indirectly: 'It's not the people I have a problem with, it's the policy'
Modern racism is also referred to as symbolic racism. This term captures the sense of modern racism's obliqueness. The measures of modern racism are correlated to

attitudes about affirmative action and immigration – in other words, issues related to policy. In organisations, the target of the racist attitude is not the people or group but something more indirect, such as aspects of the diversity policies. The distinction between types of prejudice has also been referred to as 'blatant' and 'subtle' racism.[13,14]

During the 2017/18 American football season, several players 'took the knee' when the national anthem was played. President Donald Trump tweeted:

'Wouldn't you love to see one of these NFL owners, when somebody disrespects our flag, to say, "Get that son of a bitch off the field right now. Out! He's fired. He's fired!"'

The players were protesting against the killing of African Americans by police officers, and the majority of players involved were African American. In this case, someone with racist views can express them indirectly by vehemently attacking a policy (taking the knee) rather than the group itself.

Critically, these researchers found that subtle racists do not engage in expressing negative views about minority groups – this would be socially unacceptable – but they do fail to express any positive views about these groups.[13,14]

It's worth noting that subtle prejudice isn't just confined to race. The same mechanism has been found to apply to sexism, anti-Semitism, heterosexism and attitudes towards obese people. This is a complex area, however, and it is important that we do not automatically interpret disagreement with a policy as an indicator of someone's implicit racism. For example, it is perfectly possible for someone to be in favour of greater diversity and against the setting of numerical targets. There is an increasing tendency to view those who are opposed to target-setting (to achieve greater diversity) as being against the idea of treating people fairly. This kind of position has been called 'principled conservatism'.[2] It is perfectly possible for people to agree on a goal but to disagree about how to achieve it. But it is the ambiguity of the interpretation of the attitude that provides modern racists with the cover they need. One way of distinguishing between modern racists and 'principled conservatives' is that the former find it far more difficult to express any positive views about visible minorities.

With the increasing diversity of society, it is important not to assume that racism is exhibited just by white people towards other minorities, and towards black people in particular. Research has shown, for example, that immigrant Latinos in the USA have more negative attitudes about black people than many other groups, including USA-born Latinos (63% vs 38%). Asians (Koreans, Japanese and Chinese) hold stronger anti-black and anti-Latino views than whites.[5] If we ignore the complexity of race dynamics, we fail to examine other forms of racism and to explore other options for reducing prejudice. Furthermore, we may miss the variety of attitudes and views found in different minority groups. For example, Latinos in the USA and

Asians in the UK may have a different view of affirmative, or positive, action than black people.[15,16]

It is about differences in 'values', not abilities

It is about differences in 'values', not abilities. One of the ways in which racism has become more elusive is shifts in language which seem to imply new modes of thinking. A key term here is 'values', which is increasingly used as a strategy for denoting differences between groups while apparently avoiding entrenched stereotypes. Many people see Islam as a threat to society due to its different values – despite the fact that the essential beliefs of Muslims are no different to those of any other faith.

We used to be told that some groups had superior intellectual capabilities and personality traits. Today these ideas are increasingly rejected. Instead we learn that different groups have different values. This may seem an advance – in that the concept of differing values appears to exclude comparisons between groups. But values create obstacles as surely as the old group traits – and cut both ways. Middle-class white workers may see black people as lazy and lacking a strong work ethic, but black workers may see white middle-class people as domineering and egotistical.[17] Barriers, whether built from superstitions or from values, separate 'us' from 'them'.

This account is similar to a straightforward distinction between old-fashioned and modern prejudice, but it also incorporates the idea that we exaggerate differences between groups and their cultural norms, beliefs, values, language and behaviour.

Internalised conflict: The head versus the heart

Susan Fiske's authoritative work in the field of prejudice identified how bias originates.[18] People with moderate implicit biases typically have limited direct personal experience of minority group members. They also have limited experience of constructive intergroup interactions, with most of their information about other groups obtained from the media. By these means they develop unconscious, negative associations.

These unconscious or implicit biases sit alongside, but contradict, our conscious attitudes – our constructive attempts to display greater tolerance and understanding of others. People with moderate biases, Fiske argues, will hold anti-prejudiced values. This means they may feel internal tension and conflict as their conscious beliefs fail to match their feelings. It can feel as if the heart (or the gut) is arguing with the head – though, of course, the stage for this multi-layered drama is the brain.

The potential for values to become areas of conflict within us was raised as early as 1944 by Gunnar Myrdal[19] when he was asked to investigate race in the USA. He observed that two of the USA's most deeply held values are egalitarianism and individualism. The first leads to a concern for underprivileged groups, but the second leads to the belief that individuals are responsible for creating opportunities for themselves. Myrdal believed American society was grappling with the tension between these sets of values.

This need not just be a flashpoint between people, however: this tension exists within us too. The conflict is between our explicitly held attitudes and those which may be suppressed or even implicit. It has also been found that pro- and anti-black attitudes are linked respectively to humanitarian (a care for the welfare of others) and individualistic (people are responsible for their own outcomes in life) attitudes.[20] These attitudes align conspicuously with Myrdal's American values of egalitarianism and individualism.

A consequence of the mutation of racism and these conflicting values is how we account for the continuing disparities between ethnic groups on issues such as pay, employment and housing. If these differences are not due to discrimination, then the reason must lie with the groups themselves: they must be unwilling to work hard enough or apply themselves. In turn, this leads to a disparity between how different groups view prejudice. For minorities, prejudice can be seen as a societal, systemic issue that affects their freedom and life chances. For the majority, on the other hand, racism is increasingly seen as a thing of the past, and the disparity in outcomes between groups is due to the minorities' own behaviour.[5] So if members of a particular group are not as successful as others then they should reflect on their own attitudes and behaviours, not seek to blame others. This is also known as the 'Bootstraps Model' (that is, 'They should pull themselves up by their own bootstraps, as others have done').

On the other hand, the internal conflict can lead to more positive reactions.[21] People may have genuinely positive and explicit attitudes towards another group. When such individuals find themselves thinking in stereotypes or behaving in a discriminatory fashion, they experience genuine discomfort. It was found that when some participants in a study were told they had behaved in a discriminatory fashion towards someone from a stigmatised group, such as a black person or a disabled person, they would behave in a more helpful way in subsequent interactions with that person – more so than if the person was white or able-bodied. The key here is to give the person feedback on their behaviour and give them the opportunity to learn.

Avoiding discussions about race and racism therefore means that we also avoid one possible solution to dealing with it: calling it out. For some of us, the discussion itself may be enough for a period of reflection and changes in our behaviour.

Teaching racism to our children

We also need to be wary of the assumption that racism is dying out of its own accord, as parents raise a new generation of children minded towards inclusion and tolerance. I've often heard it said that racial prejudice must be waning because our children have no issue with colour. I have heard global directors of diversity of major multinationals expressing this very sentiment: 'Our children do not notice racial differences and do not mind being with people of other colours or ethnicities and so the next generation will be free from racism.'

Unfortunately, this is not the case. The reason children do not show prejudice is because they are not born with it. But neither were we, and so our children, rather than being different to us, are like we were at that age. Racial bias is something people develop over time. And it has developed in every generation since racism was created. The Greek historian and geographer Agatharchides noted that while children might initially be alarmed by someone of markedly different colour, this feeling would soon disappear.[22] Any sense of alarm one feels on encountering a black person stops after childhood. Snowden notes that as black and white people lived together in the Greek and Roman worlds, 'there was no reason for a child or even a parent to attach special significance to differences in colour or to think that blacks were *fundamentally* different' (author's italics).

Gordon Allport,[23] who wrote the classic work on prejudice over sixty years ago, concluded that, while children do notice that people have different skin colours, they do not accord it much significance. The situation changes as they get older and acquire the belief that the colour of a person's skin means something. This pattern, which has been observed in many countries (e.g. France,[24] China,[25] the USA[26]) is a preference for people of similar colour first of all. This starts as early as four years of age. By adolescence, children not only have an in-group preference (i.e. towards people like themselves), but they are making more stereotypical assumptions about different groups.

We learn our negative out-group (i.e. people not like us) responses, therefore, via a combination of in-group preferences and negative stereotypes about minorities. The decline in children's willingness to reveal these attitudes shows that they simultaneously learn, from those around them – parents, teachers, family members – that it is not acceptable to voice them.

Interestingly, black American adults do not have such a strong in-group bias as white Americans.[28] By the age of thirteen, black Americans have far less of an in-group bias than their white counterparts[26] and these attitudes are maintained into adulthood.

Linked to these attitudes is the idea of a hierarchy of human beings. For example, Hispanic children aged five showed an in-group preference for Hispanic people over black people. No difference was found between preferences for Hispanics over whites. Although the development of the concept is influenced by familiarity, there is also an element of preference at work.

Associations between skin colour and the supposed intellectual, psychological and moral characteristics of individuals are far from obvious to a small child. These associations have to be learned. There is nothing exceptional or different about today's youngsters compared to previous generations of youngsters – except perhaps for the increasingly elaborate and detailed system of prejudices available for their consumption. We were the same when we were their age, and so were our parents, and the chain of learning stretches back through history.

Implicit and explicit prejudice begin to become noticeable by early adolescence, and continue into adulthood. Our overt behaviours and expressed attitudes may be egalitarian and tolerant, but our implicit attitudes may be the opposite.

Conclusion

Racism has evolved and mutated. The overt and obvious forms of prejudice discussed in Chapter 2 are witnessed less than they were, and it is comforting to believe that racism is becoming a thing of the past, that somehow we live in an enlightened age where judging people by the colour of their skin is no longer acceptable.

Unfortunately, this is far from the truth. Today, prejudiced attitudes are expressed in more subtle and nuanced ways, several of which have been described in this chapter. First, we can avoid any meaningful contact with the minority group. Second, racial discrimination is practised when the circumstances allow it. Third, rather than criticising a minority group, those with racist beliefs will attack a policy and use that as a means of finding an outlet for their attitudes. Fourth, we make a distinction between groups in terms of their 'values'.

For some of the points, valid claims can be made that this is not racism at all. Disagreeing with a policy (for example, on target-setting) or an action (for example, taking the knee) is not prejudiced. That is correct, of course, but the fact is that it could be, and it is this ambiguity about the position taken which demonstrates the subtlety of the behaviour.

An unwillingness to examine our own motives and attitudes often leads people to adopt a supposedly colour-blind approach. It's as if we pass legislation on ourselves and the job is done: 'I don't notice a person's colour.'[5]

Our understanding of racism needs to become much more sophisticated in order to match racism's increased subtlety and elusiveness.

1. Dovidio, J.F. & Gaertner, S.L. Aversive racism and selection decisions: 1989 and 1999. *Psychol. Sci.* **11**, 315–319 (2000).

2. Brown, R. *Prejudice: Its Social Psychology* (Blackwell, 1995).

3. Greeley, A.M. & Sheatsley, P.B. Attitudes Toward Desegregation (1971 National Opinion Research Center, Chicago Illinois).

4. Lewis, M. *The Blind Side: Evolution of a Game* (W.W. Norton & Company Inc., 2007).

5. Bonilla-Silva, E. *Racism Without Racists: Color-Blind Racism and the Persistence of Racial Inequality in America* (Rowman & Littlefield, 2010).

6. Crisp, R. *The Social Brain: How Diversity Made the Modern Mind* (Robinson, 2015).

7. Mason, D. Changing patterns of ethnic disadvantage in employment. In *Explaining Ethnic Differences: Changing Patterns of Disadvantage in Britain* (ed. D. Mason) (Policy Press, 2003).

8. Latane, B. & Darley, J.M. Group inhibition of bystander intervention in emergencies. *J. Personal. Soc. Psychol.* **10**, 215–221 (1968).

9. Dovidio, J.F., Gaertner, S.L.E., Kawakami, K. & Hodson, G. Why can't we just get along? Interpersonal biases and interracial distrust. *Cult. Divers. Ethn. Minor. Psychol.* **8**, 88–102 (2002).

10. Brief, A.P. et al. Just doing business: Modern racism and obedience to authority as explanations for employment discrimination. *Organ. Behav. Hum. Decis. Process.* **81**, 72–97 (2000).

11. Craig, M.A. & Richeson, J.A. More diverse yet less tolerant? How the increasingly diverse racial landscape affects white Americans' racial attitudes. *Psychol. Soc. Psychol. Bull.* **40**, 750–761 (2014).

12. Michaels, E., Handfield-Jones, H. & Axelrod, B. The War For Talent (Harvard University Press, 2001).

13. Meertens, R.W. et al. Is subtle prejudice really prejudice? *Public Opimon* Q. **61**, 54–71 (1997).

14. Pettigrew, T.F. & Meertens, R.W. Subtle and blatant prejudice in western Europe. *Eur. J. Soc. Psychol.* **25**, 57–75 (1995).

15. Omi, M. & Winant, H. *Racial Formation in the United States: From the 1960s to the 1990s* (Routledge, 1994).

16. Pew Research Centre. Public backs affirmative action, but not minority preferences. Available at: http://www.pewresearch.org/2009/06/02/public-backs-affirmative-action-but-not-minority-preferences/ (Accessed 10th October 2017).

17. Firat, R.B. Apathetic Racism Theory: A Neurosociological Study of How Moral Emotions Perpetuate Inequality (The University of Iowa, 2013).

18. Fiske, S.T. What we know now about bias and intergroup conflict, the problem of the century. *Curr. Dir. Psychol.* Sci. **11**, 123–128 (2002).

19. Myrdal, G. & Bok, S. *An American Dilemma: The Negro Problem and Modern Democracy* (Transaction Publishers, 1996).

20. Katz, I. & Hass, R. Racial ambivalence and American value conflict: Correlational and priming studies of dual cognitive structures. *J. Pers. Soc. Psychol.* **55**, 893–905 (1988).

21. Katz, I., Glass, D.C., Lucido, D. & Farber, J. Harm-doing and victim's racial or orthopedic stigma as determinants of helping behavior. *J. Pers.* **47**, 340–364 (1979).

22. Snowden, F.M. *Before Color Prejudice: The Ancient View of Blacks* (Harvard University Press, 1983).

23. Allport, G.W. *The Nature of Prejudice* (Addison-Wesley, 1954).

24. Salès-Wuillemin, E. et al. Linguistic intergroup bias at school: An exploratory study of black and white children in France and their implicit attitudes toward one another. *Int. J. Intercult. Relations* **42**, 93–103 (2014).

25. Xiao, W. S. et al. Individuation training with other-race faces reduces preschoolers' implicit racial bias: a link between perceptual and social representation of faces in children. *Dev. Sci.* **18**, 655–663 (2015).

26. Baron, A.S. & Banaji, M.R. The development of implicit attitudes. *Psychol. Sci.* **17**, 53–58 (2006).

27. Hirschfeld, L.A. On a folk theory of society: Children, evolution and mental representations of social groups. *Personal. Soc. Psychol.* Rev. **5**, 107–117 (2001).

28. Nosek, B.A., Banaji, M. & Greenwald, A.G. Harvesting implicit group attitudes and beliefs from a demonstration website. *Gr. Dyn. Theory, Res. Pract.* **6**, 101–115 (2002).

Chapter 4

Unconscious race bias today: The evidence

Today, there can be no doubt that people who display blatant or extreme biases are doing so intentionally. Traditional attitude surveys provide good indicators of those people's opinions. Such people do not wish to have close relationships with other ethnic groups, and believe different ethnic groups cannot relate to each other or mingle easily. It is a dog-eat-dog world in which there are winners and losers, and they believe minority group members have taken 'their' jobs or jumped the queue for benefits. They feel resentment, frustration and aggression, and they will approve of racist political organisations. They perceive threats to their identity more than most people do, and they will seek to maintain the status quo with hostile acts.[1]

Most of us are not like that. Most of us are not overt racists. But we all have unconscious bias. Today's psychologists have a remarkable array of technology at their disposal, enabling them to perform many elegant (and occasionally devious) experiments. The most iconic technique is EEG (electroencephalography), which measures the brain's electrical activity via electrodes attached to the scalp. The toolkit also contains fMRI (functional magnetic resonance imaging) scanners, which measure brain activity based on the association between cerebral blood flow and neuronal activation.

Other tools have been developed to explore unconscious or implicit attitudes and associations. Using sophisticated software to present themed images and carefully designed analytics, researchers can identify the unconscious use of stereotypes. There are a number of related tools, the most widely researched and used of which is the implicit association test (IAT). We'll return to the IAT shortly – after we've considered a rather older, simpler and more widely applied device which has repeatedly identified discrimination in many countries: the CV.

The name on the form

The term 'curriculum vitae' ('course of life'), also known as a résumé, is believed to have first been used by Leonardo da Vinci, and has been with us for nearly 550 years. Updating and burnishing our CVs is an important part of career planning, and CVs remain the principal means by which organisations attempt to judge the suitability of candidates for jobs. Applicants use their CV to demonstrate that they have the qualities required to carry out a particular job role. But a CV can say so much more – through one small detail.

Economists and psychologists have long recognised the potential use of CVs to probe whether selectors change their decisions once they are made aware of the gender, race or other distinguishing personal characteristic of a candidate. Recruiters in all reputable organisations will reject, often passionately, the very idea that they may be acting with bias when using CVs, but research reveals the opposite is true.

The methodology is well established. Organisations are sent two CVs which are identical in all respects, apart from the name of the candidate. One application form has a name indicating that the applicant is a member of the majority (or dominant) community, while the other form has a name indicating they are a minority.

The BBC carried out such an experiment in 2017 for a news programme.[2] The researchers applied for 100 job vacancies, sending two applications for each post. The CVs were identical except for the names on them: one was from Mohamed, the other from Adam.

While Mohamed was called for an interview on four occasions, Adam's strike rate was three times better, at 12. The BBC conducted similar, but slightly more elaborate, research in 2004.[3] Then they used six identical application forms. Two forms were from 'Jenny Hughes' and 'John Andrew' – white names. Another two were in the names of 'Abu Olasemi' and 'Jinka Olatunde' – black-sounding applicants. The final two applicants had Muslim names – 'Fatima Khan' and 'Nasser Hanif'. The BBC team sent the forms to 15 employers and waited to see who was invited to an interview. Twenty-five per cent of employers asked the white candidates to come in for interviews – almost double the success rate of black candidates (13%) and nearly three times that of the Muslim candidates (9%).

Other research following this approach has found similar outcomes. A study carried out in the Boston and Chicago areas used, as the BBC study did, names that were suggestive of a black person (Aisha, Jamal, Hakim) and those suggestive of a white person (Emily, Neil, Todd).[4] The white applicants received approximately 50% more invitations for an interview than the black candidates (9.7% versus 6.5%). This outcome was the same regardless of occupation, industry and company size.

The study was noted for its careful design: résumés were adjusted to the job being applied for and the contents were varied to present a range of suitability levels. High-calibre candidates were given a longer work history, good qualifications, fewer gaps in their work history, and appropriate skills and certifications. The researchers replied to 1,300 job ads with four tailored responses from a high-quality African American applicant, a low-quality African American applicant, a high-quality white applicant and a low-quality white applicant. The results showed that, in order to receive the same invitations to interview (or call-back) as a white candidate, a black applicant required an astonishing eight years more experience. The researchers also found that the implicit attitudes relating to the perceived intelligence of black and white applicants correlated with the number of African Americans called back for interview.[4]

A study carried out in Milwaukee, Wisconsin, found that white applicants with a criminal record had a greater chance of being invited to interview than equally qualified African Americans without a criminal record. Fourteen per cent of African Americans were invited to interview, with this number falling to 5% of those with a criminal record. However, white applicants with a criminal record were invited back to interview on 17% of occasions – that is, over 20% more white applicants than their black counterparts who did not have a criminal record.[6]

But that's the UK and the USA, isn't it? They each have their own problems with regard to race, don't they? You would not expect the same results in a country more at ease with itself, one that is more liberal and open-minded. Like, say, Sweden or Canada. In fact, a large research project in Sweden found similar results.[5] Researchers compared CVs of candidates with Swedish and Muslim names. The candidates with Muslim names were about 50% less likely to be invited to an interview. Recruiters who held negative stereotypes about Arabs and Muslims – naturally – were more likely not to shortlist the Middle Eastern candidates.

A study in Canada compared call-back rates in the cities of Toronto, Montreal and Vancouver for applicants with Indian, Chinese and English-sounding names. The English-named applicants received 35% more call-backs.[7]

The culture of the candidates, as implied by their résumés, made a definite difference to their reception. Other research has shown that white candidates are more likely to be given the benefit of the doubt.[8] Where a candidate was either clearly suitable or unsuitable, the chances of selection for white and black candidates appeared very similar. But for applicants who fell in the grey area, being neither clearly deserving of acceptance or rejection, white candidates had a considerably greater chance of being selected than black applicants (76% versus 45%).

We might expect HR departments to be alert to this kind of wily and cost-effective experiment, given its repeated demonstration and stark results. However, the Swedish study, like the BBC survey, was rerun after 10 years – and produced the same outcome.

Rejecting a candidate on the basis of their name certainly seems crude and out of step with our belief that we have made progress in tackling racism. A now-familiar pattern emerges: overt racism is mutating into a subtler form that slips under the radar. The Swedish study showed that prejudiced recruiters were more likely to weight criteria differently in favour of white candidates, thereby using the apparently objective machinery of the hiring process to justify their own biases.

Researchers using eye-tracking techniques found significant differences in the way information about shortlisted candidates is processed by recruiters.[9] Those with higher implicit preferences for white people spend more time looking at the negative information about black applicants than the corresponding negative details about white applicants. The implicit bias of a recruiter triggers a search for a rational reason to reject the black candidate. This research therefore provides insight not just into implicit attitudes but also into implicit motivations. It seems we make, and act on, plans prompted by our biases, even though we may be unaware that we are doing so.

Measuring unconscious bias

There are various more sophisticated instruments and methods designed to measure our implicit or unconscious bias. Some of these measure physiological data, such as heart rate, skin reactions or the electrical activity of muscle tissue (electromyography), which shows which muscles are being used (e.g. those associated with smiling or frowning). Other approaches measure reaction times to various stimuli in order to determine the mental associations we make between a particular group and a set of characteristics. The best known of these is the IAT, briefly mentioned earlier. The computer-based IAT involves several tasks. Initially, the subject is asked to sort stimuli into one of two categories. This might be an image of the words 'black' and 'white' on either side of the screen, with a central word widely associated with one of the categories. In the next stage, subjects sort according to pairs of attributes rather than labels. The third task combines the first two – so the categories combine labels with attributes. Here, subjects are asked to sort the words and images into categories like 'White/Black' and 'Black/Good'. Further stages vary the pairings and their placement on the screen. In each case, the software records the subject's reaction times.

The theory behind the IAT and its variants is that our response times will be quicker and more accurate when the characteristics we are judging match more closely with

Figure 4.1. Screenshot from test at https://implicit.harvard.edu/implicit/education.html

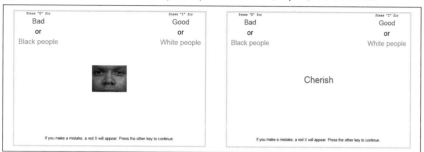

Screenshot from the Harvard Implicit Bias test at https://implicit.harvard.edu/implicit/education.html

our cognitive schemas. So, for example, people find it easier to associate the group labelled 'Elderly' with characteristics such as 'Slow'. The stimuli are presented so fast that conscious control and intervention are harder to apply. The reaction times therefore tell us whether we are making unconscious, or implicit, associations.

One of the first IAT studies showed that participants found it easier to associate black people with negative words and achievements than with positive ones.[10] Notably, the study showed that the results of the IAT did not agree with the attitudes expressed by explicit measures. This confirmed earlier studies, which revealed the same discrepancy between explicit and implicit measures of stereotyping black people, even among those who saw themselves as low-prejudiced individuals on the explicit measures.[11]

Other measures of implicit attitudes have been used to examine 'shooter bias' in police officers.[12,13] These tests reveal that police officers are more likely to assume that black people are armed, and therefore they will shoot them more often than they will shoot white people in similar circumstances. This is likely to occur even when the officers themselves do not hold explicit stereotypical views about black people. Their consciously held views therefore do not help to counteract their negative implicitly held stereotypes.[14] The tests also showed that officers shoot at *armed* white targets less frequently than they do at black targets. Their stereotyping actually puts officers in greater danger.

It's important to stress that implicit bias is a real and independent phenomenon. While we now see ourselves as more liberal, egalitarian and open-minded than we have ever been, our implicit attitudes are often directly at odds with our consciously held beliefs. As long ago as 1981, fewer than 15% of Americans could be described as being overtly racist.[15] Yet we continue to be aware of racial stereotypes, which can affect our perceptions, decisions and behaviour without our realising it. Modern forms of biased behaviour are more subtle than the overt racist acts of 50 years ago, and are more likely to emerge in actions which are less consciously controllable.

One study demonstrates this vividly.[16] Participants were asked to rate pictures of people on various dimensions, including their likeability. The results showed a pro-black bias – white subjects said they liked the black people more than the white ones. However, the participants were also connected to an electromyograph, which recorded muscular activity in their faces. These data showed that participants frowned more when shown a picture of a black person and smiled more when shown a photo of a white person – their non-verbal behaviour was an indicator of liking or disliking.

There are several under-the-radar reactions which can be measured to provide insights into our unconscious behaviours. These include the following:

- speech errors, which give an indication of nervousness

- eye contact, which tells us about trust, attraction and respect

- rates of blinking – more blinking is an indicator of tension

- the relevance of material discussed in a conversation

- the amount of time spent in conversation.[17]

None of us is immune; we are all prone to implicit biases regardless of our expressed attitudes to race. Unfortunately, since we can readily assess and adjust our conscious beliefs, it can be difficult to appreciate that we are biased at an unconscious level. We are proud of our rationality and convinced of its superiority: an overwhelming 97% of judges believe they are better than average at making unbiased decisions.[18] Research into the actual decisions judges make reveals distinct race bias.[19] This lack of self-reflection about bias – the lack of willingness to consider that racial bias is not just about other people, but about me – is one of the key obstacles to dealing with it.[20]

Implicit bias directly affects decisions and actions. Doctors with an implicit (but not explicit) pro-white bias:

- have considerably different interactions with patients

- believe black patients are less able to follow a medical regime, and think that they are experiencing less pain

- display greater verbal dominance with black patients and are significantly less patient-centred in their approach

- are less likely to recommend certain types of treatment for black patients.[21]

On the receiving end of the behaviour are patients. When faced with someone with a pro-white bias, black patients felt disrespected and had less confidence in the doctor.

We learn about racial stereotypes throughout our lives – from the people around us, the media, interactions with others, and our experiences. It's good that we are now consciously exploring their impact and challenging their meaning. But it's naïve to think we have somehow inoculated ourselves against their power. We seem to be telling ourselves that because we no longer consciously indulge such attitudes they have disappeared. The research reveals how – at a deeper, unconscious level – bias remains and continues to shape our world.

In patient–doctor interactions, for example, doctors with a pro-white bias felt they had dealt with black patients fairly and were liked by the patients. The patients themselves were less satisfied with the interactions. The self-belief of fairness acted as an impediment to the doctors' insight, awareness and openness to the very idea of bias.[22] In such contexts, doctors with a pro-white bias were more verbally dominant[23] while patients felt less respected and had less confidence in the doctor.[22]

Unconscious bias can quickly lead to self-fulfilling prophecies. If a doctor believes implicitly that their black patients are less easy to deal with, this could affect their non-verbal behaviour. The black patient notices this and responds in a negative way, thereby reinforcing the white person's view of the minority. Going beyond these automatic reactions and treating people as real, present individuals takes mental effort – and we will only put in this effort if we believe there is a problem in the first place. It's hard to recognise the cycle, let alone break it.

In the past, racist behaviour was designed to cause harm, whether physical, emotional or both. Today's racist behaviour is less likely to manifest as a desire to cause actual harm, but as a lack of willingness to help.

Dual processing theories and neuropsychology

The idea that we have two systems operating in parallel in our brains is not new. Throughout history, philosophers and scientists have theorised that people have different cognitive systems operating simultaneously. Typically, one system is seen as slow, effortful and accessible by us. The other system is fast, intuitive and not accessible.[24]

Plato suggested there were three elements to the soul: reason, spirit and appetite. Each element works in a different way and seeks to achieve different goals. Reason represents the best of us and seeks the truth. Spirit is about honour and winning, while appetite looks for superficial gratification and judges by appearance. When reason controls spirit and appetite uses judgement to achieve its goals, then harmony is achieved.[24]

Philosophers such as Aristotle, Aquinas, Descartes, Locke and Leibniz speculated widely and influentially on the workings of the human mind. Schopenhauer drew a distinction between the 'will of life' – our primitive impulses – and conscious intellect, representing the human condition as being like a strong blind man carrying a sighted lame man on his shoulders. The most famous proponent of parallel systems was Sigmund Freud, who developed a complex theory of conscious and unconscious systems. The latter, according to Freud, comprises repressed impulses and is the source of mental conflict.

Today our dual mental architecture is frequently referred to by the terms System 1 and System 2, as popularised by Daniel Kahneman and summarised in Table 4.1[24] below.

Table 4.1. The differences between System 1 and System 2.

System 1	System 2
Evolutionarily old	Evolutionarily recent
Unconscious, preconscious	Conscious
Shared with animals	Uniquely (distinctively) human
Implicit knowledge	Explicit knowledge
Automatic	Consulted
Fast	Slow
Parallel	Sequential
High-capacity	Low capacity
Intuitive	Reflective
Contextualised	Abstract
Pragmatic	Logical
Associative	Rule-based
Independence of general intelligence	Linked to general intelligence

But what's actually going on in the brain? fMRI technology helps us see how people make unconscious assessments of black and white people. Certain parts of the brain have been implicated in the process of prejudice and bias, namely the amygdala, the ventromedial prefrontal cortex (VmPFC) and the insular cortex. I will concentrate on research into the amygdala.

The amygdala is the part of the brain that reacts to fear and threat. When we receive ambiguous stimuli, this part of the brain is activated to help us decide whether to approach or avoid a situation. The amygdala is also involved in interpreting facial expressions, especially around the eyes. Research[25] has shown that this part of the brain showed greater activity in white participants when they were shown unfamiliar black faces rather than unfamiliar white faces. These faces clearly triggered a sense of threat. If the black faces were familiar, the pattern was less clear. People with high levels of anti-black implicit bias have also been found to have greater amygdala activity[26] under such circumstances, and the darker the skin tone, the greater the activity.[27]

As described in Chapter 2, many justifications were put forward to legitimise the slave trade. Africans were denigrated in any number of ways, including suggesting that they were less than human. Few people would openly endorse these views today, yet traces of these attitudes remain in our implicit attitudes. Our prejudices have found a way to survive without scrutiny. Researchers have combined different techniques to explore the subtleties of race prejudice. One example is the exposure of participants to rapid, subliminal priming images. So quickly are the images presented that the participants are not aware that they have seen them. The experiments explore how this brief exposure affects decision-making. Those primed with black faces are then presented with a new, out-of-focus image which gradually becomes clearer. Participants primed with black faces identified the out-of-focus image more quickly as being an image of apes. Those primed with white faces, or with no prime, took longer to make the identification.[28] Other researchers using fMRI technology have concluded that people with a strong anti-black implicit bias, compared to those with little or no bias, make different associations for black and white faces, representing the former as more animal-like than human.[29]

Conclusion

Humans have the ability to classify and categorise information, to reach conclusions quickly. The ways in which we classify and categorise are learned through our interactions with other people and by our absorption of the prevailing culture. According to psychologists Audrey and Brian Smedley, culture is 'external, acquired and transmissible to others'.[30 (p17)]

It's not the human brain that's at fault: it's the ideas, associations and stereotypes we acquire and pass on. We are predisposed to react, think and feel in ways that are deeply embedded. The concepts we associate with people did not exist until we created and perpetuated them – and now we are habituated to reacting in implicitly biased ways. But since we conditioned ourselves to think in these ways, we can think our way out of them – if we are sufficiently motivated to do so.

The evidence for unconscious bias reviewed in this chapter comes from a range of different sources, from the most sophisticated and expensive brain-scanning equipment at one end of the spectrum to the use of the humble CV at the other. The research shows that, whether we believe it or not, race bias – conscious or unconscious – has not gone. Unless we are prepared to acknowledge this fact, then it is going to be with us a lot longer.

The good news is that biases are malleable. Research into interventions shows that it's possible to change our biases once we are aware of them. Many different ways of reducing both implicit and explicit biases have been explored. However, before we can change our biases we need to challenge them, and this requires a willingness to engage with them, to own them, and to be open to new ways of examining our behaviour, thoughts and feelings.

Finally, I think it is worthwhile to reflect for a moment not just on what the research is telling us, but who the participants in some cases were: judges and doctors. These are highly skilled, highly trained, well-educated people. These are people who, in the main, are working in a profession they have chosen – one which provides them with not just a good living but also social standing. They are motivated to do the best for the people who come to them for assistance. Despite all this, racial bias can be detected in their decision-making as well as their interactions.

If they are biased, then why not you? Or me? It is grossly arrogant to assume that we may not be susceptible to race bias. It is complacent to believe that racial prejudice is not our problem. It is naïve, bordering on stupid, to suggest that racism is not present in society today. Indifference to these issues is the precondition for the perpetuation of racism.

1. Fiske, S.T. What we know now about bias and intergroup conflict, the problem of the century. *Curr. Dir.* Psychol. Sci. **11**, 123–128 (2002).

2. Adesina, Z. & Marocico, O. Is it easier to get a job if you're Adam or Mohamed? BBC News. Available at: http://www.bbc.co.uk/news/uk-england-london-38751307 (accessed 21 September 2017).

3. Grint, K. *The Sociology of Work* (Polity Press, 2005).

4. Bertrand, M. et al. Implicit discrimination. *Am. Econ.* Rev. **95**, 94–98 (2005).

5. Carlsson, M. & Rooth, D.-O. Evidence of ethnic discrimination in the Swedish labor market using experimental data. *Labour Econ.* **14**, 716–729 (2007).

6. Pager, D. The mark of a criminal record. *Am. J. Sociol.* **103**, 937–975 (2003).

7. The Conference Board of Canada. Racial wage gap – society provincial rankings – how Canada performs. Available at: http://www.conferenceboard.ca/hcp/provincial/society/racial-gap.aspx (accessed 21 September 2017).

8. Dovidio, J.F., Gaertner, S.L., Nier, J.A., Kawakami, K. & Hodson, G. Contemporary racial bias: when good people do bad things. In *The Social Psychology of Good and Evil* (ed. A.G. Miller) (Guilford Press, 2004).

9. Beattie, G. *Our Racist Heart? An Exploration of Unconscious Prejudice in Everyday Life* (Routledge, 2013).

10. Greenwald, A.G., McGhee, D.E. & Schwartz, J.L. Measuring individual differences in implicit cognition: the implicit association test. *J. Pers. Soc. Psychol.* **74**, 1464–1480 (1998).

11. Devine, P.G. Stereotypes and prejudice: Their automatic and controlled components. *J. Pers. Soc. Psychol.* **56**, 5–18 (1989).

12. Correll, J., Park, B., Judd, C.M. & Wittenbrink, B. The police officer's dilemma: Using ethnicity to disambiguate potentially threatening individuals. *J. Pers. Soc. Psychol.* **83**, 1314–1329 (2002).

13. Payne, B.K. Weapon bias: Split-second decisions and unintended stereotyping. *Curr. Dir. Psychol. Sci.* **15**, 287–291 (2006).

14. Graham, S. & Lowery, B.S. Priming unconscious racial stereotypes about adolescent offenders. *Law Hum. Behav.* **28**, 483–504 (2004).

15. Sue, D.W. *Microaggressions in Everyday Life: Race, Gender and Sexual Orientation* (John Wiley & Sons, 2010).

16. Vanman, E.J., Paul, B.Y., Ito, T.A. & Miller, N. The modern face of prejudice and structural features that moderate the effect of cooperation on affect. *J. Pers. Soc. Psychol.* **73**, 941–959 (1997).

17. Brown, R. *Prejudice: Its Social Psychology* (Blackwell, 1995).

18. Rachlinski, J.J., Johnson, S.L., Wistrich, A.J. & Guthrie, C. Does unconscious racial bias affect trial judges? *Notre Dame Law Rev.* **84**, 1195–1246 (2009).

19. Lammy, D. The Lammy Review: An independent review into the treatment of, and outcomes for, Black, Asian and Minority Ethnic individuals in the Criminal Justice System (https://www.gov.uk/government/publications/lammy-review-final-report).

20. Kang, J. Communications law: Bits of bias in *Implicit Racial Bias across the Law* (eds J.D. Levinson & R.J. Smith), pp.132–145 (Cambridge University Press, 2012).

21. Staats, C., Patton, C., Rogers, C. & Rudd, T. State of the science: Implicit bias review. *Kirwan Inst. Study Race Ethn.* **4**; pp 17–26 (2013).

22. Cooper, L. A. et al. The associations of clinicians' implicit attitudes about race with medical visit communication and patient ratings of interpersonal care. *Am. J. Public Health* **102**, 979–987 (2012).

23. Johnson, R.L., Roter, D., Powe, N.R. & Cooper, L.A. Patient race/ethnicity and quality of patient–physician communication during medical visits. *Am. J. Public Health* **94**, 2084–2090 (2004).

24. Evans, J.S.B.T. & Frankish, K. The duality of mind: An historical perspective in *In Two Minds: Dual Processes and Beyond* (eds J.S.B.T. Evans & K. Frankish) (Oxford University Press, 2009).

25. Phelps, E.A. *et al.* Performance on indirect measures of race evaluation predicts amygdala activation. *J. Cogn. Neurosci.* **12**, 729–738 (2000).

26. Cunningham, W.A. *et al.* Separable neural components in the processing of black and white faces. *Psychol. Sci.* **15**, 806–813 (2004).

27. Ronquillo, J. et al. The effects of skin tone on race-related amygdala activity: An fMRI investigation. *Soc. Cogn. Affect. Neurosci.* **2**, 39–44 (2007).

28. Goff, P.A., Eberhardt, J.L., Williams, M.J. & Jackson, M.C. Not yet human: implicit knowledge, historical dehumanization and contemporary consequences. *J. Personal. Soc. Psychol.* **94**, 292–306 (2008).

29. Brosch, T., Bar-David, E. & Phelps, E. A. Implicit race bias decreases the similarity of neural representations of Black and White faces. *Psychol. Sci.* **24**, 160–166 (2013).

30. Smedley, A. & Smedley, B.D. Race as biology is fiction, racism as a social problem is real: Anthropological and historical perspectives on the social construction of race. *Am. Psychol.* **60**, 16–26 (2005).

Chapter 5

The power of stereotypes

Stereotyping is the process of judging a person based on our perceptions of the group to which we believe they belong. Instead of seeing someone as a unique individual with their own personality, abilities and motivations, we view them as an example of the group.

Stereotypes are cognitive shortcuts. We take such shortcuts all the time, creating heuristic processes, or rules of thumb, by which we live our lives. Stereotypes are a form of cognitive selection based on our experiences, whether these events have occurred to us personally or are second-hand beliefs derived from others.[1] They guide the decisions we make about people, speed up the way we deal with the world, help us to make rapid decisions, and don't take up too much time or energy.

Stereotypes are easy to access, convenient to deploy and rapid in operation – what's not to like? Unfortunately, they are invariably wrong.

The apparent truth

We might like to think that stereotypes often have a germ of truth in them, and we can always find someone who conforms to a stereotype if we look hard enough. Such is the power of stereotyping that people frequently claim that stereotypes are true. In these cases, what we really mean is that stereotypes *seem* true to us – and we want to carry on using them, undisturbed by conscience and without feeling any need to question their validity. At the same time, we don't appreciate others stereotyping us, particularly when the stereotypes are negative. I met someone recently who was almost asking my permission to continue using stereotypes as he found them true and, consequently, helpful. I replied that I did not have the power to stop him but that, to be consistent about this, and to ensure he was not a hypocrite, he would also have to accept being stereotyped by others. As he was German, there were some stereotypes that he might find acceptable, but there were also some very negative ones that he would find problematic applied to himself.

The stereotypes we hold are important in the workplace because they affect the way we view people from different groups, the way we interact with one another, and the decisions we make. All of these facets of working life can be affected by our perceptions of the racial group to which we believe a person belongs.

The genesis of racial stereotypes

It is sobering and heartening to learn that we have not always carried the racial stereotypes we knowingly – or unknowingly – associate with different groups. And this reveals another paradox about stereotypes: even though we think stereotypes describe fixed attributes of a group, they are themselves malleable.

As we saw in Chapter 2, people in Ancient Greece and Rome noticed colour but did not expect a person's skin tone to communicate anything about their character.[2] The white view of black people was neither wholly positive nor wholly negative. In many instances, being black had positive associations.

Classical writers such as Pliny and Solinus praised the qualities of the Africans with whom they came into contact, noting their wisdom as well as their fame and power.[3] Herodotus tells the story of a white woman who tried to convince people around her that she was, in fact, black and a member of royalty from Ethiopia. In this story the powerful group was black, with white people seen as lower in prestige and status.[4]

By the seventeenth century, however, slavery was becoming associated with being black. In seeking to define and distinguish civilised society from the barbarian, Europeans made themselves the exemplars of civilisation. Colour was an easy way of differentiating between Europeans and non-Europeans, and so dark skin acquired negative associations. The genesis of stereotypes about black people was forensically examined by historian Kate Lowe:[5]

- The stereotype associating black skin with criminality originated with attitudes towards slaves who attempted to escape captivity. If they were caught they were branded on the cheek – a highly visible scar denoting their criminal character.

- Genuine cultural differences were interpreted as further indications of an African's stereotypical character. For example, laughter was frowned upon among the leaders of European thought. According to Erasmus, 'Only fools laugh at everything that is said and done ... The burst of laughter, the immoderate laugh which shakes the whole body ... is indecorous at any age, especially in childhood.'

- The 'laughing black' stereotype marked someone who was not only immodest, but also too stupid to recognise the degradation of their status as a slave.

- Lack of access to formal education and subsequent illiteracy only added to the stereotype of lower intelligence among black people, who were only worthy of carrying out the most menial tasks.

- Africans were also seen as inhabitants of an 'Edenic' land where they were able to get everything they needed to live on without the need to work hard.

- Societal rules regarding interactions between European men and women restricted contact between them. The rules did not apply to African female slaves, who were then vulnerable to being preyed upon by their white male owners. As a result, African women were seen as promiscuous and unable to control their sexual urges.

But Africans were still recognised for their physical courage and prowess. They were also allowed to be musicians and dancers. However, these concessions were regarded simply as manifestations of black people's uncontrollable passions, rather than skills to be admired.

Anthropologists and historians have carried out similar analyses of stereotypes of the native peoples of, for example, North America,[6] South America[7] and Australia.[8] The combination of having dark skin, not being Christian and not meeting the criteria of a 'civilised' society led to the conclusion that people from these lands were inferior to white Europeans, and so their land deserved to be taken.

The belief that people with white skin were superior to those with black skin came to influence, at a more abstract level, the associations made with the colours themselves. The colour white was linked to the desirable qualities of beauty, intellect and reliability, while black was associated with evil and depravity.[5]

Stereotypes today
Distrusting stereotypes – while clinging to them
Stereotypes come in two flavours: positive and negative. Both varieties are equally seductive and similarly toxic. They are also very loosely defined: in order to gain the speed and sense of effortlessness that stereotypes provide, we must sacrifice accuracy.

Stereotypes show consensus and contrast. Every successful stereotype is widely shared by its users and its validity is unquestioned. Characteristics appear to be meaningfully clustered, and the elements are over-generalised to ensure that as many people as possible can fit into one category. Meanwhile, the characteristics of the stereotyped group help to contrast it with other groups. This provides the basis for the formation of group hierarchies.

Although we may not consciously endorse these stereotypes today, they remain part of us; they are, to use the description of Edwin Burnett Tylor, the founder of cultural anthropology, 'survivals'.[9 (p10)] The impact of these stereotypes is still present even though outwardly we no longer openly endorse them.

One of the first studies to examine stereotypes was carried out in 1933 by psychologists Katz and Braly.[10] They gave 100 students a number of characteristics to choose from and asked them to select the five that were most applicable to different groups of people. White Americans were viewed the most favourably, being described as industrious, intelligent, materialistic, ambitious and progressive. African Americans were labelled as superstitious, lazy, happy-go-lucky, ignorant and musical. Jewish people were held to be shrewd, mercenary, inclusive, grasping and intelligent. And the Japanese were seen as intelligent, industrious, progressive, shrewd and sly. These descriptions are both wearisome and instantly recognisable.

Few of the students in the study had come into contact with people from many of these groups, yet they were remarkably consistent in their views. For example, Turkish people were seen as very religious, cruel and treacherous, despite the subjects only having a nodding acquaintance with Turkey or its people.

More recent research has demonstrated that people are less willing to express such stereotypical beliefs than they used to be. As we have seen, there has been a noticeable decline in the number of people associating negative stereotypes with minorities, as measured by explicit attitudes probed in the Bogardus social distance scale,[11] for example. But is this a real change? Or do people just hold back from expressing their true attitudes in an attempt to create a positive impression with researchers?

In one experiment, participants were elaborately hooked up to an impressive piece of machinery which they were told could measure their true feelings. A control group had no such constraints and were free to respond to the researchers in any way they wished. The participants attached to the truth-o-meter were asked to predict how the machine would respond. The researchers found that those attached to the machine revealed more stereotypical views than the control group.[12]

This study was conducted in 1971, showing that even over 40 years ago people were beginning to be wary of expressing stereotypical opinions about minorities. Since then, more sophisticated research techniques have been created, using the latest technology to help us understand how stereotypes have persisted.

One of the first studies to reveal the persistence of stereotyping was published in 1983. This study revealed how participants were able to link more positive attitudes more quickly to white people. Stereotypes were still present and operative, but they were more subtle. The stereotypes were not openly expressed, but a level of unconscious association was revealed.[13]

Research shows that while we now believe that anyone can be talented, white people are more likely to apply the more positive, achievement-related characteristics to themselves. No sharp distinctions are made; anyone can have these abilities. The distinctions we make today are those of degree, rather than being categorical. Nevertheless, white people are seen as being in a superior position.[14] In one study, participants were shown a number of pictures of black individuals. Then participants were provided with words that were either stereotypical of black people (for example, 'athletic') or counter-stereotypical ('educated') and asked to link them to the pictures they had seen. Participants chose a lighter-toned face when primed with counter-stereotypical words. Unconsciously, adjectives that were counter-stereotypical for black people (e.g. educated) were associated with paler faces. Intriguingly the researchers also found a 'skin tone memory bias'[(p7)] such that when asked to recollect an educated black man, participants made the person's face lighter.[15]

Today, people often express very positive attitudes about minorities when asked for their views. But the increasingly sophisticated research tools and methods reveal that stereotypes are fit, healthy and in no danger of extinction. They have mutated, becoming less recognisable but no less noxious.

Thinking and feeling

Stereotypes have a cognitive component and an affective, or emotional, component.[16] The cognitive aspect refers to the generalisations made about a group. The affective aspect has only been recognised more recently[17] and relates to the feelings – positive and negative – that are associated with any given group.

Researchers have also paid more attention to the affective or emotional dimension of stereotyping, most notably in the stereotype content model (SCM).[18] This model reveals the emotional aspects of a stereotype, such as competence and warmth. The factors examined by the model also include the perceived status of the group and perceived competition with the in-group. Competence refers to educational and economic success; warmth refers to the extent to which they are communal in their behaviour (that is, caring, sensitive, empathetic). Higher status predicts greater competence, while warmth is linked to lower competition with the in-group.[18]

Table 5.1 shows the feelings that are associated with the combinations of warmth and competence, and where different groups can be placed on this map (Cuddy et al. 2009).[19]

Warmth		Prejudiced	Admiration
	High	Pity, sympathy	Pride, admiration
		Disabled people, Elderly	Middle-class people
	Low	Contemptuous Prejudice	Envy, prejudice
		Contempt, disgust, Poor people, drug addicts	Envy, jealousy, Asian, feminists
		Low	High

Competence

- High competence–high warmth is associated with admiration. The groups in this category are seen as successful and they are seen as competing for resources.

- High competence–low warmth is associated with envy. Asians, Jews and feminists are in this category. On the one hand, they have high status as they are seen as educationally and economically successful. On the other, they are nevertheless seen as competing for university places and jobs. While the stereotypes about capabilities are positive, these are given a negative spin because possession of these capabilities is seen as a threat by the majority. This has implications for the progression and promotion of people from these groups – as we will see in Chapter 11.

- Low competence–high warmth. Here the groups are viewed as incompetent, and not a source of competition. Disabled people and elderly people are stereotyped in this way. Such groups are pitied and garner sympathy.

- Low competence–low warmth is associated with poor people and drug addicts. Here the feelings are contempt.

Stereotyping is not, if you'll pardon the expression, a black-and-white issue. While stereotyping is simplistic, it is also subtle. For example, poor white people may be despised and black professionals may be admired and envied. The model shows that stereotypes are not necessarily all positive or negative for any given group – they are often a mixture of both. For some minorities, positive attributes can nevertheless generate negative emotions.

We also need to recognise, however, that race is only one characteristic – we also stereotype in other ways, most notably on gender. Interactions between racial stereotypes and gender stereotypes are often ignored in books about gender and race, but I wish to explore them now.

Race and gender: clashing and overlapping stereotypes

Much research assumes that the stereotypes associated with each group apply to all individuals who belong to that group: gender stereotypes apply to all women, regardless of their race, and racial stereotypes apply to all ethnic minorities, regardless of their gender. Many organisations, and the diversity professionals within them, take a similar approach to diversity.

Establishing stereotypes for those with intersecting identities is not simply a case of adding together the stereotypes from the groups to which they belong. If it were, the stereotypes for black women, for example, would be warm, caring and sensitive (female gender stereotypes) and strong, hostile and aggressive (black racial stereotypes). This is a contradictory set of descriptions.[20]

Instead, women from ethnic minority groups have unique stereotypes associated with their dual identities. In fact, there is little overlap between female stereotypes generally and stereotypes of women from ethnic minority groups. There is also little overlap between the stereotypes of ethnic minority women and their racial group. In their research, Negin Ghavami and Letitia Anne Peplau asked participants to list ten attributes they associated with men and women from white, black, Middle Eastern, American and Latina racial groups. From these lists they generated the top 15 stereotypes associated with each group.[20]

Table 5.2: Numbers of unique and overlapping stereotypes for men and women from different racial groups out of the top 15 traits listed (taken from Ghavami and Peplau, 2012).

Racial group	Gender	No. of unique stereotypes	No. of traits that overlap with stereotypes of their racial group	No. of traits that overlap with stereotypes of their gender group
White	Men	3	10	6
	Women	2	8	6
Black	Men	4	11	1
	Women	10	5	0
Middle Eastern American	Men	3	11	2
	Women	7	4	4
Asian American	Men	5	10	1
	Women	4	9	3
Latina	Men	4	9	3
	Women	7	7	1

They found that, when compared to the stereotypes for their gender, white men and white women have the fewest unique stereotypes. To put it another way, the stereotype list for a 'man' was pretty much the same as that for a 'white man'. The same was true for a 'woman', whose stereotype list matched that for 'white woman'. This supports the view that for race *and* gender, white is seen as the norm group.

Ethnic minority men had the fewest unique stereotypes with 'man', but had a big overlap with the stereotypes of their racial group. Ethnic minority women, on the other hand, had the least overlap with the stereotypes of both 'women' and their racial group. In other words, minority women had the highest number of unique traits associated with their dual identities.

One immediate consequence of this is that when we talk about stereotypes of 'men' and 'women' we are actually describing the associations with 'white' men and women. Furthermore, when we talk about the stereotypes for a particular ethnic group we are more than likely describing the perception of the *men* from those groups, rather than women.

The pattern for Asian Americans, however, was somewhat different. The overall 'Asian American' list of characteristics was more stereotypically female in orientation. While men and women had a similar number of unique stereotypes, both also had a high number of traits that overlapped with the overall stereotypes of Asian American – which means that Asian American men are seen as more feminine than men of other ethnic groups. This observation is supported by the fact that Asian men had less overlap with the stereotypes of 'men' than Asian women did with the stereotype of 'women'.

So people with multiple minority identities have unique sets of stereotypes attached to these combined identities.[20,21]

Looking at the stereotypes associated with white, black and Asian women, research has shown that white women are typically described as communal, warm, kind, caring and sensitive, which has considerable overlap with the overall stereotypes associated with women. The traits associated with Asian women are competent, intelligent, quiet, reserved, shy and subservient. The stereotypes associated with black women include angry, loud, boisterous, strong and dominant.

Table 5.3: Stereotypes of women from different racial groups.[21,22]

White women	Black women	Asian women
Communal	Angry	Competent
Warm	Religious	Intelligent
Kind	Tough	Quiet
Caring	Loud	Reserved
Sensitive	Boisterous	Shy
Educated	Strong	Subservient
	Dominant	Mild-tempered
	Confident	Strong work ethic
	Assertive	Family-oriented
	Hostile	
	Unintelligent	

It is striking that the stereotypes for black women have least in common with traditional feminine stereotypes. In particular, the 'warmth' traits typically associated with women are lacking. In times of slavery, black women were perceived as strong, mule-like animals who were as capable of doing field work as black men. At the same time, (white) women were seen as the weaker sex. As a consequence, the stereotypes associated with black women are often masculine. Indeed some research has found that black men and women were rated as more masculine than white women and white men.[23]

There are important implications that flow from these perceptions because groups stereotyped as lacking warmth are more likely to experience harassment and discrimination.[24] However, since black women are seen as tough, strong and assertive then it is possible that any problems they encounter, such as discrimination and harassment at work, may be minimised because they will be seen as the group that is best equipped to deal with them – or they may even be blamed for causing the problems in the first place by being hostile.[21] This kind of circular reasoning is the hallmark of stereotyping.

It is difficult to obtain data directly from organisations on sensitive topics like this, but we can look at the treatment of public figures. Amnesty examined abusive tweets mentioning any of the 177 female MPs in the British parliament in the run-up to the 2017 general election. Of the million tweets they looked at, the 20 BAME (black and minority ethnic) women, despite making up only 11% of the sample, were the targets of abuse on over 40% of occasions. One MP, Diane Abbott, a long-standing, senior member of the Labour Party, was the target of 32% of the abuse aimed at

Photo of Right Honorable Diane Abbott MP
© Twocoms / Shutterstock.com

BAME women. Even with her extraordinary figures excluded, the total was still 35% for the other 19 women.[25]

The mix of traits in combination means that the same behaviour exhibited by a white woman and a black woman will be interpreted differently. For example, a white woman who is demonstrating and emphasising a point because she feels strongly about it could be seen as emotional. This behaviour is likely to be interpreted more negatively than if a white male were to act in the same way. However, views of the white woman will also be moderated by the fact that she will be seen as caring and sensitive. A black woman, on the other hand, will be viewed as loud, angry and tough. The white woman is more likely to be perceived as weak, which will lead to helping behaviours from the perceiver, whereas the black woman is likely to be perceived as threatening and hostile, and as a consequence may be avoided by others.[21] People will, I am sure, deny that they think in these ways, but black women are well aware of being stereotyped. In her book *Why I Am No Longer Talking to White People about Race*, the journalist Reni Eddo-Lodge says: 'I used to be scared of being perceived as an angry black woman. But I soon realised that any number of authentic emotions I displayed could and would be interpreted as anger. My assertiveness, passion and excitement could all be wielded against me.'[26] (p186)

Furthermore, the reasons behind perceived discrimination are also likely to vary as a function of how salient gender or race is in a given situation. When gender is made prominent, Asian women are more likely to perceive that discrimination stems from their being women, whereas when race is made salient they will see the cause of discrimination due to the fact that they are Asian.[27]

Stereotype threat

In order to communicate more effectively, we try to understand what others may be thinking and we anticipate what someone else is going to say and do. Such is the power of stereotypes that they do not only affect the feelings, perceptions and behaviours of those doing the stereotyping, but also those who are being stereotyped. Known as stereotype threat, this phenomenon was first identified by social psychologists Claude Steele and Joshua Aronson in 1995.[28] Their research revealed that our assessment of what other people think of us impacts not just our performance but our feelings and thoughts. They found that the test performance of black students can be affected by how the test is described and introduced to those taking the test.

When people are made aware of the negative stereotypes associated with the group to which they belong, the feeling that they might perform according to the stereotype creates an extra demand, which leads to impaired performance. The stereotypes about black people, as we have seen, include descriptions of their intellectual inferiority. When given the test, some students were told that the test was a measure of their intellect, and some were not. In the latter condition, when the threat was not present, black students performed considerably better than they did when it was present. The description of the purpose and function of the test made no difference to the performance of white students.

Stereotype threat shows that our environment and the expectations we believe others have of us can impair our performance. This effect does not just impact on race – studies have also shown stereotype threat associated with gender. As an anecdotal example, my wife, who is an excellent psychologist and an excellent driver, relishes the challenge of parking in a space I'll judge to be too small. But give her an audience of men, and she has been known to suddenly transform into the world's worst parker. The knowledge that others hold a stereotype about women as drivers in general, and their skill at parking in particular, negatively impacts her performance.

Sociologists have demonstrated the great power of stereotype threat by inventing status hierarchies and observing the same effects. In one study participants were told that left-handed or right-handed people were superior performers of the task they were about to carry out. 'Handedness' was further emphasised by asking them to put a brightly coloured band on their preferred wrist. Their subsequent performance matched the expectations set.[29]

The strength and versatility of stereotype threat brings a new dimension to the age-old nature/nurture debate. We are used to thinking of environmental factors as physical and, when we acknowledge the existence of environmental social factors, assuming these factors are stable and obvious. Stereotype threat is an environmental factor that negatively impacts people's performance because the 'fear of stereotype confirmation can hijack the cognitive systems required for optimal performance.'[30(p6)]

No one is immune from stereotype threat. For example, when they were told that the purpose of the study was to demonstrate how Asian people were superior at maths, white men taking a maths test recorded lower scores than Asians and other white men who performed with no threat present.[31]

Research into stereotype threat has been carried out in different countries, with different groups, and has examined different tasks.[30] Its effects can continue long after and independent of the inciting incident. Those experiencing stereotype threat feel:

- they are not being assessed by their own actions

- more harshly judged

- a sense of lower status

- others' judgements leave a permanent mark.[32]

The power of stereotype threat is strongest when people are in situations which:

- are important and have meaning to them (i.e. performance on a task taps into an aspect of our individuality, character and self-view)

- people are expecting to encounter stereotyping

- they are told that an ability being assessed is fixed and static – an indicator of absolute competence – rather than something that can be developed.[32]

For example, imagine a candidate has to take a test to get a job they really want. If the test is introduced as a measure of fixed intelligence, and where the test contains questions unrelated to anything in the application process so far, stereotype threat will be at its strongest.[32]

Although stereotype threat is universal, individuals respond to it in different ways.[33] Some people react in ways that appear to 'prove' the substance of the stereotype, while others see the threat as a challenge: they will seek to prove the stereotype wrong. But even in these situations, awareness of the stereotypes is present and is affecting the thoughts, emotions and actions of the person being stereotyped. The person is actively trying to behave in ways which are counter-stereotypical and self-conscious, and so they cannot be themselves.[30] Knowing the stereotypes that exist about any group to which we belong can, then, lead us to wonder if the person we are interacting with is viewing *us* in a stereotypical way. At the minimum, this introduces doubt into encounters and may divert attention away from the objective matter at hand.

Conclusion

Stereotypes about racial groups may be less obviously expressed than they were in the past. However, this is not because they have disappeared, but because we are more uncomfortable about sharing them in public. Stereotypes are not uniformly bad or good. Instead they are a combination of positive and negative qualities, which differ according to the group under discussion. Yet even when a minority is viewed positively in terms of its competence, stereotypes can generate feelings of envy and hostility because the minority's success is seen as a competitive threat.

In addition, too often in research studies (as well as in diversity practice in organisations) the complexity of identity is overlooked. Organisations look for a simple solution – the 'silver bullet' that will magically transform their diversity statistics. Many organisations have formulated diversity strategies that focus on gender. Some diversity practitioners take the view that gender is the most important dimension organisations need to consider, and that by improving the representation of women at senior levels, progress will also have been made on other aspects of diversity. Research shows not only that stereotypes differ by racial groups but that the distinctions are even more fine grained: we have stereotypes based on race and gender. A typical diversity strategy will adopt the strapline 'Men and women are equal, but different'. As a strategy it is monumentally stupid, based on and perpetuating the stereotypes it should be challenging. But it is worse than that: the stereotypes that such a strategy is based on are those for white men and women. In other words, race has been airbrushed out of the discussion on gender.

So, as fine as a gender diversity strategy like this may sound, it is yet another example of a 'colour-blind' approach, which ill serves minority women.

Stereotypes are known not just by those doing the stereotyping but by those being stereotyped, and this awareness affects them because, in trying to not conform to the perception, they place themselves under extra pressure. This in turn diverts energy and attention from any given task and is more likely to lead to underperformance, which in turn will reinforce the views of those who believe the stereotyping.

Whilst stereotype threat has the potential to be activated in relevant circumstances, we must also recognise that, in real-life situations, the threat is not always triggered. Stereotype threat has devastating power when it is triggered, but its operation is not inevitable.

1. Arnold, J. & Randall, R. *Work Psychology: Understanding Human Behaviour in the Workplace* (Pearson Education, 2010).

2. Shavit, Y. *History in Black: African-Americans in Search of an Ancient Past* (Routledge, 2013).

3. Snowden, F.M. *Before Color Prejudice: The Ancient View of Blacks* (Harvard University Press, 1983).

4. Onyeka. *Blackamoores: Africans in Tudor England, their Presence, Status and Origins* (Narrative Eye, 2013).

5. Lowe, K. The stereotyping of Black Africans in Renaissance Europe in *Black Africans in Renaissance Europe* (eds T. Earle. & K. Lowe) (Cambridge University Press, 2010).

6. Fleming, W.C. Myths and stereotypes about Native Americans. *Phi Delta Kappan* **88**, 213–217 (2006).

7. Grote, R. The Status and Rights of Indigenous Peoples in Latin America., Max-Planck-Institut für ausländisches öffentliches Recht und Völkerrecht (1999).

8. Bodkin-Andrews, G., O'Rourke, V., Grant, R., Denson, N. & Craven, R.G. Validating racism and cultural respect: Testing the psychometric properties and educational impact of perceived discrimination and multiculturation for Indigenous and non-Indigenous students. *Educ. Res. Eval.* **16**, 471–493 (2010).

9. Tylor, E.B. *Primitive Culture* (Harper & Row, 1958. Original work published 1871).

10. Katz, D. & Braly, K. Racial stereotypes of one hundred college students. *J. Abnorm. Soc. Psychol.* **28**, 280–290 (1933).

11. Bogardus, E.S. A social distance scale. *Sociol. Soc. Res.* **17**, 265–271 (1933).

12. Sigall, H. & Page, R. Current stereotypes: A little fading, a little faking. *J. Pers. Soc. Psychol.* **18**, 247–255 (1971).

13. Gaertner, S.L. & McLaughlin, J.P. Racial stereotypes: Associations and ascriptions of positive and negative characteristics. *Soc. Psychol. Q.* **46**, 23–30 (1983).

14. Jackman, M.R. *The Velvet Glove: Paternalism and Conflict in Gender, Class and Race Relations* (University of California Press, 1994).

15. Ben-Zeev, A., Dennehy, T.C., Goodrich, R.I., Kolarik, B.S. & Geisler, M.W. When an 'educated' black man becomes lighter in the mind's eye: Evidence for a skin tone memory bias. *SAGE Open* **4**, 1–9 (2014).

16. Firat, R.B. *Apathetic Racism Theory: A Neurosociological Study of how Moral Emotions Perpetuate Inequality* (The University of Iowa, 2013).

17. Fiske, S.T. Stereotyping, prejudice and discrimination in *Handbook of Social Psychology, Vol. 2* (eds D.T. Gilbert, S.T. Fiske & G. Lindzey) (McGraw-Hill, 1998).

18. Fiske, S.T., Cuddy, A.J.C., Glick, P. & Xu, J. A model of (often mixed) stereotype content: Competence and warmth respectively follow from perceived status and competition. *J. Pers. Soc. Psychol.* **82**, 878–902 (2002).

19. Cuddy, A.J.C. et al. Stereotype content model across cultures: Towards universal similarities and some differences. *Br. J. Soc. Psychol.* **48**, 1–33 (2009).

20. Ghavami, N. & Peplau, L.A. An intersectional analysis of gender and ethnic stereotypes: Testing three hypotheses. *Psychol. Women* Q. **37**, 113–127 (2012).

21. Donovan, R.A. Tough or tender: (Dis)similarities in White college students' perceptions of Black and White women. *Psychol. Women* Q. **35**, 458–468 (2011).

22. Rosette, A.S., Koval, C.Z., Ma, A. & Livingston, R. Race matters for women leaders: Intersectional effects on agentic deficiencies and penalties. *Leadersh. Q.* **27**, 429–445 (2016).

23. Goff, P.A., Eberhardt, J.L., Williams, M.J. & Jackson, M.C. Not yet human: implicit knowledge, historical dehumanization and contemporary consequences. *J. Personal. Soc. Psychol.* **94**, 292–306 (2008).

24. Cuddy, A.J.C., Fiske, S.T. & Glick, P. The BIAS map: Behaviors from intergroup affect and stereotypes. *J. Pers. Soc. Psychol.* **92**, 631–648 (2007).

25. Amnesty International UK. Black and Asian women MPs abused more online. Available at: https://www.amnesty.org.uk/online-violence-women-mps (accessed 11 October 2017).

26. Eddo-Lodge, R. *Why I'm No Longer Talking To White People About Race* (Bloomsbury Circus, 2017).

27. Remedios, J.D., Chasteen, A.L. & Paek, J.D. Not all prejudices are experienced equally: Comparing experiences of racism and sexism in female minorities. *Gr. Process. Intergr. Relations* **15**, 273–287 (2012).

28. Steele, C.M. & Aronson, J. Stereotype threat and the intellectual test performance of African Americans. *J. Pers. Soc. Psychol.* **69**, 797–811 (1995).

29. Lovaglia, M.J. et al. Status processes and mental ability test scores. *Am. J. Sociol.* **104**, 195–228 (1998).

30. Inzlicht, M. & Schmader, T. *Stereotype Threat: Theory, Process and Application* (Oxford University Press, 2012).

31. Aronson, J. *et al*. When White men can't do math: Necessary and sufficient factors in stereotype threat. *J. Exp. Soc. Psychol.* **35**, 29–46 (1999).

32. Steele, C.M. A threat in the air: How stereotypes shape intellectual identity and performance. *Am. Psychol.* **52**, 613–629 (1997).

33. Sackett, P.R. & Ryan, A.M. Concerns about generalizing stereotype threat research findings to operational high-stakes testing in *Stereotype Threat: Theory, Process, and Application* (eds M. Inzlicht & T. Schmader), pp. 259–263 (Oxford University Press, 2011).

Chapter 6

Race and gender: Intersections, interactions and inclusion

When identities combine – and collide

'Intersectionality! Boo! Are you scared yet?'[1] So begins one magazine article, responding to recent debates about this seemingly provocative topic. Helen Lewis playfully imagines she is being shocking just by using the word – and some people doubtless find intersectionality frightening just because of its syllable count. Knowing that it's associated with feminist theory may make it even more likely to be dismissed out of hand. However, intersectionality is both a transparently descriptive term for the phenomenon it treats and a highly useful concept.

Imagine several groups of people drawn as circles or ovals. If the resulting diagram is to be representative of real life, there will be overlaps among the figures. No one is 'just' black, or female, or Muslim, or disabled. The more distinct groups we recognise, the greater the number of potential overlaps. In the terminology of set theory, an area of overlap is called an intersection. Intersectionality is a quality or a state associated with membership of an intersection.

While society has made progress in recognising gender and minority groups, recognition of intersectionality is patchy. Indeed, much of the debate about intersectionality and its importance has so far taken place among progressive campaigners. An inability to respect overlapping identities can come from any direction. For example, in the 2017 UK general election, anti-FGM (female genital mutilation) campaigner Nimco Ali faced criticism for standing against an incumbent female Labour MP as a candidate for the Women's Equality party:

> *My critics tell me I shouldn't run against another woman at all, and particularly not another feminist, as if all women and all feminists were interchangeable. As successful as I have been as a campaigner, black and minority ethnic women like me are largely invisible: talked about and talked at.[2]*

The debate in the literature often centres around which minority group fares worse in the work environment. Is it ethnic minority women, because they have multiple subordinate identities? Or do ethnic minority men fare worse because they are seen as a threat to white male authority and power? Overall, the evidence to support either view is mixed. The research is fascinating, but simply taking race and then splitting it by gender may be an over-simplistic view of gendered race discrimination.

A more pertinent question is how dual identities overlap to create new unique subsets of stereotypes for men and women from different racial groups. How do the subsequent perceptions of these minority subgroups then influence the perceptions, judgements and decisions made about them? Understanding this will give us a clearer picture of who is likely to fare worse in any given situation, and why. People with multiple minority identities may experience distinct forms of discrimination at work. There is a complex interaction between race and gender, and each combination of race and gender needs to be explored separately to understand how it leads to discrimination.

We tend to assume that racism in organisations affects men and women equally and in the same manner. We also assume that gender discrimination affects white and ethnic minority women in the same way.[3] However, this means overlooking the interaction of race and gender. Consequently, studies of gender often ignore race, and studies of race often ignore gender.[4]

This chapter focuses on the group most frequently overlooked in race and gender research – ethnic minority women. How are they perceived? How do they fare in the workplace? And how do their experiences differ from those of white women and ethnic minority men?

It's worth stressing that I am only looking at two combined identities – race and gender – in this chapter. In real life, people have multiple identities, and so to focus on race and gender is too simplistic. Also, here I only discuss three subgroups of people: white, black and Asian. There is a wide spectrum of sub-identities within each of these groups, so we need to use some caution in applying the insights presented here. There is, as always in dealing with discrimination, the danger of accidentally introducing new forms of exclusion or dismissal alongside perspectives and techniques designed to promote inclusion and respect. The key with any model for thinking about people is to remember that it's a model – a construct that guides our thoughts and actions, but not the sole, correct and complete replacement for a sensitive and open approach to human issues.

Race and gender: different differences

Race and gender bias do share some features. Both have an impact on life experiences and access to opportunities. The impact and consequences of the bias are often the same – for example, women earn less than men and are less likely to be promoted to senior positions. The same is true for minorities when compared to the majority. Because the outcomes are often similar – and similarly negative – people often assume both -isms are the same.

Yet sexism and racism have evolved differently, and the ways in which each bias devalues people also differ. Furthermore, experiences of race and sex discrimination are not the same.

First, it is typically easier to determine a person's gender than their race. There is a clear visible biological distinction for gender, whereas there is no one set of genetic markers setting one human 'race' apart from another. How we identify and name the group a person belongs to varies depending on the culture, situation and context.[5]

Second, women are not a minority group; they are only a minority in certain situations. As a consequence, contact between men and women is inevitable, unavoidable and accepted as a fact of everyday life. Contact between people of different ethnic groups on any meaningful level is not as frequent. Many people from a majority group, both male and female, may have few friendships with anyone from a minority group. While it is practically impossible to live a life without contact with someone from the opposite sex, this could happen with regard to race.

Third, the relative lack of contact between different racial groups leads to differences in perception between racism and sexism. Whether we feel there is more sexism or racism in a situation varies depending on our race and gender. So, since white people are unlikely to experience racial discrimination, a white person may probably conclude that gender discrimination is a bigger issue than racism – they are more likely to have experienced or witnessed sexism among their white colleagues and/or know someone who has. In contrast, ethnic minorities will have been subject to more racial discrimination and so are likely to perceive racism as at least as big an issue as sexism, if not a bigger one. Since the majority of organisations are led by white men and a few white women, this may be why more time, effort and resources are directed at combating sex discrimination than racial discrimination,[3] and why organisations are more willing to take action to improve gender equality than racial equality.[6]

Fourth, the historic sources of racism and sexism are different.[3] Sexism has traditionally been perceived to come from an external source. The roles and expectations of men and women are learned from the society within which a person lives. In contrast, racism has historically been associated with internal sources – it comes from the individual.

The gender hierarchy is fixed across most cultures – typically, men have political and economic power and women are in an inferior position. Sexism is therefore more universal, with cultures typically sharing the same beliefs about women. Racism, on the other hand, is culture-specific. A person's position in the ethnic hierarchy is likely to influence the amount of discrimination they face.[5]

It can be tempting to think that the expectations a culture places on women are the same. This is not the case. The belief that came to be formed during the Industrial Revolution – that men should be breadwinners and women the homemakers – only applied to the white majority. Racial minorities, seen as of lower status, had different gender expectations forced upon them. African slaves were not allowed to take the traditional gender roles of white men and women. Black men had no opportunity to provide for their family, and black women were not exempt from hard labour or from doing men's work, unlike white women.[7]

Fifth, there is the very practical consideration that men and women are co-dependent: we need each other to exist. The acceptance that there are 'boys' jobs and girls' jobs' is an acceptance of the belief (albeit totally false and misguided[8]) that men and women have different, yet complementary, capabilities. We need one another, in other words – and as long as everyone stays in their predetermined box, contentment prevails. There is no such co-dependence between racial groups: we do not need Asian people to run convenience stores or to drive taxis. Indeed, where there is perceived to be an over-reliance on immigrants in the labour market, you can hear the cry that 'They are taking our jobs', the unsubtle whinge also being an indicator of the lack of co-dependence. Racial discrimination therefore has the potential to be unlimited – there are, in theory, no jobs that minorities should have, nor any limit on the sanctions that can be applied to them.

These important differences remind us that, while race and gender are both socially constructed notions, they are not the same. The effects generated by each set of ideas are also different. The ways in which we tackle racism and sexism have to take account of these facts.

Who fares worse? Double jeopardy

There is a commonly held belief that, owing to their dual minority identities, ethnic minority women are more likely to experience double the discrimination that single minority status individuals (such as white women or black men) suffer. This is referred to as the double jeopardy hypothesis,[9] and it treats prejudice as additive: the more minority characteristics a person has, the more discrimination they will encounter.

The white male norm hypothesis[10] also posits that, since the default social group is white men, any deviation from this norm will make people stand out. Therefore, black men and women are more noticeable than white men. The expectation would be that black women, due to their double minority status, should stand out even more than white women or black men.

Researchers have found considerable support for these two hypotheses:

- ethnic minority women reported experiencing more harassment than ethnic minority men or white men and white women[11]

- employers expect black women to be paid less than married black males and white females[12]

- black female leaders who made mistakes were penalised more severely than black male and white female leaders.[13]

Other research suggests that black and Latina women:

- earn the lowest wages[14]

- have the least authority in the workplace[15] and

- are employed in more undesirable jobs.[14,16]

From these findings, many researchers have concluded that ethnic minority women face the most discrimination in the workplace and that the discrimination is driven by their dual minority status.

On the other hand: man to man

While there is some evidence to support the double jeopardy theory, there is also a great deal of research that shows that it is black *men*, not black women, who encounter the most discrimination. This is based on social dominance theory, which suggests that power struggles between men and women are seen as less important than those between in-group and out-group males, and that intergroup conflict is a male-on-male phenomenon. White men perceive ethnic minority men as more of a threat than ethnic minority women, therefore ethnic minority men are punished for displaying agency (that is, a sense of action and purpose) and rewarded for showing deference. Black men face a backlash if they display dominance, because this threatens the power and status of white males.[17]

According to social dominance theory, there are social hierarchies in which dominant groups are valued more – they have power, wealth and high-status positions. Men, typically, have a more dominant status than women. There are also culturally defined hierarchies in which different races are placed in different positions on the social hierarchy. Structures can vary across cultures but in Western cultures white people are at the top of the hierarchy. Subordinate groups such as women and other racial groups are therefore less valued than men and white people. They have less power and wealth and take low-status roles. Members of the dominant group are more likely to be given a job interview; once interviewed, they are more likely to be hired; and once hired they are more likely to be given a higher salary, as well as being steered towards jobs with greater opportunities for promotion.[5]

Evidence for this comes from, for example, looking at pay, which is examined in more detail in Chapter 10. The wage difference between ethnic minority women and white women disappears when factors such as education are controlled for. However, the pay gap between ethnic minority men and white men remains.

Further evidence comes from a study which showed that black female leaders who display dominance are better liked and given higher status than white female leaders and black male leaders.[13] In Sweden, male immigrants reported more experiences of discrimination than female immigrants.[17] In the USA, black men are more likely to report experiencing workplace discrimination than black women.[17]

A pecking order for discrimination was also revealed in the discounts given to people making car purchases. White men received the biggest discounts, followed by white women, black women, then black men.[18]

Conclusion

While there are different conclusions that can be drawn from the data, one thing is clear: gender and race are not separate subjects. On the whole, minority women experience more discrimination than white women. The jury may still be out as to whether minority women experience more discrimination than minority men, but for me the question is irrelevant. Gender and race intersect, interact and can lead to a lack of inclusion for both minority men and women. Another conclusion that we can draw is that the experiences of white women will not be the same as those of minority women. The biggest danger in the diversity strategies of organisations is in not recognising this.

Many organisations today are building their diversity strategies around gender. It makes sense in many ways: there is considerable gender bias in organisations which operates in both blatant and subtle ways.[8] Gender stereotypes are pervasive and impact organisational life in myriad ways. However, ignoring race, or not placing any emphasis on it, means that gender strategies will be focused on white women in the workplace. Minority female experience will be seen as the same as that of white women. Progress for white women should therefore be recognised as progress for all women.

To ignore race when looking at gender policies and strategies is to take a colour-blind approach; or, to put it more bluntly, it is a manifestation of modern racism.

Gender strategies also mean recognising the discrimination that men face in the workplace; more attention is being given to allowing men to work more flexibly. This work is to be commended. Looking at bias men face, however, also needs to address the particular difficulties that minority men face in the workplace in terms of how they are perceived, stereotyped and discriminated against.

1. Lewis, H. The uses and abuses of intersectionality. *New Statesman*, 20 February (2014).

2. Ali N. I'm a Women's Equality Party candidate – here's why I'm standing against a female Labour MP. Available at: http://www.newstatesman.com/politics/june2017/2017/05/im-womens-equality-party-candidate-heres-why-im-standing-against-female-0 (accessed 21 September 2017).

3. Trotman Reid, P. & Clayton, S. Racism and sexism at work. *Soc. Justice Res.* **5**, 249–268 (1992).

4. Mirza, H.S. 'All the women are white, all the blacks are men – but some of us are brave': Mapping the consequences of invisibility for black and minority ethnic women in Britain in *Explaining Ethnic Differences: Changing Patterns of Disadvantage in Britain* (ed. D. Mason) (Policy Press, 2003).

5. Sidanius, J. & Veniegas, R.C. Gender and race discrimination: The interactive nature of disadvantage in *Reducing prejudice and discrimination: Claremont Symposium on Applied Social Psychology'* (ed. S. Oskamp), pp. 47–69 (Lawrence Erlbaum Associates, 2000).

6. Yates, C. & Sachdev, P. *Rewire: A Radical Approach to Tackling Diversity and Difference* (Bloomsbury, 2015).

7. Baxandall, R., Gordon, L. & Reverby, S. *America's Working Women: A Documentary History, 1600 to the Present* (Random House, 1976).

8. Kandola, B. & Kandola, J. *The Invention of Difference: The Story of Gender Bias at Work* (Pearn Kandola Publishing, 2013).

9. Beale, F. Double jeopardy: To be black and female in *The Black Woman* (ed. T. Cade) (New American Library, 1970).

10. Zarate, M.A. *Cultural normality and social perception. Unpublished doctoral dissertation* (Purdue University, West Lafayette, IN, 1990).

11. Berdahl, J.L. & Moore, C. Workplace harassment: Double jeopardy for minority women. *J. Appl. Psychol.* **91**, 426–436 (2006).

12. Settles, I.H. Use of an intersectional framework to understand black women's racial and gender identities. *Sex Roles* **54**, 589–601 (2006).

13. Livingston, R.W., Rosette, A.S. & Washington, E.F. Can an agentic Black woman get ahead? The impact of race and interpersonal dominance on perceptions of female leaders. *Psychol. Sci.* **23**, 354–358 (2012).

14. Aldridge, D. Black women and the new world order: Toward a fit in the economic marketplace in *Latinas and African American Women at Work: Race, Gender and Economic Inequality* (ed. I. Browne.) (Russell Sage Foundation, 1999).

15. Browne, I., Hewitt, C., Tigges, L. & Green, G. Why does job segregation lead to wage inequality among African Americans? Person, place, sector, or skills? *Soc. Sci. Res.* **30**, 473–495 (2001).

16. Spalter-Roth, R. & Deitch, C. 'I don't feel right-sized; I feel out-of-work sized': Gender, race, ethnicity and the unequal costs of displacement. *Work and Occupations* **26**, 446–482 (1999).

17. Sidanius, J. & Pratto, F. *Social Dominance: An Intergroup Theory of Social Hierarchy and Oppression* (Cambridge University Press, 1999).

18. Ayres, I. & Siegelman, P. Race and gender discrimination in bargaining for a new car. *Am. Econ. Rev.* **85**, 304–321 (1995).

Chapter 7

'One of us?' Socialisation in organisations

Getting, and succeeding in, a job is not just about doing good work. Networks, social groups, being accepted and valued within work teams – all of these things matter. *Who* you know counts for as much as *what* you know. In the workplace, the associations we make with people and the networks we belong to influence how included we feel, how others view us, and how we progress.

This chapter explores how we form groups at work and how race and colour affect who we consider to be part of our in-group. It then looks at how being perceived as part of an out-group affects the way we (mis)interpret behaviours and emotions of people from visible minorities. Being part of the white majority in organisations brings with it silent privileges, the acknowledgement of which would undermine the idea of meritocracy. Finally, I look at some of the ways in which we can achieve greater inclusion in groups and teams.

At first sight: when people meet

Imagine walking into a room where you're expecting to see a group of people you know well – perhaps they're from a department in your organisation. Instead you find you don't recognise anyone. Mildly anxious, you scan the room and spot a group of people you vaguely know, chatting to each other. You go straight over and join the group.[1]

This is an unremarkable scene: it happens all the time and it's over in seconds. But it reveals several key points about how we behave and interact with others.

Two evolutionary developments have led to the success of human beings. First, there are our powers of reasoning and our ability to understand our environment – and, with varying degrees of accuracy, to predict and prepare for future events.[2] Second, we find comfort, reassurance and security in being with people like ourselves. The anxiety we experience when encountering a group of strangers is rapidly replaced by more comforting notions of security when we find people we know, with whom we can identify and empathise. This process is at the heart of social identity learning[1, (p.118)].

Social identity learning is one of the most influential and well-researched theories in social psychology. It's also one of the easiest to recognise in action – especially in the workplace. We continuously process social information, acquiring, integrating and interpreting the streams of data in which we are immersed. For example, if we see someone with their lips pursed, eyes narrowed and brow furrowed, how we integrate and interpret this information depends on the context. If we do not know this person, then we might believe they have an unfriendly, critical attitude towards us. If, on the other hand, this is a close colleague and friend, then we're more likely to believe they are feeling agitated and anxious about something – and we may be keen to understand their predicament and offer our help.

The interpretation we place on the situation depends on our being able to process a host of factors relating to past experience as well as the context in which the behaviour occurs. So, if we do not know a person well or at all, or we perceive them to be different from people to whom we generally feel closer, we may interpret their behaviour more negatively.[1] Social psychologist Muzafer Sherif[3] conducted a famous study looking at intergroup conflict. It is sometimes referred to as the Robbers Cave study, after the Robbers Cave State Park in Oklahoma where the experiment was carried out. Eleven-year-old boys at a summer camp were split into two groups. Members of each group had time to get to know one another and then decide on the name of their group. The groups were then set a task in competition against each other, with the winners to be rewarded with a prize. Sherif and his team saw how quickly the competition, lack of knowledge of the opposing group, and rewarding of aggressive activities created an intense conflict among a random group of children.

Social identity theory (SIT)[4] built on, and advanced, Sherif's work. Henri Tajfel and John Turner, the originators of SIT, demonstrated the ubiquity and the subtlety of its effects. We make very rapid decisions about who is in the in-group and who is in the out-group. Essentially, the in-group contains 'people like me'. Tajfel and Turner defined a group as:

> a collection of individuals who perceive themselves to be members of the same social category, share some emotional involvement in this common definition of themselves, and achieve some degree of social consensus about the evaluation of their group and of their membership in it.[4 (p15)]

This is not just a process of self-definition; others also have a part to play. How non-group members view individuals and the group helps to create the group's identity, status and its prestige: some groups are deemed by observers to be 'better' than others.[5] Our behaviour, thoughts and feelings are different when we are dealing with members of our in-group or members of an out-group. This is summarised in Table 7.1.

Table 7.1. Behaviour, thoughts and feelings towards in-groups and out-groups.

Behaviour	Thought	Feeling
More generous to in-group	Exaggerate differences with out-group	Greater trust
Happier to cooperate with in-group	Think out-groups are biased against them	Greater satisfaction
Greater agreement with in-group	Think of in-group as similar	Higher commitment
Communicate more with in-group	Filter information to fit our beliefs	Greater security
More helpful to in-group	In-group success attributed to ability	More understanding
Conformity with in-group	Out-group success attributed to factors other than ability	Higher self-esteem
Approach in-group	In-group failures attributed to other factors	More empathy
Avoid the out-group	Out-group failure attributed to lack of ability	More sympathy
More open with in-group	Out-groups scrutinised and criticised more	Greater comfort

When we are interacting with our in-group we are more altruistic and cooperative. We attribute success to the group's ability, and failures to other factors. We feel more trust, comfort and security. When dealing with out-group members, the opposite patterns occur: people are less helpful, less willing to cooperate, and communicate less, and people feel more anxiety, uncertainty and mistrust.

We are very poor at processing large amounts of information, and will grasp at anything that helps to categorise people into 'us' and 'them'.[6] Today, whether we like it or not, colour and ethnicity combine to make one of the most significant ways of creating these categories.

Relational demography: believing is seeing

Emory Bogardus created the social distance scale. Developed in the 1930s[7] (book 18.2 p. 16), it describes the degree to which people are willing to have social contact with people from other social groups, including people of different ethnicity or colour. As we have noted in other chapters, attitudes have changed a lot since this scale was first created; generally, people are more willing to have people of different races and nationalities as neighbours, friends and spouses.

Although findings such as these indicate a greater degree of tolerance towards different groups, other research shows tendencies that point in the opposite direction. Where a group holds a dominant position, it is less willing to give it up or share it with others. This is known as social dominance theory.[8]

The field of relational demography takes these studies to the next level, examining how groups identify similarities and differences among their members. Factors such as race and gender are easily identifiable markers of difference, but these are surface-level differences and do not suggest that individuals necessarily have different personalities or values. Our rational brains acknowledge that people's values or abilities cannot be based purely on their skin colour. Nevertheless, we too easily assume that differences will exist on these and other dimensions. For example, a team of all-white male lawyers is not necessarily different to a team of three white male lawyers and three black female lawyers. They most likely share more in terms of professional outlook, training and class expectations than a random collection of individuals. Having defined them as lawyers, we would expect to find common values, problem-solving styles and motivations. Despite this, we will assume there are greater differences between the latter team than the former. The very fact of the objectively identified surface differences – namely colour and gender – lead us to believe there will be deeper levels of difference as well. Race and ethnicity are intimately associated with status expectations, which consequently affects how people relate to one another within teams.[9]

Even when we are presented with clear, objective and unambiguous information about a person's characteristics or talents, we prefer to judge people implicitly according to the labels we attach to them. In fact, the labels even affect *what* we are seeing.

Chapter 2 discussed Alessandro de' Medici, whose colour was not remarked upon or seen as being significant in the sixteenth century. The changing views of race and what it meant to be black led observers of his portrait to see very different, and negative, qualities in him by the nineteenth century. But that was then and this is now: that surely couldn't happen these days, could it?

Imagine you are asked to draw a picture of someone's face from a photograph. This should be drawn in enough detail so that someone who had not seen the original photo could recognise the person. Giving the person in the photo a label could surely not affect the picture that is drawn – after all, the photo is right there in front of us, it has not changed, and the task has remained the same. This is exactly what psychologists asked participants to do using an image that was deliberately ambiguous in terms of race. The pictures the participants drew differed markedly based on whether the image was described as being of a white or a black person. People saw what they wanted to see based on the label, and then drew what they believed was presented to them: believing is seeing (this was also the title of the paper the researchers published[10]).

If this kind of distortion can happen with such an apparently objective task as drawing someone's face, it's not surprising that we make similarly biased interpretations about people's speech, behaviour and shows of emotion.

When test participants are presented with identical transcripts of a discussion between team members, they believe there is more conflict and tension present when the group is described as 'diverse' rather than 'homogeneous'. Not only do we exaggerate physical differences when we are faced with diversity, but we go on to manufacture underlying divisions as well.

We don't even need to have other people present in order to generate positive or negative feelings about groups. Negative emotions can be engendered and anxieties raised simply by being told that a group we are about to meet is ethnically different.[11]

People's actions are also interpreted differently depending on whether they are seen as a member of the in-group or of an out-group. One research team showed participants several videos of people walking in ways stereotypically associated with black or white people.[12] The walking style associated with black people, called the stroll, was meticulously detailed by the researchers: exaggerated knee bend, head slightly tilted, one foot dragging. The stroll was contrasted with a standard walking style: erect posture, leg and arm swing synchronised, steady stride and straight head. Those adopting the 'stroll' walking style were rated as more aggressive, potentially more hostile and less intelligent than those using the standard style.

This finding is consistent with research about how people interpret others' emotions. In one study, participants were shown a range of faces whose expressions progressed from hostility to happiness. In the mid-range, expressions were more ambiguous. People were asked to identify when the face they were examining was no longer hostile. White faces were identified as lacking hostility significantly sooner than black faces.[13]

The way we interpret behaviour depends on who we believe is exhibiting it, and in particular whether or not they are part of our in-group. It is not actual behaviour that we are assessing, but our interpretations. In the workplace, this has a real impact on how comfortable we feel with someone and the extent to which we view them as a positive contributor to the group – or as a potential troublemaker.

We can send messages to our team-mates in very subtle ways through our non-verbal behaviour.[14] Non-verbal behaviours are more difficult to control than conscious ones, and we are usually much less aware of them. Someone might be friendly and sociable in the way they talk to another person, but their body language might reveal something else. For example, the amount of eye contact we give someone, how close we sit to another person, and our body posture all have a significant impact on whether a person feels comfortable with us or not.[15] These effects are often played out in teams. Who is invited to contribute? Whose ideas are taken up, taken seriously and taken forward? Whose contributions are recalled at the end of the meeting?

This effect was encapsulated in the experience of a black, British-born, African Caribbean energy company professional whose team leader gave him the helpful feedback that he should 'act more white'. This staff member was somewhat surprised by this advice; he had not been aware that he was behaving 'black'. In this case, the team leader did not feel comfortable with having a black person in his team, and he was interpreting his team member's behaviour in line with his own stereotypes about black people. This tells us that simply creating diverse teams, although an undoubted advance on previous practice, is not the total solution.

The silent benefits of privilege

The great advantage of being in an in-group and of being in a dominant group is that you are unlikely to be aware of any special treatment. Events like Black History Month are a subtle acknowledgement of this privilege, because for the other eleven months of the year it can be assumed that discussions about culture or history are about the dominant white group. Other privileges include being with people like you whenever you want to be; being confident that when you meet someone at work they will be the same colour as you; and not having to wonder whether the bad experience you had at work had racial undertones.[1] The greatest privilege of being in the dominant group is not having to recognise your privileges. In-group members are absolved from reflection on their unearned advantages, their smooth accession to positions of power, and their high status.

Early in 2017, John Allan, chairman of Tesco, sparked international headlines when he claimed that white men were 'an endangered species' in boardrooms and that this is an 'extremely propitious period' to be 'female and from an ethnic background, and preferably both'[16]. Lucky for him, then, that he chaired a board of nine men and three women, all white. In his view, privilege is something that minorities have, or maybe even expect. The thought that he and his board members may have been the beneficiaries of privilege was not something that even entered his pretty little head.

A rule of thumb I use is that whenever somebody maintains that their organisation does not have dominant or subordinate groups based on gender and race, they are in the dominant group. Ask those who do *not* share that person's membership and you will hear a different story – one that prominently features discrimination and a lack of power and privilege.

This is not unlike a discussion about in-groups and out-groups I had with partners of one of the 'Big Four' UK accountancy firms. One of the partners said he did not believe there were dominant groups and subordinate groups in the organisation: 'We all believe in the same firm,' he said proudly. This is a fine sentiment. Nevertheless, the partners were overwhelmingly male and all white.

People are typically surprised and offended by research showing how much we favour people like ourselves. For one thing, prejudice is bad business. It doesn't make sense in terms of productivity or performance to favour some people on a non-merit basis. This is the kind of in-group/out-group thinking which researchers find time and again, and which runs directly counter to the best interests of the organisation. But the power of this phenomenon can't be wished away. It is an important point to recognise: our instinctive urge is not to maximise overall rewards for an overarching organisation, but to maximise the difference between the in-group and the out-group.[4]

Collusion: a curious response to being in a subordinate group

We might assume that friction and tension between groups will follow naturally from the mere existence of subordinate and dominant groups. In fact, conflict is not inevitable: it arises when the dominant group feels that competition between groups is increasing.

We might expect the search for fairness within organisations, and the motivation to create equal opportunities for all, would lead minorities to seek to overturn the discriminatory system in subtle and direct ways. The standard account of the relationship between dominant and subordinate groups does not completely describe the reality of what goes on in organisations, however. In most organisations the dominant group – the one with most power – will be white and male. Men will tend to be over-represented in the most powerful functions and in senior positions. They will be more likely to be given opportunities to progress to more powerful roles earlier in their careers. Conflict can be avoided, tension reduced and calmness maintained if everyone in the organisation accepts the prevailing state of affairs. The dominant group will be happy to go along with this approach and may not even recognise that any injustices exist.

It's surprising to learn that subordinate groups may also agree to accept the status quo. The theory of system justification[17] shows that, while members of low-status groups would never explicitly accept the racial inequalities associated with the status quo, data on implicit unconscious bias shows a very different picture. High-status groups display an in-group bias, as we might expect. However, low-status groups also have a bias toward the high-status group (i.e. they display an out-group bias). People from the out-group also implicitly endorse the more negative traits associated with their group and the more positive ones associated with the dominant group. This favouring of the out-group by low-status group members is a sign of endorsement for the status quo. The result is a tendency to view the current system as good, fair, natural and even desirable. This tacit acceptance of the existing system by the minority groups themselves needs to be identified and challenged, but when minorities and women challenge the status quo they run the risk that they will be viewed more negatively and their careers negatively affected as a result.

One of the cornerstones of SIT is that we strive to maintain or enhance our self-esteem because this gives us a positive view of ourselves. Belonging to a group feeds into our sense of self-esteem. Where a group has low status, individuals can:

- try to leave the group, or show how they are somehow different from others in the group

- compare their in-group to a 'worse' group

- reframe how the group is viewed, which includes emphasising dimensions and aspects that they feel reflect well on the group in comparison to other groups.

Lower-status groups can enhance their self-esteem in these ways, but ironically these tactics involve greater denigration of other groups and can also lead to greater antagonism by the dominant group, if the dominant group can be defined in ethnic or race terms.

Doorways, not barriers: actions to improve socialisation of groups

We cannot prevent people from forming in-groups and out-groups. Even as we try to block the creation of such groups with some categories of people, we continue generating in-groups and out-groups in other contexts. For example, while many people who voted to Remain in the UK's European referendum of 2016 noted that migrants were being treated as an out-group, they were nevertheless happy to categorise those who voted to Leave as uneducated, older, working-class people who did not know what they were voting for.[18] We get rid of one out-group only to create another one elsewhere, blithely justifying, rationalising and reinforcing the new construct.

One way to help groups reduce the tendency to form in-groups and out-groups based on colour is to get people to expressly recognise the qualities that every individual brings to the team. This process helps each team member to be recognised as an individual, not simply as a category denoted by their colour, but as an individual with unique strengths, experiences and perspectives.[19]

An enhanced belief in the value of diversity helps people to see beyond the obvious, superficial differences that we can all see and be distracted by.[20] By drawing out individuals' experiences and strengths, we get the best out of any team, whether it is diverse or homogeneous.[21]

How you view the diversity of a group makes a big difference to its ultimate effectiveness. Imagine that, in a team consisting of younger and older workers, the younger people see the older people as old-fashioned or less technically savvy. The basis for tension, misunderstanding and conflict exists before the group even starts work. When younger members view older members as having experience and knowledge that can benefit them, teams are more cohesive and effective.[22] When it comes to race, a much more sensitive subject, it is important for team leaders to set the right tone: to convey that everyone has a contribution to make, and should be free to participate and to feel valued as part of the group.

The superficial differences that human beings can't help seeing must not be a barrier, but a doorway. They signal the opportunity to derive new insights into personality, attitudes, perspective and experience that will contribute to the successful completion of any group task. Research studies have consistently shown that when we achieve this breakthrough, better results follow.[23]

Making this change is a multi-stage process. The first step involves refusing to accept that colour differences are significant. The second step involves getting to know people as individuals, understanding what they bring to the team, and recognising the contribution they can make. The third step involves rejecting our habit of seeking out views that are similar to our own.

Conclusion

This chapter has looked at how we form groups and the impact this has in the workplace. Colour and ethnicity are two of the most significant ways that determine whether someone is in the in-group or the out-group. Knowing someone's colour impacts our interpretation of that person's behaviour and emotions; it also affects our levels of comfort with, and support for, that person.

One of the biggest privileges of being part of the white majority is not having to notice or acknowledge those same privileges. The good news is that it is possible to create teams that are inclusive and effective – if we are sufficiently motivated to do so.

1. Jones, J. M., Dovidio, J. F. & Vietze, D. L. *The Psychology of Diversity: Beyond Prejudice and Racism*. (Wiley Blackwell, 2014).

2. Crisp, R. *The Social Brain: How Diversity Made The Modern Mind*. (Robinson, 2015).

3. Classics in the History of Psychology – Sherif (1954/1961) Chapter 7. Available at: http://psychclassics.yorku.ca/Sherif/chap7.htm?wptouch_preview_theme=enabled. (Accessed: 20th September 2017).

4. Tajfel, H. & Turner, J. C. The social identity theory of intergroup behavior. *Psychology of Intergroup Relations* **5**, 7–24 (1986).

5. Landy, F.J. & Conte, J.M. *Work in the 21st Century: An Introduction to Industrial and Organizational Psychology*. (Hoboken, NJ: Wiley, 2016).

6. Triandis, H.C. The future of workforce diversity in international organisations: A commentary. *Applied Psychology* **52**, 486–495 (2003).

7. Bogardus, E.S.A social distance scale. *Sociol. Soc. Res*. **17**, 265–271 (1933).

8. Sidanius, J. & Pratto, F. *Social Dominance: An Intergroup Theory of Social Hierarchy and Oppression*. (Cambridge University Press, 1999).

9. Axt, J.R., Ebersole, C.R. & Nosek, B.A. The rules of implicit evaluation by race, religion and age. *Psychol. Sci*. 1–12 (2014).

10. Eberhardt, J.L., Dasgupta, N. & Banaszynski, T.I. Believing is seeing: The effects of racial labels and implicit beliefs on face perception. *Personal. Soc. Psychol. Bull*. **29**, 360–370 (2003).

11. Antonio, A. L. et al. Effects of racial diversity on complex thinking in college students. *Psychol. Sci*. **15**, 507–510 (2004).

12. Neal, L.V.I., McCray, A.D., Webb-Johnson, G. & Bridgest, S.T. The effects of African American movement styles on teachers' perceptions and reactions. *J. Spec. Educ*. **37**, 49–57 (2003).

13. Hugenberg, K. & Bodenhausen, G. V. Facing prejudice: Implicit prejudice and the perception of facial threat. *Psychol. Sci*. **14**, 640–643 (2003).

14. Dovidio, J.F., Gaertner, S.L.E., Kawakami, K. & Hodson, G. Why can't we just get along? Interpersonal biases and interracial distrust. *Cult. Divers. Ethn. Minor. Psychol*. **8**, 88–102 (2002).

15. McConnell, A.R. & Leibold, J.M. Relations among the Implicit Association Test, discriminatory behavior and explicit measures of racial attitudes. *J. Exp. Soc. Psychol*. **37**, 435–442 (2001).

16. Rawlinson, K. White men 'endangered species' in UK boardrooms, says Tesco chairman | Business | The Guardian. Available at: https://www.theguardian.com/business/2017/mar/10/white-men-endangered-species-in-uk-boardrooms-says-tesco-chairman (accessed: 22nd November 2017).

17. Jost, J.T., Banaji, M.R. & Nosek, B.A decade of system justification theory: Accumulated evidence of conscious and unconscious bolstering of the status quo. *Polit. Psychol*. **25**, 881–919 (2004).

18. Lowe, J. Pro-EU Campaigner: 'We Made Brexit Voters Feel Like Closet Racists;' Available at: http://www.newsweek.com/brexit-racists-trevor-phillips-595042. (Accessed: 10th October 2017).

19. van Knippenberg, D. & Schippers, M. C. Work group diversity. *Annu. Rev. Psychol*. **58**, 515–541 (2007).

20. van Dick, R., van Knippenberg, D., Hagele, S., Guillaume, Y.R.F. & Brodbeck, F.C. Group diversity and group identification: The moderating role of diversity beliefs. *Hum. Relations* **61**, 1463–1492 (2008).

21. Homan, A.C., van Knippenberg, D., Van Kleef, G.A. & De Dreu, C.K.W. Bridging faultlines by valuing diversity: Diversity beliefs, information elaboration and performance in diverse work groups. *J. Appl. Psychol.* **92**, 1189–1199 (2007).

22. Proudford, K.L. & Smith, K.K. Group membership salience and the movement of conflict: Reconceptualizing the interaction among race, gender and hierarchy. *Gr. Organ. Manag.* **28**, 18–44 (2003).

23. Phillips, K.W., Kim-Jun, S.Y. & Shim, S.-H. The value of diversity in organizations: A social psychological perspective. *Organ. Manag. Ser.* 253–271 (2011).

Part 3
Racism at Work

Chapter 8

Everyday racism: Micro-incivilities and how every little counts

Racial prejudice is often understood solely in terms of overtly hostile behaviours and attitudes towards other groups. Overt racist behaviour is blatant and indisputable. It can include verbal abuse, physical intimidation and assault.

But what of racist behaviour and attitudes which are subtle, apparently innocuous, and therefore not necessarily categorised as racism by those displaying or witnessing them? And, to make things even more complicated, what if the behaviour in question is not an action or a voiced opinion, but an absence or a withholding? This brings us to the area of micro-behaviours or microaggressions – a word coined by Chester M. Pierce in 1970 to describe the casual insults and dismissals he noticed white Americans aiming at African Americans.

Personally, I find the phrase too judgemental and accusatory. 'Micro-incivility', I believe, describes the types of behaviour we are talking about more accurately and also in a way that people are prepared to acknowledge, accept and possibly change. The concept of workplace incivility is documented in the psychology literature and its application. Workplace incivility is 'defined as low-intensity acts which violate the norms of respectful behaviours established in a specific setting, and whose intent to harm is ambiguous'.[1, (p11)]

On their website, the Australian Human Rights Commission refers to 'casual racism' and how its effect is to 'undermine civility'.[2] Micro-incivilities are the kinds of daily, commonplace behaviours or aspects of an environment which signal, wittingly or unwittingly, to members of out-groups that they do not belong and are not welcome. They include subtle slights or insults that are, in some respects, products of the automatic ways in which we respond to out-groups.[3] The behaviours are not blatant and are so commonplace that they suggest an almost 'mundane automaticity' in the memorable phrase of Susan Fiske.[4, (p.124)] Such behaviours include making stereotypical judgements, assumptions, embarrassing slips of the tongue, and awkward social interactions. It is ironic that we laugh at the awkwardness experienced by characters in comedy shows such as *The Office* and *Curb Your Enthusiasm*, enjoying their discomfort while ignoring the toxic social chills that we can cast in real life. Awareness of micro-incivilities and their potency alerts us to aspects of our behaviour that are more difficult to control: principally, our non-verbal behaviour and the way in which we speak.

Micro-incivilities are also referred to under the label of 'everyday racism', a term that appeared in the title of a book by Philomena Essed in 1991.[5] While terms like these attempt to convey the insidious mundanity of this kind of casual, drip-drip racism, we need to be aware that great harm can be inflicted by seemingly tiny actions, thereby making us more mindful of the effects of our behaviour and our daily interactions.

The display of micro-incivilities is widespread and generally unnoticed by the perpetrators, who do not look or sound like typical racists. In fact, the perpetrators are not some wayward, thoughtless fraction of an otherwise right-thinking population. They are you and me. We may remain in our own bubbles, assuming our interactions with others have been successful, whereas the people we have been engaging with have reached a very different conclusion. And most of us will be surprised, shocked and shamed if we are called out for practising racism unawares.

The subtlety of micro-incivility means that a white person and a visible minority person may end an interaction with very different views about how it went. People may not be aware of the dissonance between their verbal and non-verbal behaviours. The majority person concentrates on their outward behaviour, expression and language and might consider the interaction to have been very positive. But they will not be aware of their micro-behaviours: the small, but discernible, cues that signal interest, trust and respect. But in these situations the other person is taking in much more information – non-verbal cues as well as the verbal expressions of comfort and inclusion.[6,7] Some examples of micro-incivility include:

- being ignored
- being talked over
- having your authority undermined
- being constantly criticised for seemingly small issues
- having assumptions made about your honesty
- having stereotypical judgements made about your abilities.[8]

It can also include omissions – the things we do not do – such as:

- not giving eye contact
- not sitting facing a person
- not giving someone your attention
- persistently not saying someone's name correctly
- not inviting someone to speak up in a meeting.

We should not underestimate the impact of micro-incivilities. Surveys show that overt instances of racism are, although unpleasant, easier to handle than more subtle forms. Situations in which the person is not sure whether discrimination has occurred (and, if it did, whether it was deliberate or not – a situation known as attribution ambiguity) are the hardest to deal with, because the person is uncertain what their correct response should be.[9,10]

Opposing micro-incivilities

Effective teams and organisations have been found to display various proactive, positive behaviours known as organisational citizenship behaviours (OCBs). These include:

- altruism – helping a colleague
- conscientiousness – going the extra mile
- civic virtue – getting involved in community activities
- courtesy – showing consideration for others
- sportsmanship – putting up with situations that are not ideal without complaining.[11]

OCBs oil the wheels in organisations, keeping teams on track by supporting relationships and shared goals. The absence of these behaviours causes friction – between team members and in the smooth running of the organisation. Micro-incivilities can effectively invert the positive values of OCBs, leading to the withdrawal of help between colleagues (failures of altruism), a lack of politeness (suspensions of courtesy), and complaints about the behaviour of others (breakdowns in sportsmanship).

Since micro-incivilities often wield their power through absences and omissions, they may be hard to observe in real life. Failing to make eye contact with someone may not seem like a significant (in)action, but it will have an effect. Someone who avoids looking at someone else may not be aware they are doing so: the rest of the group may not be aware either, but the person who is being ignored will be acutely aware. Eye contact demonstrates trust, attraction and inclusion. By withholding eye contact, we render the other person invisible. We also unsettle them, making them uncertain about the situation and confused about why they are not being recognised as an equal.

Micro-incivilities are small, behavioural examples of bias. In one study, implicit racial bias was related to behaviours involved in interacting with others. When meeting a black person, white participants spoke less, smiled less, talked less about the task in hand, and showed more hesitation in their speech.[12]

People can also commit micro-incivilities in their speech. Believing we are saying something neutral, we can actually send mixed messages. For example, during a 2008 town hall meeting in Minnesota, a woman in the audience said: 'I can't trust Obama. I have read about him and he's not, he's not, uh – he's an Arab.' John McCain, the Republican Party candidate, was quick to interrupt: 'No, ma'am. He's a decent family man [and] citizen that I just happen to have disagreements with on fundamental issues, and that's what this campaign's all about.'

McCain may have thought he was dealing firmly with a racist statement while honouring the integrity of his opponent. But he also seemed to be saying that 'an Arab' is the opposite of 'a decent family man'.[3] (p5)

Asked about the Republican Party's views on race, Secretary of State Colin Powell made this careful – but passionate – distinction:

> I'm also troubled by, not what Senator McCain says, but what members of the party say, and what is permitted to be said. Such things as 'Well, you know that Mr Obama is a Muslim.' Well, the correct answer is 'He is not a Muslim. He's a Christian. He's always been a Christian.' But the really right answer is 'What if he is? Is there something wrong with being a Muslim in this country?' The answer is 'No. That's not America'... This is not the way we should be doing it in America.[13]

As Powell says, there's a crucial difference between 'the correct answer' and 'the really right answer'. But the need for this distinction is only brought about by the raising of an invalid question. Implicit bias, acting through micro-incivilities, can distort the public agenda, forcing individuals to defend themselves against nonsensical and irrelevant charges. To be scrupulously fair, we should note that Democrats Hillary Clinton, Joe Biden and Bill Clinton also had unfortunate moments when referring to Barack Obama, and they were not as nuanced. The Hillary Clinton campaign published a photograph of Obama wearing a turban –emphasising both his foreign-ness and Muslim-ness.[14] They then suggested that it was right that he celebrated his roots.

Biden implied that his opponent, being 'articulate and bright and clean', was unlike other African Americans.[15] Bill Clinton, seeking the support of Edward Kennedy for Hillary Clinton's bid for the White House, said that 'A few years ago this guy would have been carrying our bags'.[16] What these Obama-related examples also reveal is the significance of competition: the politicians and their representatives, Democrat and Republican, made the statements when Obama was competing against them for election.

It's instructive when people in the public eye make errors of this kind. A politician's faux pas can make them seem, at best, out of touch, or, at worst, clueless. But we mustn't lose sight of the fact that micro-incivilities form a corrosive element in the daily lives of ordinary individuals as well. The photographer Kiyun asked her friends at Fordham University in New York to tell her about their experience of micro-incivilities, and took pictures of them holding signs showing the offensive quotes or actions. Some of the pictures suggest a single, emblematic instance which stands for a lifetime of casual insult: 'This girl sitting next to me moves, to sit closer to someone she's talking to, and this white guy whispers loudly that she moved because I ... "SMELL LIKE RICE".'[17] Other examples are given but to be honest a more powerful way of learning about micro-incivilities, if you are white, is to ask minorities about their experiences. Examples I have been told about include:

- A black British woman being asked 'You look black but you're articulate and sound English. So what are you?'

- A minority female, having just joined the organisation in a very senior role, was chatting to another new joiner. A woman comes over and says 'It is wonderful to have you here and it's great you have joined us.' Except she addresses the white woman not the new senior post holder.

- A British woman of Chinese origin whose boss continually calls her Jenny. She said that whenever she receives an email which starts 'Hi Jenny' she ignores it.

And these were all collected in less than ten minutes.

Others communicate the weariness of dealing with the repetition of wilfully ignorant statements and queries: 'You don't act like a normal black person, ya know?'

I know that many readers will recoil at the suggestion that these behaviours occur in their organisation. Nevertheless, because the majority of organisations do not try to discover what the daily experiences of their minority employees are, they remain unaware of the possibility of racial micro-incivilities in their own workplaces. One prestigious law firm was willing to conduct focus groups with its minority staff and found the experience of micro-incivilities was very common. Presenting the findings back to the partners, their initial reaction was typically of disbelief, but to their credit this was soon replaced with a sense that it was up to them, the leadership, to ensure that they paid more attention to improving their minority team members' well-being.

Research into micro-incivilities tells us that the characterisation of prejudice as typically consisting of overt acts of hostility, as described by earlier generations of psychologists, needs to be updated. Those earlier researchers were not wrong – but they were describing a world that has since evolved. As society has changed, so has the expression of prejudice.

Today, someone with impeccable egalitarian values may still treat some groups unfavourably, and may not even be aware they are doing so. We can admire our 'right-on' conscious behaviour while being betrayed by our unconscious biases. After an Islamist terrorist attack, a Muslim friend told me that he had not experienced any verbal or physical abuse. However, he had been asked by several colleagues what his 'take' on the events was. When he was first asked this, he did not think too much about the question, but after he had been asked the same question several times he realised that people thought his reaction to the tragic events – as a Muslim – would somehow be different to other people's reactions, and that he might even be supportive of the attack. I have since used this example as a case study in organisations, and some white people in particular struggle at first to see where the offence lies.

There are well-established procedures in place to deal with overt prejudice in the workplace. A racist person showing overt hostility to minorities will, in most organisations, damage themselves by being disciplined and even dismissed. There is therefore a clear incentive for racists to assert themselves by using the language of inclusion while using behaviours that make some people feel more included than others – what the author Mary Jackman has referred to as the 'Velvet Glove'.[18] This need not be a deliberate strategy; we may not be aware of our own racially biased behaviour. Self-awareness and a willingness to examine our own behaviour and thinking are critical to the continued efficacy of diversity efforts.

However, a belief that an organisation has 'done' diversity can cause problems in itself. Discussions about diversity and inclusion provide some of the most fertile ground for the propagation of micro-incivilities. For example, native-born members of minorities may be asked where they are from. When they answer, they may be asked, 'No, where are you *really* from?' These situations also provide people with the opportunity to demonstrate prejudice in the act of denying it – for example, the classic claim that 'some of my best friends are black'. People may also give what they imagine to be compliments – and proof of their colour-blindness – which serve only to reinforce the superiority of their own judgement: 'I don't think of you as …'. A prevailing belief that racial equality has been achieved creates opportunities for people to avoid listening to the experiences of minorities, and even to blame them for being too sensitive.[3]

The complex and self-deceiving nature of such situations makes it difficult for those on the receiving end of micro-incivilities to be sure what is really happening, how they are feeling, and whether they can question what's taking place. Raising an issue can make you look like a spoilsport – someone who over-interprets the behaviour of others or who can't take a joke. But the defence that something was 'just a joke' serves the purposes of the maker of the offensive remark, articulating and reinforcing their belief that they are not really racist.[19]

An examination of micro-incivilities in professional cricket teams found that people either accepted the 'banter' or suffered the consequences if they complained – including being regarded as not a member of the team, thereby creating a kind of self-fulfilling prophecy.[19] This double bind – living with covert, excluding behaviour or inviting overt exclusion – understandably leads many people to downplay how they feel about micro-incivilities. This can have serious long-term consequences. Individual acts of micro-incivility have different levels of impact in the moment, but their cumulative impact over time is debilitating. Being on the receiving end of such behaviour can erode confidence and create lasting self-doubt.

One way of describing how jokes work can be found in the concept of category error. (All analyses of humour are famously humourless.) We laugh at jokes because the punchline confounds our expectations – yet the mistake is one we can understand. In the past, black Africans were sometimes given nicknames such as Blanco, which means white.[20] The joke lies in the mismatch between the appearance of the person and the meaning of the label. When you are the person who owns the appearance and must bear the label, you become a kind of walking error: an anomaly and a misfit. Every time the nickname is used, the person is reminded that they do not belong.

Today's jokes are less obvious – and no funnier. Race-based nicknames are rarely used now, but more pernicious name-based micro-incivilities thrive. Not pronouncing someone's name correctly is one example. Each time we call attention to our unfamiliarity with a name, we advertise our discomfort about people who are different to ourselves. Still, perhaps mispronouncing names is better than continually forgetting the name altogether. A friend of mine works in an organisation that prides itself on its diversity policies. Despite having been corrected on several occasions, her boss regularly calls her by the name of the only other Asian woman in the department. I am sure he finds it of little consequence and possibly even amusing. The point about 'banter' like this, in my experience, is that it is not meant to be two-way: the target is meant to laugh along with everyone else, not to reply with some witticism of their own. It is surprising how often a retort is met with a sulky: 'All right, it was only a joke.'

When you are the target of this behaviour, you're being forcibly linked to a long and ignoble tradition. When slaves arrived in Europe, their identities were taken away: languages, communities, families and religions were disregarded, along with their names. These acts of dispossession are still being re-enacted, day in, day out, by people who believe their motives are pure.

Conclusion

The behaviours described here may be 'micro', but we should not underestimate their impact. The person engaging in the behaviour may think nothing of what they are doing, if they are aware of their behaviour at all. For the person on the receiving end, however, these actions create a dilemma. How should they respond? Should they put up with it and accept that they are not accepted? Or should they call it out and risk being excluded anyway? All of us who work in groups (and leaders in particular) should try to understand how we can all become more inclusive, in order to create more powerful, more effective teams.

1. Di Marco, D., Hoel, H., Arenas, A. & Munduate, L. Workplace incivility as modern sexual prejudice. *J. Interpers. Violence* (2015). doi:10.1177/0886260515621083.

2. Casual racism FAQs. Australian Human Rights Commission. Available at: https://www.humanrights.gov.au/our-work/race-discrimination/projects/casual-racism-faqs (accessed 11 October 2017).

3. Sue, D.W. *Microaggressions in Everyday Life: Race, Gender and Sexual Orientation* (John Wiley & Sons, 2010).

4. Fiske, S.T. What we know now about bias and intergroup conflict, the problem of the century. *Curr. Dir. Psychol. Sci.* **11**, 123–128 (2002).

5. Essed, P. *Understanding Everyday Racism: An Interdisciplinary Theory* (Sage Publications, 1991).

6. Gaertner, S.L. & Dovidio, J.F. The subtlety of White racism, arousal and helping behavior. *J. Pers. Soc. Psychol.* **35**, 691–707 (1977).

7. Dovidio, J.F., Kawakami, K., Johnson, C., Johnson, B. & Howard, A. On the nature of prejudice: Automatic and controlled processes. *J. Exp. Soc. Psychol.* **33**, 510–540 (1997).

8. Noon, M., Blyton, P. & Morrell, K. *The Realities of Work: Experiencing Work and Employment in Contemporary Society* (Palgrave Macmillan, 2007).

9. Waters, M.C. & Kasinitz, P. Discrimination, race relations and the second generation. *Soc. Res. (New. York).* **77**, 101–132 (2010).

10. Barrett, L.F. & Swim, J.K. Appraisals of prejudice and discrimination. In *Prejudice: The Target's Perspective* (eds J.K. Swim & C. Stangor) (Academic Press, 1998).

11. Arnold, J. & Randall, R. *Work Psychology: Understanding Human Behaviour in the Workplace* (Pearson Education, 2010).

12. McConnell, A.R. & Leibold, J.M. Relations among the Implicit Association Test, discriminatory behavior and explicit measures of racial attitudes. *J. Exp. Soc. Psychol.* **37**, 435–442 (2001).

13. Bhuyan, A.Z. Powell rejects Islamophobia. OnFaith. Available at: www.onfaith.co/onfaith/2008/10/19/powell-rejects-islamophobia/103 (accessed 5 November 2017).

14. MacAskill, E. Clinton aides claim Obama photo wasn't intended as a smear. *The Guardian*. Available at: www.theguardian.com/world/2008/feb/25/barackobama.hillaryclinton (accessed 5 November 2017).

15. Thai, X. & Barrett, T. Biden's description of Obama draws scrutiny. CNN.com. Available at: http://edition.cnn.com/2007/POLITICS/01/31/biden.obama/ (accessed 5 November 2017).

16. Lizza, R. Let's be friends. *The New Yorker*, 10 September 2012. Available at: https://www.newyorker.com/magazine/2012/09/10/lets-be-friends (accessed 5 November 2017).

17. Nigatu, H. 21 Racial microaggressions you hear on a daily basis. Buzzfeed, 9 December 2013. Available at: https://www.buzzfeed.com/hnigatu/racial-microaggressions-you-hear-on-a-daily-basis?utm_term=.blw71mLWx4#.mjxDPjpa1W (accessed 5 November 2017).

18. Jackman, M.R. *The Velvet Glove: Paternalism and Conflict in Gender, Class and Race Relations* (University of California Press, 1994).

19. Burdsey, D. That joke isn't funny anymore: Racial microaggressions, color-blind ideology and the mitigation of racism in English men's first-class cricket. *Sociol. Sport J.* **28**, 261–283 (2011).

20. Lowe, K. The stereotyping of Black Africans in Renaissance Europe. In *Black Africans in Renaissance Europe* (eds T. Earle & K. Lowe) (Cambridge University Press, 2010).

Chapter 9

Employment and access to organisations

This and the following two chapters focus on specific key processes within organisations, and the way that racial bias impacts them. This chapter explores gaining access to organisations: that is, attraction, recruitment and selection methods. Chapter 10 looks at progression within organisations and examines biases in areas such as performance management, pay and promotion. Chapter 11 on leadership looks at the issues that visible minorities face when they are viewed and assessed as potential leaders.

I begin this chapter with an overview of minorities in the labour market.

The divided world of employment

The field of employment can be usefully divided into primary and secondary labour markets. Primary markets are composed of large, profitable and well-capitalised companies. These organisations maintain their own internal labour market structures which impact pay, promotion and conditions. This makes the primary labour market comparatively isolated from the wider competitive jobs landscape. At the lower tiers, people may have skills and expertise that are highly specific to the firm which employs them. This may provide greater security for the employee – until technology or market conditions make their skills and knowledge redundant.[1]

The secondary labour market is distinguished by its more fluid, informal and insecure nature. Opportunities in this market tend to be for lower-graded skills, especially manual activities. The secondary labour market contains proportionally more women and minorities than the primary market. It also tends to be more seasonal and oriented to part-time, temporary and zero-hours contract work. Although work in the secondary market is inherently insecure, people with transferable skills may have an advantage over people in the primary market who have company-specific skills.[1]

The concentration of minorities in the secondary labour market is a pattern found in many countries, including the UK, the USA, France, Germany and Switzerland.[2] Migrant labour sourced in the secondary labour market has clear attractions for employers. This is not new.[3] Migrants accept poorer working conditions primarily because they are focused on earning a living and may not intend to stay in their adopted home. They may also see the work which they can obtain as being better than the alternative options available to them in their country of origin.

Minority groups are disproportionately affected during a recession, with an unemployment rate typically twice the rate of the white population – and up to three times more for minority women, an effect referred to as 'hypercyclical'.[4 (p112)]

Jobs in the secondary labour market are precarious. Research carried out in 2017 by the Trades Union Congress (TUC) on the UK's 3.1 million black, Asian, and minority ethnic (BAME) employees showed that nearly a quarter of a million were in temporary jobs or on zero-hours contracts that do not guarantee workers a minimum number of hours in any given week.[5] Black workers in particular faced insecurity at work, and were more than twice as likely as white workers to be in temporary and zero-hours work, the research found. One in eight black workers were employed on that basis, compared with one in 20 white workers.

While minorities tend to be concentrated in the secondary labour market some groups, most noticeably Indian and Chinese people in the UK, are better represented in the professions.[6] However, even within the professional groups, there is a pay gap between majority and minority members, and there are still very few minorities at senior levels in organisations.

Minorities working in the primary labour market can find themselves confined to restricted fields, thereby importing a sense of minority exclusion into the mainstream world of work. These areas may include human resources (HR), support roles, community relations positions or jobs focusing on minority customers and markets.[7]

The focus on gender tends to be on women entering male-dominated areas. This makes sense as the male-dominated occupations are on average better paid, with higher perceived status. Occupational segregation is one of the main reasons for the gender pay gap, as opposed to women being paid less than men for doing the same job.[8] Women tend to take jobs involving care or service, whereas men dominate in STEM (science, technology, engineering and mathematics) roles, as well as blue-collar roles, which place an emphasis on strength.[8]

It has been suggested that the stereotypes that exist about groups lead employers to identify those people who would be best suited to work in lower-paying positions, with few benefits and greater job insecurity. As a consequence, if we see men in female-dominated roles it is more than likely that they will be minority men.

One important psychological consequence of this is the effect that working in a female-dominated role has on minority men. Contrary to the commonly held stereotype, black men working in caring roles, for example, see themselves as more 'caring' than white men.[8] White men working in such roles are more likely to receive unsolicited invitations to work in more highly paid, 'gender-appropriate' roles. Informal networks operate to enable white men to gain better paid employment.[8] This has been called the 'gendered racial hierarchy'.[8 (p740)]

Discrimination in employment continues to be a measurable phenomenon, with 67% of black people in the USA reporting discrimination when applying for jobs.[9] While being on the receiving end of derogatory comments may more commonly be the experience of black people, around one-third of white people say they have heard such things being said.[9] Further evidence that racism continues to operate comes from the finding that children of immigrants in European Organisation for Economic Co-operation and Development (OECD) countries report higher levels of discrimination than their parents.[2]

Racial discrimination is not, as I tire of hearing from some clients in continental Europe, an 'Anglo-Saxon' problem. It is ironic that, to dismiss the idea of racism in their own country, they resort to a patronising, Eurocentric excuse. I met with a group of nearly 100 future leaders (all white and mainly male) from an engineering company in Paris recently to discuss the topic of bias. Subsequently, I was given the feedback that, while they enjoyed the session, in future they would appreciate it if I did not refer to gender or race bias since it did not 'fit with the French sensibility'. I had managed to get this hyper-masculine group of men to discover their sensitive souls simply by talking about the possibility of them being biased. I almost felt sorry for them.

Minority groups' differing experience of discrimination is reflected in the different patterns of self-employment among groups.[1] According to analysis reported in the Economist, 44% of new businesses registered in Germany in 2015 were founded by immigrants, up from 13% in 2003. In all, about one-fifth of people engaged in entrepreneurial activity were born abroad. The reporters commented on how immigrants' disadvantages pushed them towards self-reliance in their new home:

Entrepreneurship among immigrants stems partly from difficulty gaining access to the regular labour market. Many start-ups in the past decade were launched by Eastern Europeans whose countries had been admitted to the European Union but who did not yet enjoy full working rights in other EU states. Self-employment offers better prospects for ambitious immigrants, says Mr Leicht: 'Their incomes rise faster, they tend to do things more in line with their qualification and discrimination is less of a problem.' Applicants with foreign-sounding names find it harder to get job interviews with German firms. In a survey of migrant entrepreneurs by KfW, a German development bank, a third said they saw no other way to make a living.[10]

In the UK, self-employment is higher than average among some minority groups than for the population as a whole. This is often taken as an indication of a group's entrepreneurial outlook. However, it is just as likely that individuals went into self-employment due to the discrimination they faced when working as employees.[11]

The African Caribbean community in the UK has the lowest rates of self-employment, largely because African Caribbean people are over ten times more likely to be turned down by banks for start-up capital than white people and five times more likely to be turned down than Asian people.[12] Similar systemic effects are seen in the USA where the more black and Hispanic people work in an occupation, the lower the salary is. Analysis of US Census data shows that white men earn 25% more than black and Hispanic men.[13]

This situation is reflected in significant differences in attitude about a number of race-related policies. For example, in the USA approximately half of the white population think that policies designed to counteract past discrimination, or affirmative action, should be eliminated, but only 6% of black people agree with this statement. Furthermore, while over half the white population believe a lot of progress has been made in race relations, less than a third of black people share this opinion. All groups believe in the American dream, but it is clear that, for many black people, their colour is a significant obstacle to realising that dream.[14]

Learn to earn

Because of their impact on employment, I want to take a brief look at education and race. Minorities typically spend a greater proportion of their income on their children's education than the majority population. Nevertheless, some minorities perform better in the education system than others. In the UK, people of Indian and Chinese origin perform particularly well, and are more likely than the white population to attend university. Students of Pakistani and Bangladeshi origin do less well, as do those of Caribbean heritage.[15,16]

Much attention has focused on the reasons for the lower attainment of some minority groups. Two principal reasons have been advanced: racism in teachers, and pupils' reaction to that racism. Some teachers have reported being afraid of, and intimidated by, young black males. Their fear leads them to interpret behaviour more negatively when it is displayed by young black people.[15] Similarly, students' speech patterns can affect teachers' views of them and can lead to different expectations of European Americans, African Americans, and Asian and Latina students.[17] At the same time, implicit stereotypes reinforce the belief that black pupils have lower academic potential.[18]

In response to the racism they face, black students find strength in unity, but this can move focus and energy away from their academic studies. Some groups find it harder to avoid anti-scholastic influences in their communities. It has been found that other black students disparage those who want to succeed academically and say they are 'acting white'. This analysis works only up to a point: the groups most likely to be victims of bullying and harassment at school, Asians and Chinese pupils in the UK (and also in the USA), are most likely to achieve academic success.[15]

When it comes to education, ethnicity may be its own social capital. There is evidence that minority groups must pay more to obtain the same educational opportunities as their majority peers. In the UK, university candidates of Indian heritage are two and a half times more likely to come from fee-paying schools than white candidates; Chinese candidates are five times more likely. This is despite the fact that the average income of minority parents is lower than that of the population of white parents. Academic success is emphasised more in some communities than others. The sense of purpose is maintained by providing not just encouragement and discipline, but also extra tuition.[15]

Certainly, the motivation to obtain qualifications is rational – qualifications do improve the chances of gaining a better job. In fact, in the UK, minorities are 50% more likely to go to university than their white peers. However, they are less likely to attend the more prestigious universities, they are more likely to be part-time students, and they are more likely to be mature students – particularly Caribbean women. Some researchers found that minorities need to get better results than white students to obtain places at more prestigious universities.[19] Minorities also tend to attend universities close to where they live. Generally speaking, once all other variables have been controlled for, new universities in the UK tend to respond more favourably to minority applicants.[15]

Attraction, recruitment and selection

Gaining access to organisations is an obstacle to visible minorities, so it is necessary to examine recruitment and selection processes in more detail.[12]

Every selection process has seven aspects:

1. Discrimination – in the sense of 'recognition and understanding of the difference between one thing and another' (*Oxford English Dictionary*). It refers to identifying the candidates who best meet the selection criteria.

2. Validity and reliability – the effectiveness and robustness of the process.

3. Legality and fairness – there should be little or no adverse impact i.e. a significant disparity in selection ratios between different groups.

4. Convenience and practicality.

5. Cost and development time.

6. Applicant reactions – candidates should feel, regardless of whether or not they are selected, that the process was fair and job-related.

7. Evaluation – data gathered from running the process can be used to determine how successful the process was in meeting its goals.

From my experience of working with recruiters, I would reorder and annotate the list as follows:

1. Cost – to be kept to the absolute minimum.

2. Convenience – the lowest possible administrative burden.

3. Information – success rates are useful and we might look at feedback.

4. Discrimination – it would be good, on the whole, to recruit people who will best fit with the organisation.

5. Legality and fairness – it would be bad to break the law or to be seen acting unfairly.

6. Applicant reactions – huh? They want a job, don't they?

7. Validity and reliability – it takes forever to develop a demonstrably effective process, so let's just carry on doing what we've always done and hope for the best.

Despite their insistence that People Are Our Greatest Asset, too many organisations want a recruitment process that is, above all, quick, cheap, and easy to operate. The more involved aspects, such as ensuring that the qualities being examined are actually required for the job, or that the process is fair, are given pretty short shrift (in my experience). It's not surprising that those involved in recruitment and selection take shortcuts. (I include 'executive search firms' here – which in many instances well deserve their 'head-hunter' label.) Many recruitment professionals demonstrate a lack of professionalism which, in any other line of work, would get them thrown out of the industry body. I believe that, in the world of recruitment and selection, the bar is so low that virtually any behaviour is considered acceptable as long as the right number of people are selected for a job as quickly as possible. Poor professional standards in recruitment play a large, and central, part in the continuing under-representation of minorities in many organisations. The mismatch between the make-up of labour market pools and organisations tells us that, at the very least, recruitment professionals are not taking the time to seek the best candidates from the available population.

I must also conclude that an overwhelming concern with cost and convenience is the main reason why even well-resourced major organisations refuse to use selection methods which have lower adverse impact but which also take longer to develop and administer. Slogans about 'valuing diversity' and logos of diversity awards make cheap, upbeat website content. But these materials distract from the fact that most large organisations show little genuine concern about fairness for minorities in the area that matters most – the way they choose who to recruit to the organisation.

Attracting diversity

Networks are a key means of attracting people to apply for jobs, and providing information about opportunities and guidance about whether or not they should apply. Immigrants and their children may lack both networks and an understanding of the way the labour market operates. These communities place greater emphasis on formal educational qualifications. But contacts are also important and, without them, immigrants and their children are at a disadvantage. This is true in all OECD countries, as has been shown by extensive research.[2] At first glance we might think this is simply because networks provide information about opportunities, but the research also found that networks play a role in assessing the suitability of candidates and even in letting employers know about the availability of potential candidates.

Networks may be informal, but they can be highly effective means of recruitment. Employee referrals and word-of-mouth recommendations have a kind of built-in guarantee of suitability, because the recommender is often a trusted individual – an insider. The recommender takes a certain amount of responsibility for the success of the appointment, so if performance problems arise then the recommender will be summoned for 'a quick word' and may be less trusted in future. Research has shown that minorities and women respond less well to such referral methods, preferring more formal selection procedures.[20]

The personal touch can make a huge difference. Generally speaking, when they recruit, managers tend to select people of the same ethnic background as themselves. This is often partly due to their limited contact with people from other ethnic groups. But the personal dimension is not restricted to the business of establishing contact or passing on a recommendation. It also includes knowing how to approach an employer, how to respond to employers, how to complete an application form – in short, having the knowledge to navigate the selection process.[2]

Organisations which refer to diversity in their recruitment advertisements, brochures and websites are viewed more positively by minority applicants than those which do not.[20] Every organisation must invest in its public image but potential candidates, especially women and minorities, pay more attention to the messages that originate from external sources. Media stories that exemplify an organisation's commitment (or lack of) to diversity count for a lot more than mere imagery. No matter how clever and slick a recruitment advertisement is, its effectiveness will be undermined each time the press reports on a case of discrimination. The other area that is important is the personal experiences of friends and relatives working for the organisation. The word-of-mouth element therefore acts as a way of deciding whether an employer is even worth considering.[21]

Furthermore, minority candidates tend to use the selection procedure as an indicator of what it might be like to work for an organisation. The more considerate and careful the process, the more likely a minority candidate is to continue with their application. However the longer the process and the more stages it has will result in more minorities withdrawing.[22,23,24] This effect may also be connected to the fact that, because they expect, not unrealistically, to experience racial discrimination, minority candidates apply for more jobs than white candidates. The higher withdrawal rate may partly be due to casting a wider net, which inevitably includes less appealing roles, employers and industries.

Shortlisting

The low professional standards of recruiters are most clearly demonstrated in their decision-making during shortlisting. As described in chapter 4, the discrimination that recruiters reveal at this stage of the selection process has proven to be a boon to researchers wishing to demonstrate how bias can impact decisions. The OECD summarised and collated this research to demonstrate how universal the findings are.[25] Some organisations are now going down the route of removing names from

CVs. It may be effective, but it shows a lack of trust in recruiters. I suspect that this is becoming an attractive option because it is cheaper than training recruiters to do their jobs better.

A potentially useful course of action would be to have recruiters evaluate several CVs at the same time. When this procedure was followed, less gender bias was present than when recruiters examined each CV in turn. Joint evaluation, it is suggested, triggers a more analytical and reasoned approach to assessment, whereas separate evaluation is more intuitive.[26]

Selection tests

According to the British Psychological Society (BPS), a selection test is:

> *an assessment procedure designed to provide objective measures of one or more psychological characteristics. These include abilities, attitudes, attainments, interests, beliefs, personality and so on. The important feature of psychological tests is that they produce measures obtained under standardised assessment conditions which have known reliability and validity.*[27 (p14)]

The critical feature of the test, as this definition notes, is that it is standardised: that is, the nature and conduct of the test are as similar as possible whenever the test is used. Those taking the test should be given the same instructions, questions and completion time. Tests of ability and intelligence, however, pose a real conundrum for psychometricians and recruiters alike – at least, they should. Repeated studies have found they are valid, reliably predicting performance in a role. In fact, the more complex the role, the better the predictive power of these tests seems to be.[28] On the other hand, differences in scores are regularly observed between white people and minorities. [29,30,31]

The adverse impact of tests has been noted for several decades, and led to a decline in their use in the 1970s as well as calls for their general abolition. Yet over the past 30 years there has been an explosion in their use.[12] It is proving very difficult to square this particular circle: the adverse impact of tests competes with their predictive ability. The issue, in my experience, is seen differently by academics and practitioners, with the former being more likely to explore adverse impact and discrimination issues. But then, we have to ask whether this situation is any different to that of a scientist working in any commercial field – cosmetics, for example. There's a product to sell and, as long as it does what it says on the tin, is it really the responsibility of the scientists to tell the consumer about any drawbacks of their products – unless specifically mandated by some law? So it is with test publishers: they need busy, hard-pressed recruiters to purchase their product. Buyers are looking to improve the quality of their new recruits with the straightforward application of a patented, fool-proof method that looks fair. The standardisation of the product ensures that everyone experiences the same test in exactly the same way under the same conditions: 'we treat everyone the same, so we must be fair.' This is a flawed argument, and its promotion by my fellow psychologists makes it even more disheartening to me.

The failure to address the contradiction at the heart of standardised testing, whether by intellectual omission or commercial pressure, means there is a continuing mismatch between the statements that 'tests show adverse impact' and 'tests are good predictors of how someone will perform in a job'. Unless the source of the paradox is tackled, broad interpretations of test results will be nonsensical. For example, one pair of authors felt the gap between impact and prediction could only be explained by a difference in intelligence between black people or Latinos and white people – an inescapable, genetic difference. Their conclusion, in other words, amounted to a return to the race-based theories of the past.[32] Other psychologists have attempted to explain the gap in terms of environmental factors, including early life experiences such as prenatal care and child nutrition.[33]

Research into stereotype threat takes a different approach to the nature/nurture debate, suggesting there is 'something in the situation itself' which holds minority groups back from achieving their true potential.[34] Research into the content of such tests has revealed little overt bias, but analysis of the knowledge required to answer particular questions and the language in which questions are couched *does* show a bias. A study called the Black Intelligence Test of Cultural Homogeneity[35] measured knowledge of ghetto slang. The resulting measure, known as BITCH, showed how it's possible to create a test biased towards young black people, which can then be deployed to ensure that white people score less well. The complementary Cultural/Regional Uppercrust Survey Test measure (aka CRUST) is a recipe for building tests that are biased towards those from the upper classes.[36] Provocatively, French psychologists have argued that a principal reason for the development of intelligence tests was the desire to keep the lower classes in their place following the threats to the social order posed by the French Revolution.[37]

Test publishers are generally liberal-minded people who are concerned about issues of diversity and inequality. But they are also prepared to set these concerns aside when focusing on commercial concerns. If this situation is to change, recruiters in organisations – and their leaders – need to state clearly that the status quo is not good enough. As long as they continue to accept the unacceptable, we will have to assume the purchasers need to believe the tests are completely objective and that trying alternative methods to produce more equitable outcomes would amount to preferential treatment. It's hard not to think that the age-old stereotypes about the inferiority of minorities are simply being perpetuated under the cloak of 'science'. Science tells us tests have adverse impacts, but tests are valid, therefore tests are fair.

Good practice with regard to selection tests is well established. The steps are:

- carry out a detailed job analysis
- choose tests at a level that is appropriate for the role
- choose methods which are reliable, valid, and have the lowest adverse impact
- train your assessors and provide guidance to prospective candidates
- establish clear decision-making rules for the use of the tests
- carry out validation studies.[38]

We cannot assume that best practice is necessarily followed all the time. For example, the Commission for Racial Equality (CRE) found that only 8% of organisations carried out any sort of validation of their processes. It concluded that the use of validity data was not sufficient to justify a test if there was adverse impact. This advice was produced more than 20 years ago. Has it been widely and consistently followed?

The CRE also identified aspects of selection which could contribute to perceptions of stereotype threat, most noticeably in situations where minorities were the only non-white people at a testing event. The authors observed that 'ethnic minority candidates sometimes say that being the only ethnic minority person in a group can affect the way others relate to you and how you yourself behave'.[38 (p33)]

The usual advice is to choose selection techniques with good validity and low adverse impact. Reviews of selection processes have shown it is possible to meet these criteria – if recruiters can motivate themselves to do so. As long as recruiters' primary focus remains on cost and administrative ease, the problem of adverse impact will not be reduced, let alone resolved.

Performance simulation tests, work sample tests and situational judgement tests seek to assess job-related skills more directly than aptitude tests, and they have low adverse impact.[39,12] Assessment centres have better predictive validity because, when well designed, they measure different aspects of the job as well as assessing different competences. However, the evidence for adverse impact in assessment centres is mixed, with some studies showing reduced subgroup differences and others finding as much adverse impact as with other processes.[40]

Interviews

Interviews are not just widely used, but are often considered to be the most important part of any selection process. Untrained interviewers, especially, form a first impression of a candidate within one-tenth of a second of meeting them.[41] Negative information is given more weight than positive information. After the first four or five minutes, the interviewer's initial decision is unlikely to change. These first impressions are based on our cognitive biases. We rapidly assign people to mental pigeonholes – and we are often wrong about them. Unstructured interviews carried out by untrained interviewers have been found to be the most biased, as the rapid assessments to which we are all prey have free rein.

Larger organisations often have formal selection criteria that describe the qualities and characteristics required of a prospective jobholder. These criteria will be used to guide all aspects of the selection process, from advertising the role to making the final decision. This, at any rate, is the theory. In practice, selectors are usually looking for something slightly different than the formal criteria. I know this because I often play a trick on selectors. I ask them, 'What are you *really* looking for?' The answer is generally a list of competences or terms like 'chemistry', 'impact' and 'presence' – and, by far the favourite answer given by untrained selectors regardless of organisation, 'personality'.

Needless to say, these terms are not found in any reputable set of formal criteria. As measures, they are so vague that they are worse than useless. In one organisation where the interview process was showing adverse impact, an analysis of interview notes showed interviewers were making decisions purely based on 'personality'. Candidates were marked as having either a 'good' or 'bad' personality. (Whatever your understanding of the word 'personality', it's unlikely you think it comes in only two flavours.) Even more intriguing were the interviewers' attempts to determine how much personality a candidate had. Quantities such as 'lots' and 'not much' were cited. I still wonder about those candidates who were viewed as having 'no personality' – although I wonder more about the interviewers.

The interview setting encompasses much of the territory covered by psychological research and theories relating to attraction. We are drawn to people who are like us on many dimensions, including gender and race. Attraction and perception similarity are also based on attributes such as interests, education and experience.[42] Race and gender act as proxies for these other dimensions of similarity: they are obvious markers of difference and so can be used as a means of perceiving whether people share our interests. The feeling that someone is similar to you leads to greater feelings of attraction.[43]

Perceived similarity is just as important as *actual* similarity. In an interview context, we do not necessarily have the time, ability or motivation to discover whether perception matches reality. Perceptions can lead to self-fulfilling prophecies in the way candidates are treated, assessed and appraised. Typically, selectors and organisations talk about the importance of 'fit'. Fit is a wonderfully slippery concept, being both concrete and abstract. People know what they mean by 'fit', but somehow find it difficult to articulate it to others. This is because fit is an emotional, rather than a rational, judgement. It is the feeling you have when you recognise that someone shares your values and interests. However, 'fit' also carries connotations of race and gender, as previously discussed.

'Fit' can mean different things to different interviewers. There is cultural fit with the organisation – the extent to which candidates share interests and personality styles with the rest of the team. Then there is individual fit: how similar are you to the interviewer? If selectors feel candidates are different from themselves, the selectors' feelings towards the candidates are less warm. Research in professional services firms found fit was a powerful factor in selection decisions.[44]

How warmly they feel towards a candidate affects the ways interviewers respond to the replies of a candidate. The way candidates present themselves in an interview certainly has an impact on the selector's decision. Two types of impression management technique have been examined in the context of interviews. Self-promotion, where people focus on their accomplishments, was found to be more effective than ingratiation, where the interviewer is paid compliments and common areas of interest and agreements are sought. However, both techniques were found to be effective.[45] The stereotypes that exist for minority groups means that self-promotion behaviour is more likely to be mis-interpreted when minorities employ them.[46]

The attraction an interviewer feels towards a candidate who is similar to themselves is revealed in their interactions, especially non-verbal behaviour such as smiling, discussing more social topics, showing signs of interest in the other person, and sitting closer to the candidate. Negative indicators include errors in speech, hesitation and reduced eye contact.[47]

Biases do not only impact immediate decisions; they can also affect the way people recall an interview. In one study, interviewers were asked to recollect candidates a week after the interviews. Despite the fact that black and white candidates had been selected in equal numbers, interviewers 'remembered' the black candidates as having given less intelligent responses than white candidates.[48]

The impact of race and gender in access to organisations

When it comes to gaining access to organisations, the interaction between race and gender is powerful and disruptive. The seemingly straightforward task of categorising people according to their gender is greatly influenced by how we also perceive their race. For example, we find it harder to categorise black women as either 'black' or 'female' than we do white women or black men.[49,50,51] We also find it harder to categorise Asian males as 'men' than we do to categorise Asian females as 'females'.[52] So, for example, when the gender of a face is ambiguous, people are more likely to categorise black people as male and Asian people as female.

These findings suggest that race interferes with the gender categorisation process because – without people necessarily being aware of it – racial stereotypes are gendered. In one study, for example, people had to write 700 words about a college senior who was either black, Asian or white. The gender of the person they were to write about was not specified. They found that the gender pronoun (he, she, him, her) was more likely to be female when people wrote about an Asian college senior. In contrast, when writing about a black college senior the pronouns were more likely to be male.[53]

What impact does the gendering of race have in the workplace? In this case, racial stereotypes, together with masculine/feminine stereotyping of the group, will influence whether or not someone is deemed suitable for an occupation.

Someone may be rejected because of the occupational prototype attached:

- to their racial group
- to their gender, or
- to people of their racial group and gender.

Matching by racial stereotype

In the first case, there is a matching process between the stereotypes about a person's racial group and the prototypes associated with any given role – this helps us to determine that somewhat indefinable quality referred to as 'fit'. For example, the prototypes of sales occupations are more closely aligned to the stereotypes associated with white people who are perceived to be social, whereas the prototype of an engineer is more closely aligned to the stereotypes of Asians – for example, that they are good at maths.[54]

Matching by gender stereotype

In one survey, people were asked to assess the masculinity and femininity of 30 sports. The results were used to look at the number of black and Asian athletes taking part in each sport. Sports categorised as masculine were likely to have significantly more black athletes competing in them, whereas sports categorised as feminine had significantly more Asian athletes participating in them. So, whether a racial group is perceived to be masculine or feminine seems to influence the race of the person selected for each sport – and also whether or not they perceive themselves to be suitable for the sport.[54]

This point also applies to stereotypes about 'men's work' and 'women's work'. Some roles are perceived as male-typed (e.g. builder, surgeon, engineer) and others are deemed to be female-typed (e.g. nurse, midwife, secretary). When asked to review job applications from an Asian, black or white male or female candidate seeking the position of a librarian (a female-typed role) or a security guard (a male-typed role), the Asian applicant was most likely to be selected for the librarian position, whereas the black applicant was most likely to be selected for the security guard position. There is a match between the perceived gender of an occupation and the perceived gender of a race.[55,56]

Matching by race and gender stereotype

Third, we have the combination of race and gender. It has been found that how a job is described influences which racial group is deemed to be a better match for the job. Describing the job using stereotypically feminine traits led to the Asian candidate being more likely than the black candidate to be selected for the job. In contrast, describing the same job with stereotypically masculine traits led to the black candidate being more likely to be selected.

The leadership prototype powerfully limits the opportunities of minorities, since being white is a key facet.[57] In addition, the gender we associate with a racial group has been shown to influence the types of leadership role for which black and Asian candidates are selected. Asian candidates are more likely to be selected for leadership roles requiring stereotypically feminine traits, whereas black candidates are more likely to be selected for leadership roles requiring stereotypically masculine traits. The actual gender of the candidate does not influence these outcomes.[56]

Conclusion

There are no excuses for poor recruitment and selection processes. The overall philosophy that companies should adopt is well known and is outlined at the start of this chapter. In practice, the seven principles are subverted by a potent mix of bias and unprofessionalism.

Attracting a diversity of candidates requires companies to pay attention to the diversity messages conveyed in their marketing to prospective candidates. That is a good place to start, but is not sufficient. Minority candidates will form an impression of an organisation based on factors other than recruitment messages. These will include the professionalism of the recruiters; the apparent integrity of the process; the media coverage of diversity and discrimination in the organisation; and what they learn about the organisation from friends and relations who already work there.

As well as the philosophy, the practice of recruitment and selection is also well established and has changed little over several decades. The issue therefore is not what to do, but why do people, in particular HR departments, not follow the rules?

In addition, stereotypes about race and gender affect perceptions about who we may deem suitable for a particular role. Some minorities may be considered better able to carry out some roles than candidates from other minority groups. The intersection between race and gender means that the process of assessing 'fit' is different for each minority group.

1. Grint, K. *The Sociology of Work.* (Polity Press, 2005).

2. OECD. Labour market integration of immigrants and their children: Developing, activating and using skills in *International Migration Outlook 2014* (OECD Publishing, Paris, 2014).

3. Doeringer, P.B. & Piore, M.J. Internal Labor Markets and Manpower Analysis. (Harvard University, Massachusetts Institute of Technology, 1971).

4. Jones, T. *Britain's Ethnic Minorities.* (London: Policy Studies Institute, 1993).

5. Insecure work and Ethnicity Report. (TUC. Available at: https://www.tuc.org.uk/research-analysis/reports/insecure-work-and-ethnicity. (accessed 2 June 2017).

6. Mason, D. Changing Patterns of Ethnic Disadvantage in Employment in *Explaining Ethnic Differences: Changing Patterns of Disadvantage in Britain* (ed. Mason, D.) (Policy Press, 2003).

7. Sue, D.W. *Microaggressions in Everyday Life: Race, Gender and Sexual Orientation.* (Wiley, 2010).

8. Yavorsky, Jill, E., Cohen, Philip, N. & Qian, Y. Man Up, Man Down: Race-Ethnicity and The Hierarchy Of Men In Female-Dominated Work. *Sociol.* Q. **20**, 733–758 (2016).

9. Kawakami, K., Dunn, E., Karmali, F. & Dovidio, J.F. Mispredicting affective and behavioral responses to racism. *Science.* **323**, 276–278 (2009).

10. Immigrants are bringing entrepreneurial flair to Germany. Available at: https://www.economist.com/news/europe/21716053-while-native-germans-are-growing-less-eager-start-businesses-new-arrivals-are-ever-more. (accessed: 21st September 2017).

11. Clark, K. Ethnic minority self-employment. *IZA World Labor* (2014). doi:10.15185/izawol.120.

12. Arnold, J. & Randall, R. Work Psychology: *Understanding Human Behaviour in the Workplace.* (Pearson Education Limited, 2010).

13. Cokley, K., Dreher, G.F. & Stockdale, M.S. Toward the Inclusiveness and Career Success of African Americans in the Workplace in *The Psychology and Management of Workplace Diversity* (eds. M.S. Stockdale & F.J. Crosby) (Oxford: Blackwell, 2004).

14. Bonilla-Silva, E. *Racism Without Racists: Color-Blind Racism and the Persistence of Racial Inequality in America.* (Rowman and Littlefield, 2010).

15. Modood, T. Ethnic Differentials in Educational Performance in *Explaining Ethnic Differences: Changing Patterns of Disadvantage in Britain* (ed. Mason, D.) (Policy Press, 2003).

16. GOV.UK Ethnicity facts and figures. Available at: https://www.ethnicity-facts-figures.service.gov.uk/. (Accessed: 10th October 2017).

17. Tenenbaum, H.R. & Ruck, M.D. Are teachers' expectations different for racial minority than for European American students? A meta-analysis. *J. Educ. Psychol.* **99**, 253–273 (2007).

18. van den Bergh, L., Denessen, E., Hornstra, L., Voeten, M. & Holland, R.W. The implicit prejudiced attitudes of teachers: Relations to teacher expectations and the ethnic achievement gap. *Am. Educ. Res. J.* **47**, 497–527 (2010).

19. Boliver, V. How fair is access to more prestigious UK universities. *Br. J. Sociol.* **64**, 344–364 (2013).

20. Newman, D.A & Lyon, J.S. Recruitment efforts to reduce adverse impact: Targeted recruiting for personality, cognitive ability and diversity. *J. Appl. Psychol.* **94**, 298–317 (2009).

21. Kandola, B., Wood, R., Dholakia, B. & Keane, C. *The Graduate Recruitment Manual.* (Gower, 2001).

22. Ryan, A.M., Sacco, J., McFarland, L. & Kriska, S. Applicant self-selection: Correlates of withdrawal from a multiple hurdle process. *J. Appl. Psychol.* **85**, 163–179 (2000).

23. Schmit, M.J. & Ryan, A.M. Applicant withdrawal: The role of test-taking attitudes and racial differences. *Pers. Psychol.* **50**, 855–876 (1997).

24. Ones, D.S. & Anderson, N. Gender and ethnic group differences on personality scales in selection: Some British data. *J. Occup. Organ.* Psychol. **75**, 255–276 (2002).

25. Nisen, M. & Yanofsky, D. Rich countries and the minorities they discriminate against, mapped – Quartz. Available at: https://qz.com/304296/rich-countries-and-the-minorities-they-discriminate-against-mapped/. (Accessed: 10th October 2017).

26. Bohnet, I., School, H.K., Van Geen, A. & Bazerman, M.H. When Performance Trumps Gender Bias: Joint Versus Separate Evaluation. Faculty Research Working Paper Series. *Manage. Sci.* **62**, 1225–1234 (2016).

27. European Test User Standards for Test Use in Work and Organisational settings. (The European Federation of Psychologists' Associations. http://www.eawop.org/uploads/datas/10/original/European-test-user-standards-v1-92.pdf?1297020028. (2005).

28. Ones, D.S. & Viswesvaran, C. Job-specific applicant pools and national norms for personality scales: Implications for range-restriction corrections in validation research. *J. Appl. Psychol.* **88**, 570–577 (2003).

29. Schmidt, F.L. & Hunter, J.E. The validity and utility of selection methods in personnel psychology: Practical and theoretical implications of 85 years of research findings. *Psychol. Bull.* **124**, 262–274 (1998).

30. Bertrand, M. et al. Implicit discrimination. *Am. Econ.* Rev. **95**, 94–98 (2005).

31. Sackett, P.R., Borneman, M.J. & Connelly, B.S. High stakes testing in higher education and employment: appraising the evidence for validity and fairness. *Am. Psychol.* **63**, 215–227 (2008).

32. Herrnstein, R.J. & Murray, C. *The Bell Curve: Intelligence and Class Structure in American Life.* (Free Press, 1994).

33. Outtz, J.L. & Newman, D.A. A Theory of Adverse Impact in *Adverse Impact: Implications for Organizational Staffing and High Stakes Selection* (ed. J.L. Outtz) 53–94 (New York: Routledge, 2010).

34. Inzlicht, M. & Schmader, T. *Stereotype Threat: Theory, Process and Application.* (Oxford University Press, 2012).

35. Williams, R.L. The BITCH-100: A Culture-Specific Test. (Washington University, St Louis. Mo, 1972).

36. Herlihy, B. Watch out, IQ myth: Here comes another debunker. *Phi Delta Kappan* Vol. **59**, 298 (1977).

37. Croizet, J. & Millet, M. Social Class and Test Performance: From Stereotype Threat to Symbolic Violence and Vice Versa in *Stereotype Threat: Theory, Process, and Application* (eds. M. Inzlicht & T. Schmader) (Oxford University Press, 2011).

38. Commission for Racial Equality. *Towards Fair Selection: A Survey of Test Practice and Thirteen Case Studies.* (1993).

39. Robbins, S.P., Judge, T.A. & Campbell, T.T. *Organizational Behaviour.* (Pearson Education Limited, 2010).

40. Dean, M.A., Bobko, P. & Roth, P.L. Ethnic and gender subgroup differences in assessment center ratings: A meta-analysis. *J. Appl. Psychol.* **93**, 685–691 (2008).

41. Willis, J. & Todorov, A. First impressions: Making up your mind after a 100ms exposure to a face. *Psychol. Sci.* **17**, 592–598 (2006).

42. Byrne, D. & Griffitt, W. Interpersonal attraction. *Annu. Rev. Psychol.* **24**, 317–336 (1973).

43. Tajfel, H. & Turner, J.C. The social identity theory of intergroup behavior. *Psychology of Intergroup Relations*. 7–24 (1986).

44. Rivera, L.A. Hiring as cultural matching: The case of elite professional service firms. *Am. Sociol. Rev*. **77**, 999–1022 (2012).

45. Ellis, A.P.J., West, B.J., Ryan, A.M. & DeShon, R.P. The use of impression management tactics in structured interviews: A function of question type? *J. Appl. Psychol*. **87**, 1200–1208 (2002).

46. Bergsieker, H.B., Shelton, J.N., Richeson, J.A. To be liked versus respected: divergent goals in interracial interactions. *J. Personal. Soc. Psychol*. **99**, 248–264 (2010).

47. McConnell, A.R. & Leibold, J.M. Relations among the Implicit Association Test, discriminatory behavior and explicit measures of racial attitudes. *J. Exp. Soc. Psychol*. **37**, 435–442 (2001).

48. Frazer, R.A. & Wiersma, U.J. Prejudice versus discrimination in the employment interview: We may hire equally, but our memories harbour prejudice. *Hum. Relations* **54**, 173–191 (2001).

49. Goff, P.A., Thomas, M.A. & Jackson, M.C. 'Ain't I a woman?': Towards an intersectional approach to person perception and group-based harms. *Sex Roles* **59**, 392–403 (2008).

50. Sidanius, J. & Veniegas, R.C. Gender and race discrimination: The interactive nature of disadvantage. *Reducing Prejud. Discrim*. 47–69 (2000).

51. Thomas, E.L., Dovidio, J.F. & West, T.V. Lost in the categorical shuffle: Evidence for the social non-prototypicality of Black women. *Cult. Divers. Ethn. Minor. Psychol*. **20**, 370–376 (2014).

52. Johnson, K.L., Freeman, J.B. & Pauker, K. Race Is Gendered: How covarying phenotypes and stereotypes bias sex categorization. *J. Pers. Soc. Psychol*. **102**, 116–131 (2012).

53. Schug, J., Alt, N.P. & Klauer, K.C. Gendered race prototypes: Evidence for the non-prototypicality of Asian men and Black women. *J. Exp. Soc. Psychol*. **56**, 121–125 (2015).

54. Sy, T. et al. Leadership perceptions as a function of race-occupation fit: the case of Asian Americans. *J. Appl. Psychol*. **95**, 902–919 (2010).

55. Williams, J.C., Phillips, K.W. & Hall, E.V. Tools for change: Boosting the retention of women in the STEM pipeline. *J. Res. Gend. Stud*. **6**, 11–75 (2016).

56. Galinsky, A.D., Hall, E.V. & Cuddy, A.C. Gendered races: Implications for interracial marriage, leadership selection, and athletic participation. *Psychol. Sci*. **24**, 498–506 (2013).

57. Rosette, A.S., Leonardelli, G.J. & Phillips, K.W. The White standard: Racial bias in leader categorization. *J. Appl. Psychol*. **93**, 758–77 (2008).

Chapter 10

Progress in organisations: Performance and pay

Chapter 9 looked at gaining access to organisations. This chapter looks at how minorities progress in organisations once they have been selected to join. The chapter focuses on how performance is assessed, managed and rewarded.

Performance management

At root, all performance management systems share the same core features:

- reviewing past performance against set objectives

- establishing objectives for the forthcoming period

- evaluating personal development needs

- creating an individual development plan.

Every organisation's system will have its own bells and whistles, but all are built around this well-established core. Problems, therefore, usually stem not from the system itself but from the way individual managers review their direct reports. Five areas are described here:

- appraisal ratings and anti-minority bias

- appraisal ratings and pro-white bias

- assessment of capabilities and development

- attributing success

- stereotype threat and organisational climate.

Appraisal ratings and anti-minority bias

Managers' judgements will be influenced by factors which were discussed in Chapter 9 and which can be seen in operation in organisational processes already:

- stereotypes of different minority groups

- performance expectations leading to self-fulfilling prophecies

- greater scrutiny of out-groups and members' performance, in particular focusing on their negative aspects

- providing less developmental support to minority group members.

Overall, there is a general tendency for managers to evaluate someone who is similar to them more favourably than someone in a minority group.[1,2]

It is difficult to obtain performance management ratings data for most organisations. However, some public information is available. In the USA, a process exists for the appointment of new judges which in the first instance involves the White House, in conjunction with other interested parties (e.g. the Justice Department, the senators from the state with the vacancy), drawing up a shortlist of potential candidates. This shortlist is then passed to the American Bar Association and each candidate is assessed against three criteria: integrity, professional competence, and judicial temperament. A review of the ABA's Judicial Performance revealed that minorities and women were receiving lower ratings than white men. Female and minority judges were more likely to be rated as 'not adequate', whereas white males' performance was likely to be assessed as 'more than adequate' and this occurred even when candidates were matched by qualifications and experience. Part of the problem was identified as the lack of transparency in the process.[3]

Knowing someone's race impacts how we view their performance. In one study, law firm partners were given reports to assess. All received the same report, but details about the ethnicity of the author were varied. More errors were identified in the report when the partners thought it had been submitted by a minority than when they thought the author was white.[4] We must note that spotting errors is not in and of itself a bad thing. Indeed, it's clearly important for a partner to identify mistakes in a report before it is sent to a client. The problem is not the detection of errors made by the minorities, but failing to recognise the quality of the report writing. Also, mistakes made by white lawyers were less likely to be identified. Ironically, this meant that poorer-quality work was more likely to be presented to clients by white lawyers than minority ones. It also reveals a pattern identified in other research: that assessors spend more time looking for mistakes, faults and negative information for minority people than for majority ones. In addition, it shows that managers in organisations are prepared to accept poorer work from white employees.

Finally, where performance is ambiguous – on a borderline between categories – employers tend not to give minorities the benefit of the doubt.[5]

Appraisal ratings and pro-white bias

Whenever organisations look at performance data and find discrepancies on racial grounds – an exercise that is not carried out widely or often – an investigation will usually be launched to discover why minorities are scored lower than their white colleagues.

In reviews that we have carried out for organisations over the years, we have found the problem was not just the under-scoring of minorities, but also the over-scoring of the majority. Most people assume that minorities are being discriminated *against* in such performance management systems, but we must recognise and respond to the possibility of bias *towards* the majority.

The minority ratings may be accurate – they may be examples of the system's rigorously correct application – but the majority ratings are inflated. The assumption behind the search for a solution is that the scores for minorities must be incorrect in some way, which reveals the belief that the assessments for the majority are correct. This assumption needs to be questioned, so that pro-white bias becomes a possibility that can be explored.

Assessment of capabilities and development

The in-group bias, as opposed to out-group hostility, described above may account for the fact that minorities feel they do not receive, or have access to, development opportunities at work. The relative lack of development opportunities is intimately related to career progression. Visible minorities, particularly men, are more likely than white men and some white women to be in lower-paying roles with limited opportunities for advancement.[6]

It has also been found that minorities are less likely to be given timely and accurate performance feedback by managers.[7,8] This happens partly because managers are wary about giving negative feedback for fear of being accused of discriminatory behaviour, but it may also reflect a lack of concern about improving the person's performance and developing them further.

Lack of development opportunities is often cited by minorities as one of the reasons they leave organisations, but not receiving timely feedback means that performance issues which could have been remedied earlier escalate until they become more serious. Minorities are less likely to receive immediate feedback, particularly when it is negative. At the end of the year at formal performance evaluations, many minority employees are surprised by the low rating they have received. The lack of robust, constructive and supportive feedback may ensure that line managers avoid a potentially difficult conversation, but does little to help minorities improve their performance as early as possible. Giving negative feedback, it could be argued, is not easy regardless of the person's ethnicity, but studies reveal that white team members are more likely than minorities to be given feedback on their performance.[8]

The stereotypical strengths associated with different groups have also been examined to see how difficult people think they are to develop. Capabilities stereotypically associated with black people (e.g. being athletic) were seen as easier and quicker to develop than those associated with white people (e.g. being well read). When black people are successful in areas they are not generally associated with, they will not be given credit for having the necessary skills. Other reasons will be produced to account for their success, as the work on attributions has revealed.[9]

Many organisations say they want people to 'challenge', and 'to speak to truth to power'. These are very fine and important principles that are nevertheless easier to say than to do. While it may be hard for many people to practise these ideals, it is even harder for people from minorities to challenge others' views. When the challenge comes from a minority person, rather than a white person, there is an increased possibility that people's views will become even more entrenched than they were before being challenged.[9] In a performance appraisal situation this could mean that minorities are seen as lacking in the skills of persuasion, whereas the real reason is bias in people with whom they are communicating. The developmental need lies not with the minority, therefore, but with their colleagues.

One tool that is used to provide performance data on an individual is 360-degree feedback. Again, however, it has been found that when customers give this type of feedback, it is often more negative for visible minorities.[10] The system can operate as a channel for racial bias, as often the feedback is anonymous.

The concept of 'voice' in the workplace – having your views heard and appreciated – is an important factor in feeling valued and secure in your work. This sense of appreciation enhances self-esteem and assists with learning and development. Minorities are more likely to work in an environment which is psychologically 'unsafe', and which does not enhance self-esteem. This has consequences for the self-development of minorities, who lack the safety net created by the support of others, most notably team leaders, and so are less likely to put themselves forward for more challenging roles and projects. This in turn leads minorities to be seen as lacking potential for more senior roles.[10]

The other complicating factor in challenging in organisations is that ingratiation is one of the most effective ways to improve your performance rating from your boss.[11] Ingratiation includes complimenting your boss, agreeing with their decisions, and sharing similar hobbies. Visible minorities are treated more warily, however, when they adopt these tactics.[10]

The assessment of capabilities has an impact in terms of the development opportunities that people receive. When compared to white staff, minorities were more concerned about the quality of their personal development. Minorities were more likely to report that line managers blocked them being given meaningful career development. This did not necessarily include formal training, but did include temporary promotions and more challenging assignments. Line managers would most often give 'budget restrictions' as one of the most common reasons for this. The only times when minorities felt pressurised to take up a development opportunity was when some form of affirmative, or positive, action programme was taking place.[8]

Affirmative, or positive, action programmes should be part of any diversity programme, and can include training or mentoring for under-represented groups. Usually, in my experience, these are run on a short-term basis with a much smaller budget than mainstream programmes. Minorities attending the events were often happy with the content, and more concerned with the perceived status of the event. Furthermore, while they experienced pressure from line managers to attend such programmes, they were also criticised by colleagues for attending.[8]

Attributing success

Attributions play a key part in evaluating performance. When a black leader is seen as successful, their success is attributed to factors other than their decision-making or leadership skills. But when their team fails, this is seen as a failure of leadership; that is, evidence of incompetence. Research[12] was conducted on quarterbacks in American football, a game that focuses huge amounts of attention on this role. Successful white quarterbacks were more often praised for their intelligent play and strategic understanding of the game. Successful black quarterbacks were more likely to have their athleticism acknowledged.

The prevailing pro-white leadership bias has the remarkable power not only to affect decisions about the future but also to rewrite history. Someone with a pro-white leadership bias is likely to assume a white leader has leadership traits, even though they have not observed these traits.[13,14] Any gaps or discrepancies in a person's leadership performance are filled in or explained away more favourably for a white leader than a minority one.[8] Our default behaviour is to rearrange the facts to fit our stereotypes (and agree with the standard prototypes) rather than question our unconscious working assumptions.

In her review of the fairness of performance management systems, the psychologist Joanna Wilde[10] found that race bias operated in subtle and significant ways. For example, people were rated, implicitly, on different criteria depending on which ethnic group they belonged to. White staff were evaluated against criteria associated with 'high standards', Asian staff on diligence and accuracy, and black staff were assessed against criteria related to leadership, being a team player and timekeeping. The interpretation of a person's behaviour, and the results achieved, differed according to the ethnicity of the employee. Where a black person succeeded, this would be attributed to non-leader related qualities, whereas failure was deemed to be due to not having leadership attributes. The same outcome was found on interpreting timekeeping. Being late had no impact on the appraisal ratings for white staff but had a significant impact for black staff, not just on their ratings but on their opportunities for progression.

Stereotype threat and organisational climate

Whenever minorities feel their ethnicity may affect the way they are viewed and that their ethnicity is judged accordingly to stereotypes, the possibility of stereotype threat exists. Anxiety about conforming to a negative stereotype then impairs their performance. Stereotype threat is most likely to occur when

- the employee cares about the task or job

- the tasks are challenging

- the stereotypes associated with a group are relevant in the situation (e.g. carrying out an intelligence test) and

- the work environment seems to reinforce stereotypes.[15]

The first two of these conditions are often seen as positives: we want employees to care about their work and to want to be challenged appropriately at work. It is the work culture and climate, therefore, that determine whether performance is enhanced or eroded.[16]

Success in a role is not just about how an individual performs. Support from others is critical, whether it comes from the line manager or other team-mates. Research shows that, when under pressure, minorities were less likely to receive help and assistance from their co-workers and were more likely to be more interpersonally distant from them, making the minority feel less included. In addition, when minorities received negative feedback they were less likely to be supported by majority colleagues.[17]

All of these factors interact and can occur on a regular basis in the workplace. While performance evaluations may show a bias towards the in-group, the extent to which a person feels included, valued and supported also has an impact on whether others help them to improve.

Sometimes the way an organisation sees and describes itself can be used as a convenient screen to hide its biases. For example, one business in South Africa described its culture as 'high-performance'. This was reinforced by performance systems that explicitly sought high standards for its people. But this high-octane talk was also used to explain why black people did not succeed. The stereotypes of black people, which would impact their performance, were choked in the language of achievement and ambition.[18]

The same investigation found that even when successful black people were hired, it was assumed they would not reach the required performance standards. Ironically, given the bold statements about its culture, underperforming black staff were not given the feedback they needed to develop and improve. The reason given was that they must be 'equity employees' (hired to fulfil a quota) and therefore little could be done about their performance. The same factors applied to black employees who were successful in their role and were promoted – the prevailing assumption was that they would not succeed.[18]

On a positive note, minorities in organisations that demonstrate an active commitment to diversity feel more comfortable and have more positive intentions to remain in the organisation.[7,19] This suggests that diversity activities help to create a culture which contributes to the security, self-esteem and retention of minorities. It becomes a self-reinforcing cycle: organisations actively commit to diversity, which then generates reciprocal commitment among their minority employees.

Pay

There is a long history of minorities being paid less than white people – colonialism and slavery being the most extreme examples. Analyses of pay by race have been carried out in several countries, and the results are striking because of their similarities. Generally speaking, in every walk of life, in every craft and profession, minorities as well as white women have consistently experienced lower pay than white men. Although education can help to close the gap between visible minorities and the majority population, in every country where this type of research has been conducted, a difference in pay is still evident. Here I will examine some macro-economic data using race pay gap data from the UK, USA and Canada.

After this, I look at how race and pay play out in organisations and provide examples from the BBC and global professional services firm PwC. The chapter ends by examining the gender and race pay gap in one organisation, to provide a more detailed picture of the ways in which they interact.

National race pay gap analyses
Example 1: race pay gap in the UK

In the UK, research published by the Fawcett Society,[20] a charity that campaigns for gender equality and women's rights, stated 'that the gender pay gap in Britain is shaped by racial inequality'. Looking at data from the 1990s to the 2010s, the researchers concluded that while progress has been made, 'large ethnic gender pay gaps remain'. The Fawcett Society research looked at gender pay gaps for women compared to white British men, and also examined gender pay gaps within ethnic groups. The results reveal the complexity of interpreting intersectional studies. For white British women working full time, the pay gap between equivalent white men is 13.9%, favouring white men. White Irish women, on the other hand, earn 17.5% more than white British men. White Irish men earn more than white British men but 3.7% less than white Irish women. Chinese women earn 5.6% more than white British men, but 11.5% less than Chinese men. Compared to white British men, the pay gaps are largest for black African women (19.6%) and Pakistani/Bangladeshi women (18.4%). The gap for black Caribbean women was 5.5%. Black Caribbean women also earned 8.8% more than black Caribbean men.

The highest earning groups per hour, working full time, were:

- Chinese men (£18.32)
- white Irish women (£18.04)
- white Irish men (£17.39)
- Indian men (£17.13)
- Chinese women (£16.21)
- white British men (£15.35).

The lowest earning groups, working full time, were:

- black Caribbean men (£13.34)
- Pakistani/Bangladeshi men (£13.25)
- white other women (£13.20)
- black African men (£13.04)
- Pakistani/Bangladeshi women (£12.52)
- black African women (£12.34).

The report concludes that the results 'are a reflection of racial as well as gender inequality' and recommends 'a rethink of women's economic inequality'.[20] (p19)

Analyses of graduates' experiences has found that minorities are less likely to be employed six months after graduating. Three and a half years post-graduation, 'differences in earnings, especially for women, tend to become larger, which could indicate that ethnic minority graduates experience less career progression than their white British peers'.[21] (pi)

Example 2: race pay gap in the USA

In the USA today, the pay gap between white and black males between the ages of 20 and 50 is between 25% and 40%, depending on industry sector. Even when educational levels and skill levels are taken into account, a significant pay gap remains.[22] In 2015,[23] white men earned, on average, $21 per hour. Apart from Asian men, who earned, on average, $24 per hour, all other groups earned less than white men. White and Asian women earned less than men of their group: $17 and $18 per hour respectively. White and Asian men earn more than women of any ethnicity, but the gap has narrowed most for white women and white men, and for Asian women and Asian men (by between 22 and 27 cents since 1980). By contrast, black women narrowed the gap by only 9 cents over the same period and Hispanic women by an even more meagre 5 cents.[23]

Even the barely perceptible progress of black and Hispanic women is more than that achieved by black and Hispanic men, who saw no change in the pay gap between white men. The corresponding figures for black and Hispanic men were $15 and $14 per hour respectively. Women from the black and Hispanic groups earned the least of any group: $13 and $12 per hour respectively.

Taking education into account reduces, but by no means closes, the gap. White college-educated men earned, on average, $32 per hour. All college-educated women, as well as black and Hispanic college-educated men, earned approximately 80% of the white male figure. Asian men was the only group to exceed the figure for white men, earning $3 per hour more. Some of these differences can be attributed to variation among sectors, but this raises the question of why pay varies across sectors. Discrimination is seen as a factor in the pay differences – by minorities at least. When asked if they agreed with the statement 'Blacks in the USA are treated less fairly than whites in the workplace', 22% of white respondents agreed, as did 38% of Hispanics and 64% of black respondents.[23]

Example 3: race pay gap in Canada

In Canada, research conducted by the Conference Board of Canada[24] found that Canadian university-educated visible minorities earned on average 12.6% less than their Caucasian peers. There were significant differences between the visible minorities, however. The range went from 31.7% less than Caucasians for people of Latin American heritage to 3.7% more for those of Japanese heritage.

For every dollar earned by their Caucasian peers:

- Latin Americans earned 68.3 cents
- Filipinos earned 79.5 cents

- black people earned 80.4 cents

- multiple visible minorities earned 81.1 cents

- West Asians (e.g. Afghani, Iraqi, Iranian people) earned 82 cents

- other visible minorities 'not included elsewhere' earned 82.4 cents.

Analysis of the racial pay gap by gender in Canada, revealed an inconsistent picture: four provinces had a race gap that was wider for women, and in four others the race pay gap was wider for men.

The national data, wherever we choose to look, reveals clear 'big picture' macroeconomic trends, regarding race and pay. Data from individual organisations is, not surprisingly, harder to obtain, but there have been a few instances where the veil has dropped. The BBC recently found itself at the centre of controversy when it was forced to reveal the pay of its top stars and performers.[25] Much attention was focused on the salary differences between men and women, with a group of high-profile performers and presenters writing an open letter to the BBC's Director-General demanding action to close the gender pay gap. However, as writer and broadcaster Afua Hirsch pointed out, far less attention was given to the ethnic pay gap, as shown by the lack of diversity among the most highly paid group. As Hirsch argued, 'a renewed focus on gender inequality can still leave questions of race inequality languishing in the dark'.[26]

As these individuals are highly recognisable it is not too onerous to identify them as either white or minority. Pay was given in bands of £50,000, so whilst this analysis is not exact, the pattern is highly revealing. On average:

- White males earned £370,534

- White females earned £268,964

- Minority males earned £249,999

- Minority women earned £209,999

The highest earning white male earned up to £2,249,999 – four and half times more than the highest earning white female (£499,999), seven and a half times more than the highest paid minority male (£299,999) and nine times more than the highest paid minority female (£249,999).

In other words, the BBC does not just have a gender pay gap, it has a substantial race pay gap too.

Another example is that of global professional services firm PwC, which revealed a race pay gap of 13% between BAME staff and white staff. The gap is almost as big as the firm's gender pay gap, which is 14%. The bonus gap was a whopping 35%.

The firm's senior partner said 'the pay gap is entirely driven by the fact that there are more non-BAME staff in senior higher-paid roles and more BAME staff in junior administrative roles'.[27]

At an even more micro level, it has been found that black waiters received fewer tips than their white colleagues, even though they were rated as providing a better service.[28] Most surprising, perhaps, is the finding that black customers tipped white servers more than they tipped black servers. The motivations of the white and black customers revealed an interesting difference. Whereas white customers may have been responding unknowingly, black customers gave larger-than-usual tips to white servers to demonstrate to the white servers that they were in a position to tip more, countering the stereotype that African Americans are in need of assistance and sympathy.

Economists[29] and sociologists[6] have known for some time that occupational segregation is one of the main factors behind the race pay gap (the same is true of the gender pay gap).

The question that needs to be asked is why this is the case. Part of the answer is the stereotyping of different groups. As discussed in Chapter 9, minority men are more likely than white men to be found in female-dominated roles. While marginally more women are entering male-dominated professions, there is little movement in the opposite direction. Men in female-dominated roles are more likely to be minorities than white men.

So, one conclusion that can be drawn from PwC's statement is that people are in fact being paid the same, regardless of race; they just happen to be doing different jobs. The confidence behind this assertion can only really be supported if a more complex intersectional statistical analysis is conducted.

It takes courage for an organisation to examine pay data, not just by gender but also by race. Few companies have the nerve to do it. After all, why open up another can of worms when equality campaigners themselves seem not to be interested? Psychologist Joanna Wilde had the rare opportunity to conduct a detailed statistical analysis of pay by race, gender and disability in one organisation, and her results are revealing.[10] When she looked at the size of the pay gap, based on averages only:

- The largest pay gap was between part-time and full-time workers (10%).

- The second largest pay gap was between men and women (just under 10%).

- The third largest pay gap was between those with disabilities and those without (5%).

- The smallest gap was between BAME and white people (2%).

Another, much deeper, analysis of the data led to a significantly different pattern emerging:

- Being black had the most negative impact on pay (10%).

- Being female had the next biggest impact (5%).

- Being Asian had no impact on pay.

- Being disabled had no impact on pay.

- Being part-time had a positive impact on pay (+3%).

This shows how superficial analyses can lead to obvious, but incorrect, conclusions. Pay inequality is not just a gender issue. To ignore race inequality is a further manifestation of modern racism. Taking a more complex, intersectional approach to pay shows that what we may believe is not necessarily true. The pattern of gender and race pay inequality is not the same in every country, but one thing is clear: hierarchies do exist and they reveal themselves most clearly when we have the courage to examine them.

Conclusion

Organisations are keen to judge people by their performance and reward them according to their achievements. Leading organisations say they do their best to live up to these values, although most recognise that they can always do better. But while the best organisations are ever more systematic in assessing and evaluating performance, bias still penetrates these processes. When discrepancies are found in appraisal and reward systems, it's often the evaluation procedure that's blamed. In fact, the systems deployed by many organisations will be based on the same well-established principles.

Rarely are organisations willing to countenance the fact that the problem is the people operating the processes. None of us is as objective as we believe we are. None of us wants to believe that the judgements we make about people at work are affected by their colour. This leads to minorities being stereotyped (which roles would be best suited to them?). As a consequence, minorities are more likely to be found in roles which have fewer opportunities for progression and which pay less. Men working in female-dominated roles will more likely be from a minority group.

The people operating these systems can be supported by proper training and briefings to conduct processes with the care, attention and accuracy needed. Chapter 12 describes in more detail the actions they can take. Showing managers the outcomes of the decisions they have taken helps to raise awareness of biases and will encourage greater fairness in the future.

Performance evaluations, career development and line manager support are all crucial ingredients in determining who is viewed as having the potential to progress into more senior positions in organisations – and this is explored in Chapter 11.

1. Sacco, J.M., Scheu, C.R., Ryan, A.M. & Schmitt, N. An investigation of race and sex similarity effects in interviews: A multilevel approach to relational demography. *J. Appl. Psychol.* **88**, 852–65 (2003).

2. Powell, G.N. & Butterfield, D.A. Exploring the influence of decision makers' race and gender on actual promotions to top management. *Pers. Psychol.* **55**, 397–428 (2002).

3. Sen, M. How judicial qualification ratings may disadvantage minority and female candidates. *J. Law Court.* **2**, 33–65 (2015).

4. Reeves, A.N. Written in black and white: Exploring confirmation bias in racialized perceptions of writing skills. *Yellow Pap. Ser. Nextions* (2014).

5. Dovidio, J.F. & Gaertner, S.L. Aversive racism and selection decisions: 1989 and 1999. *Psychol. Sci.* **11**, 315–319 (2000).

6. Yavorsky, J., E., Cohen, P., N. & Qian, Y. Man up, man down: Race ethnicity and the hierarchy of men in female dominated work. *Sociol. Q.* **20**, 733–758 (2016).

7. Davidson, M. *The Black and ethnic minority woman manager: Cracking the concrete ceiling.* (Paul Chapman Pub. Ltd, 1997).

8. Wyatt, M. & Silvester, J. Reflections on the labyrinth: Investigating black and minority ethnic leaders' career experiences. *Hum. Relations* **68**, 1243–1269 (2015).

9. Shoda, T.M., McConnell, A.R. & Rydell, R.J. Having explicit-implicit evaluation discrepancies triggers race-based motivated reasoning. *Soc. Cogn.* **32**, 190–202 (2014).

10. Wilde, J. *The Social Psychology of Organizations: Diagnosing Toxicity and Intervening in the workplace.* (Routledge, 2016).

11. Westphal, J.D. & Stern, I. Flattery will get you everywhere (especially if you are a male caucasian): How ingratiation, boardroom behavior, demographic minority status affect additional board appointments at U.S. companies. *Acad. Manag. J.* **50**, 267–288 (2007).

12. Carton, A.M. & Rosette, A.S. Explaining bias against black leaders: Integrating theory on information processing and goal-based stereotyping. *Acad. Manag. Journal* **54**, 1141–1158 (2011).

13. Lord, R.G. & Maher, K.J. Perceptions of leadership and their implications in organizations. Applied Social. Psychology Organisational Settings. 129–154 (Lawerence Erbaum Associates, Hillsdale NJ 1990).

14. Lord, R.G., Brown, D.J., Harvey, J.L. & Hall, R.J. Contextual constraints on prototype generation and their multilevel consequences for leadership perceptions. *Leadersh. Q.* **12**, 311–338 (2001).

15. Steele, C.M. A threat in the air: How stereotypes shape intellectual identity and performance. *Am. Psychol.* **52**, 613–629 (1997).

16. Roberson, L. & Kulik, C.T. Stereotype threat at work. *Acad. Manag. Perspect.* **21**, 24–40 (2007).

17. Del Carmen Triana, M., Porter, C.O.L.H., Degrassi, S.W. & Bergman, M. We're all in this together ...except for you: The effects of workload, performance feedback and racial distance on helping behavior in teams. *J. Organ. Behav.* **34**, 1124–1144 (2013).

18. Nkomo, S. Moving from the letter of the law to the spirit of the law: The challenges of realising the intent of employment equity and affirmative action. *Transformation* **77**, 122–135 (2011).

19. Jones, J.M., Dovidio, J.F. & Vietze, D.L. *The Psychology of Diversity: Beyond Prejudice and Racism.* (Wiley Blackwell, 2014).

20. Breach, A., Society, F. & Yaojun, L. Gender Pay Gap by Ethnicity in Britain – Briefing. (2017). https://www.fawcettsociety.org.uk/gender-pay-by-ethnicity-britain.

21. Zwysen, W. & Longhi, S. Labour market disadvantage of ethnic minority British graduates: University choice, parental background or neighbourhood? Non-technical summary (2016) https://www.iser.essex.ac.uk/research/publications/working-papers/iser/2016-02.pdf.

22. Calvó-Armengol, A. & Jackson, M.O. Networks in labor markets: Wage and employment dynamics and inequality. *J. Econ. Theory* **132**, 27–46 (2007).

23. Patten, E. Racial, gender wage gaps persist in U.S. despite some progress | Pew Research Center. Available at: http://www.pewresearch.org/fact-tank/2016/07/01/racial-gender-wage-gaps-persist-in-u-s-despite-some-progress/ (accessed: 21st September 2017).

24. The Conference Board Of Canada. Racial Wage Gap – Society Provincial Rankings – How Canada Performs. Available at: http://www.conferenceboard.ca/hcp/provincial/society/racial-gap.aspx (accessed: 21st September 2017).

25. BBC pay: How much do its stars earn? – BBC News. Available at: http://www.bbc.co.uk/news/entertainment-arts-40653861 (accessed: 23rd November 2017).

26. Hirsch, A. Let's not lose sight of the BBC's shameful ethnic pay gap | Media | The Guardian. Available at: https://www.theguardian.com/media/2017/aug/06/lets-not-lose-sight-of-the-bbcs-shameful-ethnic-pay-gap (accessed: 21st September 2017).

27. PwC publishes its BAME pay gap. Available at: https://www.pwc.co.uk/press-room/press-releases/PwC-publishes-BAME-pay-gap.html (accessed: 5th October 2017).

28. Brewster, Z.W. & Lynn, M. Black-white earnings gap among restaurant servers: A replication, extension and exploration of consumer racial discrimination in tipping. *Sociol. Inq.* **84**, 545–569 (2014).

29. del Río Olga Alonso-Villar Coordinator, C., Rodríguez Míguez, E., Groups, E. & Alonso-Villar, O. The Evolution of Occupational Segregation in the: Gains and Losses of Gender- Race/ethnicity Groups The Evolution of Occupational Segregation in the: Gains and Losses of Gender. (1940).

Chapter 11

Race and leadership: The frosted glass ceiling

Organisations like to stress their distinctiveness, not just from their direct competitors but also from organisations in completely different sectors: they are more profitable, more efficient, best at service provision, have the greatest customer feedback, and so on. When it comes to racial diversity, however, organisations – from widely differing sectors and with varying requirements for skills, qualifications and experience – follow a distinctive pattern. Typically and simply, organisations are more diverse at entry level, but become more white and male the further up the organisation's hierarchy you go. This can be seen in the three case studies which examine very different sectors – football, accountancy and movie-making – yet which have very similar outcomes. This pattern, I suggest, will hold true in many other sectors, and the higher the status of the profession the more this will be the case.[1] Minority employees who are recruited into organisations for their talents and abilities seem not to possess the right attributes to be promoted into leadership roles.

Research has established conclusively that minorities are grossly under-represented in leadership positions,[2,3] despite the fact that many minorities have better than average educational qualifications.[4] While much attention is given to the private sector, it would be wrong to assume that the public sector has a better track record – the lack of representation of visible minorities at the higher levels in organisations can be seen everywhere.

This chapter looks at our images and expectations of leaders – the leadership prototypes – and at how these interact with stereotypes of minority groups to produce exclusionary outcomes. By examining the intersections of gender and race, we can see how current strategies to address gender in leadership do not take race into account, and may now even be part of the problem. First, though, the chapter discusses the significance of networks, and how these not only impact decisions but also self-image.

The impact of networks

Chapter 7 looked at the impact of socialisation processes in organisations and how we establish in-groups and out-groups. Being white in an organisation means that you will, on the dimension of skin colour, look like most people you encounter. This becomes an advantage in terms of how your performance is evaluated, the development opportunities you will have, and the networks you have access to. Here I am referring to the informal relationship patterns that become established in organisations. Being part of a network, having contacts and being known to key people are all important in getting a job and progressing in a career.

One of the most notable features about research into the career progression of minorities is the prominence that is given to the operation of informal networks. People in the network – part of the dominant group – will not even recognise the importance of their network: not having to acknowledge your privilege must surely be the biggest privilege there is. Minorities notice, though, because they are excluded.[5] The tendency for people to create network ties with similar people is referred to as *homophily*.[6] Homophily occurs on socio-demographic dimensions that are considered significant in any society, and being part of an influential and dominant network carries significant benefits, including:

- access to information

- access to resources

- meeting influential people

- supportive relationships.[6]

Networks also have a significant effect on our identity: they help to shape who we are.[6] Because networks contain people who look similar to us, and are like-minded, they reinforce, without too much effort, what a leader looks like[7] – and, just as critically, what a leader *does not* look like. Self-perception and self-image have been recognised as key factors in the development of leaders. People who see themselves as a leader begin to act like a leader: they seek opportunities to develop themselves as a leader and they promote themselves as a leader. This is based on feedback not just from others but also on what we tell ourselves. The more someone sees themselves as a leader and the closer they 'fit' with the leadership prototype, the more leadership nominations they receive.[8] However, while minorities in organisations can see how others benefit from self-promotion, it is not a strategy that works for them.[9]

In terms of leadership aspirations and ambitions, being in a dominant network brings advantages and benefits:[10]

- Leadership nominations will come from within the network – those who are not part of it will be excluded.

- People look out for one another: 'you scratch my back and I'll scratch yours.' If I nominate someone for a leadership role I will expect that person to support me in the future.

- There is a subtle acknowledgement that everyone must have their turn and must be given the opportunity to lead.

- People support one another in their careers and development as leaders.

Being popular in the network also has an impact, as those with better ties and relationships with others receive more nominations.[10] Networks are powerful not just for the social ties that are created but also the influence they have on people's careers prior to becoming a leader, on who gets to be nominated for leadership roles and even the perception of oneself as a leader.

One consequence of being outside the dominant network is that more formal groups will be created for the out-groups. These come in a variety of guises, most commonly networks or employee resource groups, such as Gender Networks, Minority Resource Groups or Employee Resource Groups. Organisations like initiatives like these, fitting as they do under the banner of 'Look How Wonderful We Are!'. Minorities themselves are more sceptical about such groups. While recognising the support they receive from others in the group, they are also aware of the backlash they receive from white colleagues for attending meetings.[11] The other impact of such groups is to emphasise the leadership prototype to its members by reinforcing the implicit perception that they do not fit the bill as a leader.

I was once asked to meet with the Minority Network of a British media organisation, which I was delighted to do. I had been invited to talk on the topic of career development, and at this evening event about 60 or 70 people had turned up. For my opening statement I wanted something both provocative and amusing, so I began with: 'You do realise, of course, that in terms of your career development, you are networking with the wrong people.' I half achieved my goal, as this generated much provocation and no amusement: was I questioning the legitimacy of this group? Did I not recognise the difficulties they had had in establishing this group in the first place? Was I saying that they needed to change?

Initially taken aback, I reminded them that I was there to discuss career development, and while I understood the mutual support the group provides, that would not help them much in being promoted. And yes, if they wanted to progress further in their careers they would perhaps need to do things differently.

As minorities see informal networks as unfair,[12,9] and self-promotion as an unusable option, their response will often be to work harder and expect their efforts to be recognised.[9] Unfortunately, in organisations things do not always work like that, as the people who are promoted are those who get noticed and who are well networked. The acclaimed management Professor Fred Luthans extensively examined and researched who is promoted – which was his measure of a person's success. In detailed studies, he found that being effective as a manager was not the same as being successful as measured by the speed of promotion. He concludes: 'Successful managers spend relatively more time and effort socialising, politicking, and interacting with outsiders [to their team] than did their less successful counterparts.' And that 'networking seems to be the key to success … rather than being effective'.[13 (p461)]

In 2017, Deloitte took the decision to replace its Employee Resources Groups with Inclusion Councils in a bid to involve more white men in 'the conversation'.[14] This decision recognises that perhaps traditional diversity strategies, which have had an extraordinarily long shelf life, given their limited success, need to change. Not everyone was convinced there was a need to change, however. PwC stated they believed their ERGs 'provide more leadership opportunities to their members'.[14] Both positions miss the point. The ERGs are neither the problem, nor are they the solution: they are a symptom. Exclusion from influential networks leads out-groups to network with similar people[11] (displaying homophily), thereby exacerbating the divisions. In turn, such groups do not, on their own, improve the chances of being promoted, because the out-groups remain on outside influential networks, but they do provide the organisation with cover when challenged about their commitment to diversity.

What does a leader look like? Leadership prototypes in action

Leadership categorisation theory suggests that, whether we realise it or not, we all have a picture in our heads of what a leader is, and looks like. These views operate vertically and horizontally. The vertical has three levels: superordinate, basic and subordinate. At the superordinate level, we distinguish broadly between those who are and are not leaders. At the basic level, we distinguish between types of leader, such as business, government or military leaders. At the subordinate level, we go into further detail: for example, a military leader could be army, navy or air force.[15] These distinctions are important as we see more women running charities than private sector businesses. This is despite the fact that, having been involved in selecting and developing leaders in these different sectors, the qualities required are the same. Stereotypes, in this case those relating to gender, have an impact on our evaluation of leadership.

Leadership prototypes and how we expect leaders to act

Leadership prototypes give us an idea of how we expect a leader to *act*. We associate certain attributes and behavioural traits with people we consider to be leaders: providing direction, taking action, being determined (or, to put it another way, being agentic). People who consistently seek information and who are less conscientious are not seen as leaders. This is widely echoed in movies, where heroes negotiating complex situations are often provided with a sidekick who asks the questions.

We use the leadership prototypes we carry in our minds to compare the behaviours and traits of people we see around us. The closer the match between what we observe and what we believe, the more we regard that person as a leader. People can also be judged by their results – the more the success of a team can be attributed to an individual, the more likely it is we will view that person favourably.[16]

Agency has two dimensions: competence and dominance.[17,18,19] The competence category is made up of the traits related to a person's ability to do their job, such as being capable, skilful, intelligent and efficient. But leadership is not just about being competent; it is also about being prepared to take charge, having power over others and being assertive. The dominance category also consists of traits that enable the person to gain leadership positions, and includes behaviours such as assertiveness, boastfulness and competitiveness. Here, I will translate these into the leadership model our psychology practice uses and refer to competence as thought leadership and dominance as task leadership.[20]

As well as the dimensions of dominance and competence, leaders have to be able to engage others, to motivate and energise them. People leadership, as I refer to it, is seen as the least important by many organisations, no matter what they may say publicly. Bullying and autocratic behaviour are overlooked as long as he (and I use 'he' deliberately here) achieves results.

Leadership prototypes and what we expect a leader to look like

Leadership prototype research also reveals that not only do we have expectations about how a leader should act, we also have a picture in our minds of what a leader should *look* like, and we implicitly expect leaders to be white and male. Related to this, we also tend to see the attributes associated with leaders (what many organisations refer to as their 'leadership model') more readily in white men than in minorities and women. This applies to attributes such as visionary, strategic, determined and challenging.

Recent examination of the role of leadership prototypes and race has consistently found a pro-white leadership bias. When people were given information about the demographic composition of a company, but not the identity of its leaders, participants expected leaders to be white and subordinates to be from a minority.[21]

It is important to note that this effect is a pro-white bias, not an in-group bias. For white people, the bias is an in-group preference because the in-group is white. But minorities also show the same pro-white bias.

Attributing success

Attributions also play their part in ideas about leadership. As discussed in Chapter 10, when a black leader is seen as being successful, their success is attributed to factors other than their decision-making or leadership skills. But when their team fails, this is seen as a failure of leadership: that is, evidence of incompetence.

As mentioned in Chapter 10, the prevailing pro-white leadership bias has the remarkable power not only to affect decisions about the future but also to rewrite history. Someone with a pro-white leadership bias is likely to assume that a white leader has leadership traits – even if they have not observed these traits themselves. Any gaps or discrepancies in a person's leadership performance are filled in or explained away more favourably for a white leader than a minority one.[16,22] Our default behaviour is to rearrange the facts to fit our stereotypes rather than to question our unconscious working assumptions.

Prototypes and team member perceptions

Leadership prototypes do not just affect decisions about who might be considered a leader now, and who has the potential to be one in the future; they also affect how subordinates respond to leaders, both verbally and non-verbally.

Leaders use verbal and non-verbal signals to show they are in charge. Verbally a leader will make it known that they are in charge: 'I am the boss.' Non-verbal signs include physically taking up more space. These signals need the acceptance of team members for genuine acceptance to occur. Verbally this will be an acknowledgement that 'You are the boss'. Subordinates tend to have more constrained body language when they are with prototypical leaders – they keep their distance. This is a respectful way of behaving, which accepts and acknowledges the leader's role and status within the group. Subordinates display acceptance and acknowledgement behaviours more when with leaders who most closely match the leadership prototype.[23] Minorities who achieve leadership positions will therefore find it harder to be accepted as the leader by the team's members.

A member of staff's confidence and competence can easily be eroded by colleagues who choose to communicate their non-acceptance of a minority person's position. One study found that white subordinates could undermine their black manager by contacting other white managers.[24]

Prototypes and self-perception

Pro-white bias, which is at play even among minorities, has an impact on minorities and their self-perception. If minorities have a pro-white leadership bias, this can blind them to their own potential leadership qualities, causing them to take themselves out of contention for leadership positions.[25] This kind of self-withdrawal is important when we consider diversity in leadership. If you don't see yourself as a leader, this has a direct impact on your behaviour and it has an effect on the way you are perceived, reducing your chances of being nominated for a more senior leadership position.[10] If you see yourself as a leader, however, this encourages you to be more proactive. Since proactivity is generally recognised as another important behavioural trait in leaders, a positive self-image can be self-reinforcing.[25] Proactivity is also related to goals and career ambitions: more proactive people are more likely to apply for promotion or to seek involvement in novel projects.[26]

Leadership prototypes can have an effect not only on the decisions that those in power make about the suitability of minorities to be leaders, but on the decisions that minorities make about themselves. Out-group members are less likely to receive the quiet words of encouragement that provide individuals with a boost of confidence to put themselves forward for that promotion, or challenging assignment.[27] Failure to support staff is not an overt act of commission but a silent act of omission – one which goes unremarked but which has very tangible effects.

In my work as a psychologist, I have met many minorities in roles that did not come anywhere near matching their true capabilities. They could have taken on more challenging roles but they never received the support – mentoring, coaching, sponsoring – that would have enabled them to progress.

Race, gender and leadership

Leadership prototypes also play a significant role in explaining why there are so few women in senior positions in organisations. Not only do we expect leaders to be white, but we also expect them to be male. In this section I will summarise how race and gender stereotypes interact –and determine who is seen as having the potential to be a leader.

There are two types of stereotype: descriptive and prescriptive. Descriptive stereotypes are those traits we believe describe the key characteristics of a particular group. For example, women are stereotypically associated with warmth and the communal traits needed to fulfil 'home-making' roles – such as being caring, helpful and sensitive – whereas men are associated with the agentic traits needed to succeed in the workplace – being competent, assertive, dominant and decisive. Discrimination can occur when women are considered for male-type roles since the traits they are associated with are at odds with those believed to be required for success in many key organisational positions.[28] This sense of 'lack of fit'[29] or tendency to 'think manager, think male'[30] means women fare worse than their male counterparts when pay, performance evaluation and promotion are considered.[31,28]

Prescriptive stereotypes are the traits we believe different groups *should* demonstrate. For example, women are expected to show compassion and warmth towards others, and men are expected to be decisive, strong and determined. Women who step outside traditional roles or display traits associated with male stereotypes, such as self-promotion, competitiveness and assertiveness, are likely to be seen as less socially appealing,[32] counter-communal,[33] selfish, devious and hostile towards others.[34] This can be seen most clearly in the treatment of women politicians, who are criticised for not conforming to female stereotypes: the former Australian Prime Minister Julia Gillard, Hillary Clinton, and British Prime Minister Theresa May.[35]

Just as racism has mutated over recent years, so has sexism. Its most stunning transformation in organisations has been to take the stereotypes of men and women and turn them into strengths: men are decisive and task-focused; women are caring and empathetic. The argument in many businesses is no longer that men and women are equal. Instead we are 'equal but different'. The proponents of EBD (as I like to call it) see themselves as progressive, whereas they are in fact are deeply conservative, dressing up and perpetuating age-old stereotypes in language that is acceptable to modern audiences. The other major problem with EBD is that it takes a colour-blind approach that works to the disadvantage of minorities. Depressingly, at the forefront of this mutation are many diversity professionals.

Much of the work on gender stereotypes, as described above, has been conducted with white men and women. Importantly, the degree to which a woman is judged for lacking competence or penalised for behaving in a manner which goes against prescribed stereotypes greatly depends on the race of the woman being considered.[19]

To examine and synthesise the research on race, gender and leadership I shall use the model used in the psychology practice in which I am a partner. This has three components: task leadership, thought leadership and people leadership.[20] Task leadership relates to the setting and achieving of ambitious goals, accepting responsibility, creating plans, overcoming problems and setbacks. Thought leadership relates to technical competence and expertise, creating strategies, having vision, being innovative and enabling creativity in others. People leadership relates to inspiring others, being inclusive, creating effective teams and being able to empathise.

It is important to emphasise again that the following is *not* a description of the actual strengths and weaknesses of each group, but the stereotypes.

White people

Stereotypical views of white men: strong on task and thought leadership. Weak on people leadership.

Stereotypical views of white women: strong on people leadership. Weak on task and thought leadership.

The stereotypical view of white men fits the leadership prototype more closely than any other group. They are seen as task leaders (getting the job done) and thought leaders (possessing the ability to be visionary and inspiring). Team members also carry the prototypes in their head, so they respond in more respectful and accepting ways to people who fit the prototype best, i.e. white men. White males, however, are seen as weaker on people leadership, being viewed as less empathetic and caring.

White women are stereotypically seen as lacking in competence, capability and intelligence, and therefore do not fit the requirements of leadership positions as they fail on both the task and thought dimensions. If a white woman shows any form of power-seeking behaviour (such as ambition, self-promotion or assertiveness), she is likely to be penalised. Such behaviour threatens the social hierarchy and thus the balance of power between men and women. A social backlash then hinders her progression in the workplace. Women are forced to walk a tightrope between being perceived as competent but not liked, or being liked but not seen as competent.[36]

In the workplace, white women who present ideas in an assertive manner are less liked (by men and women) and are perceived as less trustworthy and less able to influence male listeners than men or less assertive women.[37] Women leaders are also evaluated more negatively than male leaders when they discipline staff[38] or use intimidation to achieve their goals.[39] Men are also more willing to work with 'nice' women (those who, for example, accept the salary they are offered and don't try to negotiate a higher one). When a man tries to negotiate his salary, this has no impact on the willingness of other men to work with him.[40,18]

Asians

> *Stereotypical views of Asian men: strong on thought leadership. Weak on task leadership and people leadership.*
>
> *Stereotypical views of Asian women: strong on thought leadership. Weak on task leadership and people leadership.*

The traits stereotypically associated with Asians are competent, intelligent, quiet, reserved, shy and subservient. The stereotypes are more 'female' in orientation and they apply to both genders – or, to put it another way, Asian men are seen as more female than men from other groups. Both Asian men and women are therefore stereotyped as having strengths in thought leadership and are more likely to be accepted in roles requiring technical expertise. Asian women in such roles may need to prove themselves less than white or black women. Research has found, for example, that people are less surprised by seeing an Asian woman in a scientist role than they are by seeing a white woman or a black woman. Asian women matched the prototype of 'scientist' better than women of other groups.[41]

Asian men and women are both seen as lacking in task and people leadership, because the stereotypes see them as subservient, helping and supporting others but not taking charge. Asians who conform to this stereotype are more likely to be socially accepted and liked than those who go against the stereotypes. As we can see, going against the stereotype has negative consequences.[42] Asians – both men and women – who display dominance experience more racial harassment at work than Asians who are not dominant, or other minorities who display dominance in the workplace. This means that Asians will be well represented in areas such as IT, engineering and accountancy teams, but not in leadership roles.[43,25]

But this view of Asian people is not new: while lascars, from the seventeenth century onwards, were admired for their sailing abilities, they were seen as incapable of captaining ships. Capable Indian soldiers were never seen as leaders. During the Empire, leadership roles in the Indian Civil Service were almost exclusively held by the British.[44]

One would think that having thought leadership viewed as a strength would be a good thing. In the USA, Asians have been referred to as 'model minorities' because of, among other things, their educational success. In practice, because they are a minority in the workplace, there is an edge. The Stereotype Content Model[42] shows that Asians are looked at with envy, their competence being seen as a threat to the more dominant group. If Asian people were also allowed to display dominance, they would be a significant threat to existing power structures.[45]

Being stereotypically viewed as introverted, with a tendency to be more comfortable with people like themselves, Asians are seen as lacking people skills.[46] Because Asian women are also expected to be shy and quiet, they are likely to be penalised severely if they display dominance behaviours. An assertive Asian woman who violates dominance expectations is often perceived as a 'dragon lady': a woman who is untrustworthy, manipulative and conniving. Such women are more likely to be harshly criticised.[47,36] When Asian women conform to the stereotype they are more socially accepted and will gain access to social networks and advance in their careers. However, while conforming to the stereotype may be advantageous in the short term, in the longer term it means that Asian women will be seen as not fitting the leadership prototype.

We led a workshop in an American bank which involved a case study about two candidates being considered for a role. One of the imaginary candidates was white, the other Chinese. Other information was provided about both candidates. Who did the participants decide to appoint? The typical response, much to the annoyance of employees of Chinese heritage, was that the choice depended on the nature of the role. For a quantitative job (one requiring a high level of numeracy skill) participants chose the Chinese candidate: a stereotypically conscientious 'mathlete' to fit right into the backroom. If the role under discussion was in sales, participants chose the white candidate.

Black people

> *Stereotypical views of black men: Weak on thought leadership, task leadership and people leadership.*
>
> *Stereotypical views of black women: strong on task leadership. Weak on thought leadership and people leadership.*

Based on these stereotypes, the main challenge for black men and women is to have their thought leadership and general competence recognised.

The strengths stereotypically associated with black men are related to aspects such as athleticism, strength and musicality, none of which are relevant to the leadership prototype. As the football case study, 'Race at the Rovers', shows, these skills are only relevant for playing the game, not for running it, either as coaches or administrators, nor even for leadership roles on the pitch itself. The stereotypes of black men as aggressive and hostile[48] means that they are seen as lacking people skills. When showing dominance in the workplace for task leadership, they are more likely to be seen as a competitive threat to white men in particular and will be judged more harshly as a result.[49]

The position for black women is different in a number of ways. Research has shown black women to be somewhat invisible in the workplace, and so they are less likely to be considered for career-enhancing opportunities. A series of recent reports by Catalyst identifies recognition as a key barrier encountered by ethnic minority women.[12] While white women are also seen as lacking competence, it is easier and quicker for them to have their contributions at work recognised than it is for black women. Black women often report that they have to prove themselves *more* than white women.

Black women are also seen as having strengths in the task leadership domain, but this is because the stereotypes associated with them are more masculine. For example, black women are more likely to be matched to leadership positions when the position is described as 'masculine' as opposed to 'feminine'.[50] Because of this, black women who display dominance are judged as more likeable and more hireable than similar white women[51] and are less likely to be subject to the social backlash experienced by white and Asian women when they display assertive, dominant behaviours.[18] However, there does seem to be a limit to the task leadership that black women are allowed to display. Black women are allowed to be assertive in order to get things done – but not to get ahead.[18]

While we may accept that black women have the requisite dominance traits of a leader, because they are seen as less competent, they have less leeway when they make mistakes. Consequently they are less likely to be given the benefit of the doubt or a second chance if they make a mistake. Black women are more likely to lose more ground than a white man when they make a mistake: imperfect performance highlights the lack of 'fit' between them and the role they occupy.[52]

Conclusion

Stereotypes about different minority groups have an especially powerful impact when they are combined with leadership prototypes. We expect leaders to be agentic, which is a blend of thought and task leadership. The leadership prototype research also reveals that we have expectations – implicit as well as explicit – about what a leader should look like. Basically, he should be white and male.

The picture becomes more complex when we consider race and gender. The way men and women from different ethnic groups are stereotypically perceived is not the same. Much of the organisational dialogue on gender takes the stereotypes associated with white women and men and applies them to all minorities. At diversity conferences, I have heard it said that there is little diversity in gender; it is only men and women. This approach reduces diversity to a discussion about gender, effectively marginalising race.

In fact, there are different stereotypes associated with women of different ethnic groups, and this has a considerable impact on the assessments made of their potential to be leaders. White women are stereotypically viewed as being less competent than men on thought and task leadership but have compensating, and complementary, qualities in their ability to relate to others. Asian men and women are seen as technically able and intelligent but more passive (i.e. strong on thought leadership but weak on people and task leadership). Black women are stereotypically seen as having strengths in task leadership but not in thought or people leadership. Black men are stereotypically seen as being weak in all three areas.

Why there are so few minorities in leadership roles is because of our views about what a leader should be like and our stereotypes about different groups. Both of these factors need to be properly acknowledged before they can be addressed.

Having minorities in leadership roles is important for organisations as well as for minorities. It means organisations can make the most of their available talent – a benefit which cannot be underestimated. For minorities, seeing people like themselves in anti-stereotypical positions helps to create positive role models and can also help to reduce stereotype threat.[53]

The organisational climate matters as well. Open cultures which value diversity are appreciated more by minorities than by the majority.[54,55] This could be because white employees view 'being different' as a quality associated with minorities. More open cultures are more attractive to potential job applicants[56,57] and companies with an open culture generally have better employee retention rates.[27]

The popular diversity approach based on the philosophy that 'men and women are equal but different' seeks to take the stereotypes associated with men and women and turn them into some sort of advantage. But these views and perceptions only apply to white men and women, not to those of different minority groups. It is enormously ironic that policies like these do not reduce race and gender disparities in organisations, but may actually contribute to them. Because these approaches are colour-blind, they perpetuate the attitude that racism is no longer a feature of our organisations, which helps to maintain our indifference to its presence.

1. Leslie, S.-J., Cimpian, A., Meyer, M. & Freeland, E. Expectations of brilliance underlie gender distributions across academic disciplines. *Science*. 16 Jan 2015: Vol. 347, Issue 6219, pp. 262-265. DOI: 10.1126/science.1261375. http://science.sciencemag.org/content/347/6219/262.

2. Berman, J. Soon, not even 1 percent of Fortune 500 companies will have black CEOs. *Huffington Post*. Available at: www.huffingtonpost.com/2015/01/29/black-ceos-fortune-500_n_6572074.html (accessed 5 November 2017)

3. McGregor Smith, R. Race in the workplace. Issues faced by businesses in developing black and minority ethnic (BME) talent in the workplace. The time for talking is over. Now is the time to act. Race in the workplace. https://www.gov.uk/government/uploads/system/uploads/attachment_data/file/594336/race-in-workplace-mcgregor-smith-review.pdf (2017).

4. Saggar, S., Norrie, R., Bannister, M, Goodhart, D. Bittersweet Success? Glass ceilings for Britain's ethnic minorities at the top of business and the professions https://policyexchange.org.uk/wp-content/uploads/2016/11/PEXJ5011_Bittersweet_Success_1116_WEB.pdf (2016).

5. Ibarra, H. Race, opportunity, and diversity of social circles in managerial networks. *Acad. Manag. Journal* **18**, 673–703 (1995).

6. Smith, J.A., Mcpherson, M. & Smith-Lovin, L. Social distance in the United States: Sex, race, religion, age, and education homophily among confidants, 1985 to 2004. *Publ. Am. Sociol. Rev.* **793**, 432–456 (2014).

7. Shondrick, S.J., Dinh, J.F. & Lord, R.G. Developments in implicit leadership theory and cognitive science: Application to improving measurement and understanding alternatives to hierarchical leadership. *Leadersh. Q.* **21**, 959–978 (2010).

8. Van Knippenberg, B., Van Knippenberg, D., De Cremer, D. & Hogg, M.A. Research in leadership, self, and identity: A sample of the present and a glimpse of the future. doi:10.1016/j.leaqua.2005.06.006.

9. Wyatt, M. & Silvester, J. Reflections on the labyrinth: Investigating black and minority ethnic leaders' career experiences. *Hum. Relations* **68**, 1243–1269 (2015).

10. Emery, C., Daniloski, K. & Hamby, A. The reciprocal effects of self-view as a leader and leadership emergence. *Small Gr. Res.* **42**, 199–224 (2011).

11. Ibarra, H., Kilduff, M. & Tsai, W. Zooming in and out: connecting to individuals and collectivities at the frontiers of organizational network research. *Organ. Sci.* **16**, 359–371 (2005).

12. Bagati, D. Women of color in professional services series 1. http://www.catalyst.org/system/files/Women_of_Color_in_U.S._Law_Firms.pdf.

13. Luthans, F. *Organizational Behavior: An Evidence-Based Approach*, 12e (McGraw-Hill, 2011).

14. Green, J. Deloitte thinks diversity groups are passé. Bloomberg. Available at: www.bloomberg.com/news/articles/2017-07-19/deloitte-thinks-diversity-groups-are-pass (accessed 5 November 2017).

15. Lord, R.G., Foti, R.J. & De Vader, C.L. A test of leadership categorization theory: Internal structure, information processing, and leadership perceptions. *Organ. Behav. Hum. Perform.* **34**, 343–378 (1984).

16. Lord, R.G. & Maher, K.J. Perceptions of leadership and their implications in organizations in: J. Carroll (ed), Applied Social Psychology and organisational settings. 129–154 (Lawrence Erlbaum Associates, Hillsdale NJ., 1990).

17. Rudman, L.A. & Glick, P. Prescriptive gender stereotypes and backlash toward agentic women. *J. Soc. Issues* **57**, 743–762 (2001).

18. Livingston, R.W., Rosette, A.S. & Washington, E.F. Can an agentic Black woman get ahead? The impact of race and interpersonal dominance on perceptions of female leaders. *Psychol. Sci.* **23**, 354–358 (2012).

19. Rosette, A.S., Koval, C.Z., Ma, A. & Livingston, R. Race matters for women leaders: Intersectional effects on agentic deficiencies and penalties. *Leadersh. Q.* **27**, 429–445 (2016).

20. Duff, S. *iLead toolkit box set: People, Task and Thought Leadership*. (Pearn Kandola Publishing, 2015).

21. Rosette, A.S., Leonardelli, G.J. & Phillips, K.W. The White standard: Racial bias in leader categorization. *J. Appl. Psychol.* **93**, 758–77 (2008).

22. Lord, R.G., Brown, D.J., Harvey, J.L. & Hall, R.J. Contextual constraints on prototype generation and their multilevel consequences for leadership perceptions. *Leadersh. Q.* **12**, 311–338 (2001).

23. De Rue, D.S. & Ashford, S. Who will lead and who will follow? A social process of leadership identity construction in organizations. *Acad. Manag. Rev.* **35**, 627–647 (2010).

24. Nkomo, S. Moving from the letter of the law to the spirit of the law: The challenges of realising the intent of employment equity and affirmative action. *Transformation* **77**, 122–135 (2011).

25. Festekjian, A., Tram, S., Murray, C.B., Sy, T. & Huynh, H.P. I see you the way you see me: The influence of race on interpersonal and intrapersonal leadership Perceptions. *J. Leadersh. Organ. Stud.* **XX**, 1–18 (2013).

26. Lent, R.W. & Brown, S.D. Integrating person and situation perspectives on work satisfaction: a social cognitive view. *J. Vocat. Behav.* **69**, 236–247 (2006).

27. Wilde, J. *The Social Psychology Of Organizations: Diagnosing Toxicity And Intervening In The Workplace*. (Routledge, 2016).

28. Heilman, M.E. & Eagly, A.H. Gender stereotypes are alive, well, and busy producing workplace discrimination. *Ind. Organ. Psychol. Perspect. Sci. Pract.* **1**, 393–398 (2008).

29. Heilman, M.E. Sex bias in work settings: The Lack of Fit model. *Res. Organ. Behav.* **5**, 269–298 (1983).

30. Schein, V.E. A global look at psychological barriers to women's progress in management. *J. Soc. Issues* **57**, 675–688 (2001).

31. Cejka, M.A. & Eagly, A.H. Gender-stereotypic images of occupations correspond to the sex segregation of employment. *Personal. Soc. Psychol. Bull.* **25**, 413–423 (1999).

32. Rudman, L.A., Johnson, K., Julian, S., Phillips, E. & Zehren, K. Self-promotion as a risk factor for women: The costs and benefits of counterstereotypical impression management. *J. Pers. Soc. Psychol.* **74**, 629–645 (1998).

33. Heilman, M.E., Wallen, A.S., Fuchs, D. & Tamkins, M.M. Penalties for success: Reactions to women who succeed at male gender-typed tasks. *J. Appl. Psychol.* **89**, 416–427 (2004).

34. Glick, P., Diebold, J., Bailey-Werner, B. & Zhu, L. The two faces of Adam: Ambivalent sexism and polarized attitudes toward women. *Personal. Soc. Psychol. Bull.* **23**, 1323–1334 (1997).

35. Kandola, B. & Kandola, J. *The Invention Of Difference: The Story Of Gender Bias At Work*. (Pearn Kandola Publishong, 2013).

36. Williams, J.C. Double jeopardy? An empirical study with implications for the debates over implicit bias and intersectionality. *Harvard J. Law Gend.* **37**, 185–242 (2014).

37. Carli, L.L. Gender and social influence. *J. Soc. Issues* **57**, 725–741 (2001).

38. Brett, J.F., Atwater, L.E. & Waldman, D.A. Effective delivery of workplace discipline: do women have to be more participatory than men? *Gr. Organ. Manag.* **30**, 487–513 (2005).

39. Bolino, M.C. & Turnley, W.H. Counternormative impression management, likeability, and performance ratings: The use of intimidation in an organizational setting. *J. Organ. Behav.* **24**, 237–250 (2003).

40. Bowles, H.R., Babcock, L. and Lai, L., It Depends Who is Asking and Who You Ask: Social Incentives for Sex Differences in the Propensity to Initiate Negotiation (July 2005). KSG Working Paper No. RWP05-045. Available at SSRN: https://ssrn.com/abstract=779506 or http://dx.doi.org/10.2139/ssrn.779506.

41. Williams, J.C., Phillips, K.W. & Hall, E.V. Tools for change: Boosting the retention of women in the STEM pipeline. *J. Res. Gend. Stud.* **6**, 11–75 (2016).

42. Cuddy, A.J.C., Fiske, S.T. & Glick, P. The BIAS map: Behaviors from intergroup affect and stereotypes. *J. Pers. Soc. Psychol.* **92**, 631–648 (2007).

43. Sy, T. et al. Leadership perceptions as a function of race–occupation fit: The case of Asian Americans. *J. Appl. Psychol.* **95**, 902–919 (2010).

44. Visram, R. *Asians in Britain: 400 Years of History.* (Pluto Press, 2002).

45. Kamenou, N. & Fearfull, A. Ethnic minority women: A lost voice in HRM. *Hum. Resour. Manag. J.* **16**, 154–172 (2006).

46. Lin, M.H., Kwan, V.S.Y., Cheung, A. & Fiske, S.T. Stereotype content model explains prejudice for an envied outgroup: Scale of anti-Asian American stereotypes. *Personal. Soc. Psychol. Bull.* **31**, 34–47 (2005).

47. Ono, K. & Pham, V. *Asian Americans and the media.* in (Polity Press, 2009).

48. Lowe, K. Introduction: The Black African Prescence in Renaissance Europe in *Black Africans in Renaissance Europe* (eds T. Earle & K. Lowe) (Cambridge University Press, 2005).

49. Sidanius, J. & Pratto, F. *Social Dominance: An Intergroup Theory of Social Hierarchy and Oppression* (Cambridge University Press, 1999).

50. Galinsky, A.D., Hall, E.V. & Cuddy, A.J.C. Gendered races: Implications for interracial marriage, leadership selection, and athletic participation. *Psychol. Sci.* **24**, 498–506 (2013).

51. Richardson, E., Phillips, K.W., Rudman, L.A. & Glick, P. Double jeopardy or greater latitude: Do Black women escape backlash for dominance displays? (submitted publ. 2011) Ridgeway, C. L. Gender, Status and Leadership. *Journal of Social Issues*, **57**, 627-655.

52. Brescoll, V.L., Dawson, E. & Uhlmann, E.L. Hard-won and easily lost: The fragile status of leaders in gender-stereotype-incongruent occupations. *Psychol. Sci.* **21**, 1640–1642 (2010).

53. Gündemir, S., Homan, A.C., de Dreu, C.K.W. & van Vugt, M. Think leader, think white? Capturing and weakening an implicit pro-white leadership bias. *PLoS One* **9**, e83915 (2014).

54. Arends-Toth, J. & Van de Vijver, F.J.R. Multiculturalism and acculturation: Views of Dutch and Turkish-Dutch. *Eur. J. Soc. Psychol.* **33**, 249–266 (2003).

55. Hehman, E. et al. Group status drives majority and minority integration preferences. *Psychol. Sci.* **23**, 46–52 (2012).

56. Perkins, L.A., Thomas, K.M. & Taylor, G.A. Advertising and recruitment: Marketing to minorities. *Psychol. Mark.* **17**, 235–255 (2000).

57. Pager, D. The use of field experiments for studies of employment discrimination: Contributions, critiques and directions for the future. *Ann. Am. Acad. Pol. Soc. Sci.* **609**, 104–133 (2007).

Case Studies

Notes on the case studies: Race at the Rovers, The Count and Oscar

In many ways the case studies were the starting point of this book. The examination of three very different occupational arenas was deliberate, as I wanted to explore how, on a topic like race, different they were.

I found that they were remarkably similar. Each has, understandably a racist past, but with changing public attitudes, the introduction of anti-discrimination legislation and application of equality and diversity policies, positive change in the employment of minorities took place.

The obvious acts of discrimination of the past, however, have been replaced with more subtle, indirect and obscure ways of discrimination. In all three areas it can be seen that the progress of minorities is primarily at the entry level: there are now more black footballers and minority accountants.

As people progress through their careers the opportunities for further advancement slow down for minorities. Black footballers are far less likely to become coaches, accountants are less likely to become partners or even directors.

Stereotyping of minorities is clearly in operation in terms of broader career choices. Black men – athletic and powerful – are footballers, Asians – educated and good with numbers – are accountants.

Research examining stereotypes in football reveals the frustrations experienced by Asian footballers. They feel they are not given a chance because they are stereotyped as lacking strength and character.

Black people can, on the other hand, be seen as less intellectually capable, so not only are they not seen as competent enough to be accountants, they are less likely to be given leadership roles even on the field of play itself. Our analysis of the English Premier and Football Leagues up to 2015, showed that on average only about 15% of black players were appointed as captain, despite the fact that 25% of players were black.

'Oscar' shows us the subtle but powerful impact about the ways in which we appraise, recognise and reward talent and personal endeavour. The members of the Academy, who would no doubt espouse egalitarian values, nevertheless displayed a distinctly pro-white bias in their nominations. Note this bias is not necessarily anti-black, but more likely to be pro-white.

In addition, it also shows how a small, possibly unconscious, pro-white bias becomes magnified if enough people in a large body of people hold it.

'Oscar' also shows that public discussion and debate can help enough people to become more aware and question their own attitudes and behaviour.

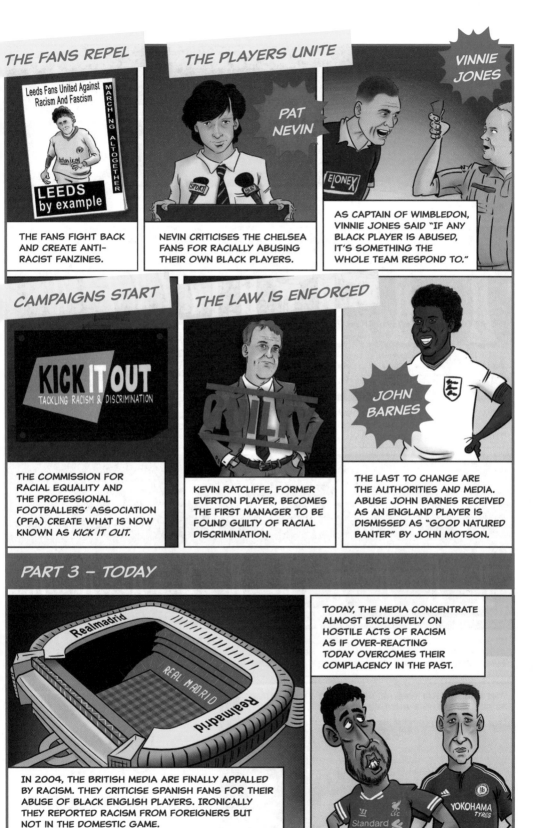

THE FANS REPEL

Leeds Fans United Against Racism And Fascism

MARCHING ALTOGETHER

LEEDS by example

THE FANS FIGHT BACK AND CREATE ANTI-RACIST FANZINES.

THE PLAYERS UNITE

PAT NEVIN

NEVIN CRITICISES THE CHELSEA FANS FOR RACIALLY ABUSING THEIR OWN BLACK PLAYERS.

VINNIE JONES

AS CAPTAIN OF WIMBLEDON, VINNIE JONES SAID "IF ANY BLACK PLAYER IS ABUSED, IT'S SOMETHING THE WHOLE TEAM RESPOND TO."

CAMPAIGNS START

KICK IT OUT
TACKLING RACISM & DISCRIMINATION

THE COMMISSION FOR RACIAL EQUALITY AND THE PROFESSIONAL FOOTBALLERS' ASSOCIATION (PFA) CREATE WHAT IS NOW KNOWN AS *KICK IT OUT*.

THE LAW IS ENFORCED

KEVIN RATCLIFFE, FORMER EVERTON PLAYER, BECOMES THE FIRST MANAGER TO BE FOUND GUILTY OF RACIAL DISCRIMINATION.

JOHN BARNES

THE LAST TO CHANGE ARE THE AUTHORITIES AND MEDIA. ABUSE JOHN BARNES RECEIVED AS AN ENGLAND PLAYER IS DISMISSED AS *"GOOD NATURED BANTER"* BY JOHN MOTSON.

PART 3 – TODAY

Realmadrid

TODAY, THE MEDIA CONCENTRATE ALMOST EXCLUSIVELY ON HOSTILE ACTS OF RACISM AS IF OVER-REACTING TODAY OVERCOMES THEIR COMPLACENCY IN THE PAST.

IN 2004, THE BRITISH MEDIA ARE FINALLY APPALLED BY RACISM. THEY CRITICISE SPANISH FANS FOR THEIR ABUSE OF BLACK ENGLISH PLAYERS. IRONICALLY THEY REPORTED RACISM FROM FOREIGNERS BUT NOT IN THE DOMESTIC GAME.

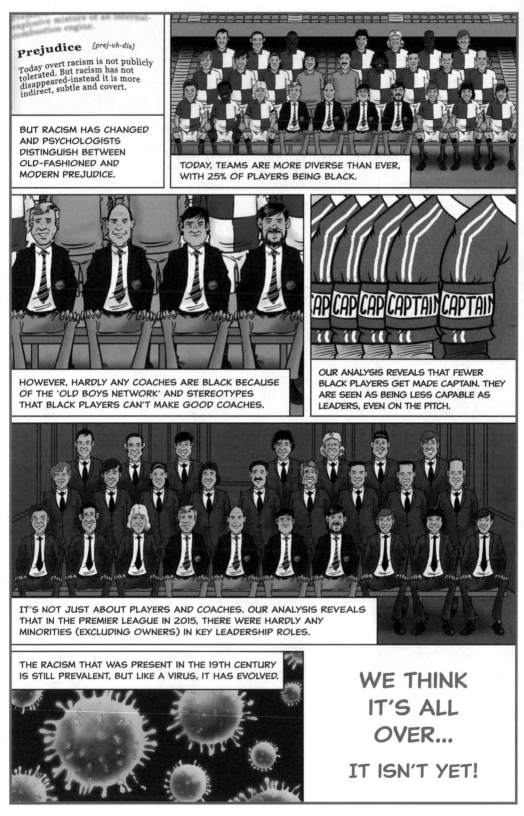

Prejudice [prej-uh-dis]
Today overt racism is not publicly tolerated. But racism has not disappeared-instead it is more indirect, subtle and covert.

BUT RACISM HAS CHANGED AND PSYCHOLOGISTS DISTINGUISH BETWEEN OLD-FASHIONED AND MODERN PREJUDICE.

TODAY, TEAMS ARE MORE DIVERSE THAN EVER, WITH 25% OF PLAYERS BEING BLACK.

HOWEVER, HARDLY ANY COACHES ARE BLACK BECAUSE OF THE 'OLD BOYS NETWORK' AND STEREOTYPES THAT BLACK PLAYERS CAN'T MAKE GOOD COACHES.

OUR ANALYSIS REVEALS THAT FEWER BLACK PLAYERS GET MADE CAPTAIN. THEY ARE SEEN AS BEING LESS CAPABLE AS LEADERS, EVEN ON THE PITCH.

IT'S NOT JUST ABOUT PLAYERS AND COACHES. OUR ANALYSIS REVEALS THAT IN THE PREMIER LEAGUE IN 2015, THERE WERE HARDLY ANY MINORITIES (EXCLUDING OWNERS) IN KEY LEADERSHIP ROLES.

THE RACISM THAT WAS PRESENT IN THE 19TH CENTURY IS STILL PREVALENT, BUT LIKE A VIRUS, IT HAS EVOLVED.

WE THINK IT'S ALL OVER...

IT ISN'T YET!

Race At The Rovers

House of Commons Culture Media and Sport Committee. Racism in Football: Second Report of Session 2012–13. London: The Stationery Office Limited, (2012).

Sport People Think Tank. Ethnic minorities and coaching in elite level football in England: A call to action. 2014. Available from: http://www.farenet.org/wp-content/uploads/2014/11/We-speak-with-one-voice.pdf.

Regis C. *My Story: The Autobiography of the FIrst Black Icon of British Football.* (Andre Deutsch, 2010. p. 257).

Burdsey D. Race, ethnicity, and football: persisting debates and emergent issues in Burdsey D, editor. (Routledge, 2011. p. 287). Available from: https://www.routledge.com/Race-Ethnicity-and-Football-Persisting-Debates-and Emergent-Issues/Burdsey/p/book/9780415882057.

Burdsey D. They think it's all over ...it isn't yet! The persistence of structural racism and racialised exclusion in twenty-first century football in D. Burdsey, editor. *Race, Ethnicity and Football: Persisting Debates and Emergent Issues*. (Routledge, 2011).

Williams J. "Dark Town" and a "Game for Britishers": Some notes on history, football and race in Liverpool in D. Burdsey, editor. *Race, Ethnicity and Football: Persisting Debates and Emergent Issues*. (Routledge, 2011).

Vasili P. *Colouring Over The White Line: The History Of Black Footballers In Britain*. (Mainstream Publishing 2000. p. 208).

Onuora E. *Pitch Black: The Story of Black British Footballers*. (Biteback Publishing, 2015).

Williams J. *Reds: Liverpool Football Club – The Biography.* (Mainstream Publishing, 2010).

THE COUNT

THE JOURNAL OF RECORD FOR 'YOUR NOBLE PROFESSION –
THE WORD 'COUNT' IS PART OF YOUR TITLE' – MAX BIALYSTOCK.

THE COUNT SPECIAL EDITION

Race and the accountancy profession

Historical cost: An inglorious past

None of us can completely escape our past and that truth applies to our profession.

Most professions completely excluded minorities until the early 1960s. The accounting profession was no exception, being exclusively dominated by white males. In the USA, African Americans were virtually barred from becoming certified public accountants (CPAs).

In the 1980s the situation in the UK regarding the employment of minorities was so dire that the regulatory body at the time, the Commission for Racial Equality, launched a formal investigation. The CRE found that white graduates were three times more likely to be appointed to posts than minority candidates overall. At the interview stage, white candidates were twice as likely to be offered a role.

The USA took the first pivotal step by passing the Civil Rights Act in 1964, which outlawed employment discrimination and acted as a catalyst to diversify the profession. Organisations such as the American Institute of CPAs set up scholarships, doctoral fellowships and career development seminars to encourage people from ethnic minorities into accountancy. Initiatives such as these led to slow progress from the mid-1960s onwards.

Today, populations are changing with the proportion of visible minorities increasing. Despite these societal changes, diversity issues persist in the workplace. This special edition of The Count looks at the progress that has been made in our profession on racial equality and the challenges that still remain. Research has highlighted two distinct categories of workplace discrimination: access discrimination and treatment discrimination.

Access discrimination:
An audit of selection

Access discrimination means discriminatory practices that prevent individuals from visible minorities from having equal access to a given profession, simply on the basis of their minority status.

In the context of the accountancy profession, this type of discrimination can occur at more than one stage of entry: acceptance onto university courses (especially Russell Group institutions) and recruitment into a professional organisation.

A comparison of statistics from the Higher Education Statistics Agency shows growth in the percentages of ethnic minority students studying and graduating from accounting degrees in the past decade. In 2000/01, 28.9% of accountancy qualifiers were of ethnic (non-white) origin. By 2012/13, this had risen to 43.9%. These figures are comparable to those from the USA, where the number of minorities studying accountancy is also 43%. Whilst direct comparisons are not straightforward, The Count's analysis reveals that of the Big Four accountancy firms, only KPMG recruit minorities in comparable numbers.

Double-entry discrimination

The shortfall in recruiting minorities may be due to a continued reliance on students from the top universities. Although some progress has been made in diversifying student populations, under-representation continues to be most apparent in Russell Group universities, where black and Asian state school applicants are less likely to receive offers than equivalently qualified white peers from private schools.

While the top universities claim they are objective in their decision making, contradictory findings have cast doubt on this. Durham University researchers found that university applicants with the same A-level grades were equally likely to apply to Russell Group universities, regardless of their ethnic background. However, those from black, Pakistani and Bangladeshi backgrounds were shown to be significantly less likely than white applicants to be offered a place at Russell Group universities, even when they had achieved the same exam grades at A-level.

Firms' reliance on elite schools (e.g. the Russell Group in the UK) and the lack of interest in students from other universities reflects a belief that some degrees are better than others, an outcome not dissimilar from American accountancy firms not trusting qualifications obtained by students at black colleges. Minorities are less likely to enter the top universities and so are less likely to enter accountancy firms despite being as motivated, engaged and confident as white students; in other words, double entry discrimination.

Although racism in professional settings may no longer be blatant, often it has simply taken on a more sophisticated form. Six months after graduating, minorities are more likely than white graduates to be unemployed. The universities which have the highest number of accountancy students employed after graduation are also those with lower numbers of minorities.

Despite the increase in minorities being recruited into firms, the numbers do not stack up well compared to the numbers studying accountancy. It has been suggested that potential recruits from minorities could be discouraged from entering the profession due to a lack of appropriate role models. A lack of ethnic minorities in senior positions tells new starters that success for minorities in accounting is unlikely, if not impossible. Potential recruits have been known to self-deselect on the grounds of anticipated future rejection.

This could leave them feeling demotivated from the outset, especially if they believe the absence of role models to be an indicator of limited prospects in the profession.

Depreciation over time: Treatment discrimination

Once in a firm minorities report being stereotyped and that they are judged by their ethnicity rather than on their performance, something known as treatment discrimination. Substantial survey and anecdotal evidence suggests that, once inside the door, the minority professional is frequently subject to treatment discrimination, including unfair assignment of projects and stunted upward mobility in the organisation.

A lack of social capital

Studies of accountancy firms show that minorities feel compelled to hide their 'difference' in order to claim a right to equality in the workplace. Research over many years shows that minorities feel that being the 'other' in a workplace had a negative impact on their chances of promotion or professional advancement.

Some of the most common stepping stones to discrimination are misattributions and stereotypes concerning minorities, while minority women reported being stereotyped more than men or white women. Other factors reported regularly include:

- Being given less challenging assignments
- Having good performance attributed to factors other than ability
- Not having access to the informal networks in the firm.

Assignment to less challenging projects has immediate and long-lasting effects on an individual's career because such projects allow the development of skills, the formation of professional networks, and the development of relationships with clients. All of these factors impact a person's visibility, promotions and, ultimately, consideration for appointment to partner.

Declining goodwill

A survey of black accounting graduates and successful black accountants showed a significant relationship between perceived treatment discrimination and job satisfaction. Subtle forms of discrimination, feelings of marginalisation and a lack of sense of belonging ultimately push black professionals to leave firms.

Personal Accounts: Two minorities tell their stories

Two visible minorities told The Count of their experiences working in major accountancy firms.

Person 1. I had worked for this firm for over a decade and a half having joined mid-career from the public sector. I enjoyed working there. It was a big firm with a lot of opportunities. One senior partner gave me some great opportunities and for a while my career seemed to be going places. I was promoted to partner – one of the very few black people to achieve this. I was given responsibility for a core area of the firm and people said I did a great job.

The election of a new senior partner and things led to changes, but that's to be expected. I was given responsibility for developing new business among minorities. I wasn't overjoyed as it felt like a demotion and I wondered if I was being pigeon-holed into an area where the firm thought having a black face would help. Anyway I did it for a few years and decided I needed a change as my career, which at one stage seemed to be going somewhere, had stalled. I realised that in all my years with the firm I had never been given P&L responsibility.

I met with the senior partner (yet another one) to discuss my career. I thought it could be a very constructive discussion and was looking forward to it, as I hadn't had a conversation like this for quite a few years.

Within minutes of the meeting starting it was clear he had no interest in me or my career. He looked at his watch, stared out of the window (the view is amazing from his office) and the subject quickly changed to his family.

That was it for me. With my experience and loyalty I had expected to be treated with a modicum of respect. He wasn't interested and I realised that my time here was up.

I resigned soon after.

Person 2. I am not an accountant by background and I was brought in to develop a new line of business. My boss, a partner, was fantastic. He encouraged, challenged, supported, – I could not have asked for more from him. He is older than me, successful, and white. On the surface you'd think I, as an Asian man from a working-class background would have little in common. In fact we shared the same values about achievement, diversity and fairness.

Anyway, after a couple of years, the results of our area were so good that I was put onto partner track. Then, following a reorganisation, I was given a new boss – a partner who had a track record on gender diversity. It started reasonably well. Then I noticed I was being called out more often by her for work that she didn't consider good enough. Occasionally she would have a point but mostly it seemed pretty trivial to me. I became disillusioned and was certainly not enjoying work any longer. My self-confidence was affected and I could not figure out what was going on. She then took me off partner track saying I lacked the qualities to be promoted.

I was thinking of quitting but following advice from friends I decided to tell my old boss what was going on. My performance was looked at by others and they concluded that I was doing very well and that the assessments made of me were unsupported by evidence.

The upshot is that I have moved boss once more and I feel that my performance is again being recognised for what it really is. It just goes to show how important having a fair-minded boss is.

The Big Four? More like the largish one, the small two and the tiny one

The highest reaches of the accountancy profession remain an almost exclusive domain of the white male. While direct comparisons are difficult, as firms present their data in different ways, one thing is clear: KPMG have the highest proportion of partners who are from a minority group, with 11%. They are followed by PwC and EY on 7% and Deloittes on 5%. KPMG also recruit the highest number of minorities into their organisation.

But Deloittes should not worry as they seem to pick up the highest number of awards for their diversity efforts.

Race and pay: Voluntary disclosure by PwC

Big Four firm PwC took voluntary disclosure to a new level when they decided to reveal an analysis they conducted on race and pay. The results showed a 14% pay gap between white and minority staff which widened to an enormous 38% for bonus payments. The issues, said PwC, are structural as minorities tend to occupy the lower status jobs and so are paid less. The results are consistent with other research that shows that minorities do not progress to more senior roles due to stereotyping and lack of access to mentors and networks. This is a bold step by PwC, which usefully sheds light on an issue which tends to be totally ignored. It is to be hoped others follow their example.

THE COUNT'S CONCLUSION ON RACE EQUALITY IN ACCOUNTANCY FIRMS: A WORK-IN-PROGRESS

There can little doubt that accountancy firms are taking diversity a lot more seriously than they did in the past – but that may not be saying much. Despite the increase in the numbers of graduates taken on this is still not, with the exception of KPMG, in line with the numbers of minorities studying accountancy at university.

The progression to partner is as tortuous and laboured as ever for minorities. The issues, despite what the firms may claim, have not changed much, if at all, and remain: stereotyping, a biased view of leadership capabilities and lack of support for development for minorities. The indifference to race equality is there for all to see and as a consequence we can only conclude that it remains a work-in-progress. The boldness PwC have shown in being transparent is significant and is a more honest approach than seeking diversity awards.

IMAGES OF LEADERS – A LACK OF BALANCE?

A content analysis of the annual reviews of the UK's Big Four accounting firms in order to analyse their representation of race and gender. Images of white men dominated the reports (81% of images), three reports failed to feature images of minorities alone, and two had no images showing blacks and whites together. Ethnic minorities are more likely (30%) to be portrayed as other stakeholders, rather than partners, employees or clients, while 90% of images of senior management figures in a firm show exclusively white people. Only 3% were exclusively people of colour.

The Count

Atewologun D, Sealy R, Vinnicombe S. Revealing Intersectional Dynamics in Organizations: Introducing "Intersectional Identity Work." Gender, Work Organ. (2016) May 1 [cited 2017 Oct 6];23(3):223–47. Available from: http://doi.wiley.com/10.1111/gwao.12082.

Bagati D. Women of Color in Professional Services Series | 1 Women of Color in Professional Services Series. [cited 2017 Oct 7]; Available from: http://www.catalyst.org/system/files/Women_of_Color_in_U.S._Law_Firms.pdf.

Boliver V. How fair is access to more prestigious UK universities. Br J Sociol. 2013;64(2): 344–64.

Lewis A.M. "Counting black and white beans": Why we need a critical race theory of accounting. Eur J Contemp Econ Manag. (2015) 2(2):1–13.

Moyes G.D., Williams P.A., Quigley B.Z. The relation between perceived treatment discrimination and job satisfaction among African American accounting professionals. Account Horizons (2000) Mar 9 [cited 2017 Nov 21];14(1):21–48. Available from: http://aaajournals.org/doi/10.2308/acch.2000.14.1.21.

Kyriakidou O, Kyriacou O, Özbilgin M, Dedoulis E. Editorial: Equality, diversity and inclusion in accounting. Crit Perspect Account (2016) Mar [cited 2017 Nov 22];35:1–12. Available from: http://linkinghub.elsevier.com/retrieve/pii/S104523541500129X

Saggar S, Norrie R, Bannister M.D.G. Bittersweet success?: Glass ceilings for Britain's ethnic minorities at the top of business and the professions. (Policy Exchange Institute, 2016).

<u>OSCAR</u>

Written by

Abigail Burdess

Based on research by Professor Binna Kandola and Kulraj Bains

INTERIOR, WAREHOUSE, EARLY MORNING.

Stepladders, rolled up red carpet, tools... a warehouse shelf with a row of Oscar statuettes. Work overalls flash past. An Oscar statuette begins to wobble, to totter, then it falls, into the next. One by one, the Oscars fall like dominoes into...

A vast can of whitewash. A hand lifts the Oscar, its gold turned white.

> CARETAKER (OFF SCREEN)
> How's this happened?!?

INT, THE INVESTIGATOR'S KITCHEN, MORNING.

February 2016. An untouched cup of coffee cools on the kitchen counter. Andy, 40, the investigator, watches – reflected in his spectacles – the TV screen. On it, action hero Will Smith is smiling charmingly.

> INTERVIEWER
> Jada's said she's boycotting. So will you be attending the Oscar ceremony this year?

On screen, Will smiles ruefully.

> WILL SMITH
> No. My wife's not going. It would be awkward to show up with Charlize...

Andy's wife, Elaine (23) beautiful, enters, carrying laundry.

> ELAINE
> Honey, could you remember to pick up the...

Andy turns to her. She is silenced by the look on his face.

> ELAINE (CONT'D)
> What is it?

Andy gestures to the TV.

> ANDY
> Will. He's boycotting the Oscars. Along with Jada Pinkett-Smith and Spike Lee.

The laundry falls from Elaine's hand.

> ELAINE
> What? But why?

ANDY

Every single nominee this year was white.

Elaine is shell-shocked.

ELAINE

I don't believe you.

Andy hands Elaine a copy of the LA Times. A picture of Cheryl
Boone-Isaacs, African American, 69, stunning. The headline reads:
'Academy President "heart-broken and frustrated" by lack of
diversity.'

ELAINE (CONT'D)

But why? Why are the Oscars so white?

On screen, Will is explaining...

WILL SMITH V/O

...the nominations reflect the Academy. The Academy reflects the
industry, and then the industry reflects America.

ANDY

I don't know. I don't know. But I'm going to find out...

CUT TO:

INT. INVESTIGATOR'S OFFICE DAY.

A chaotic office. Sam, 48, Andy's boss, graying, rumpled, has his
feet on a large desk strewn with papers. Andy plucks nervously at
the copy of the LA Times.

SAM

Ask all you like but I'm telling you, they'll never give you those
ethnicity stats! The Academy's a secret club of 6,000 industry
professionals – they would never publicly disclose their
membership!

ANDY

Well, I know that now.

Sam sees a copy of the LA Times in Andy's hand.

SAM

Wait a minute...Didn't the LA Times blow this whole thing wide open
back in 2012? I've got a copy in here somewhere...

Sam indicates a massive pile of old newspapers.

ANDY

I've got a better idea.

Andy takes out his laptop.

CUT TO:

INT. ANDY'S HOME, NIGHT.

Andy's bespectacled profile is outlined in the glow of his computer screen – Andy scans the LA TIMES data: Black filmmakers 2% – Latino filmmakers – 1%. Academy 94% white. Andy's mouth falls open.

ANDY

(under breath)

Oh my God.

Andy yawns. Elaine appears at the doorway in a nightgown.

ELAINE

You coming to bed?

ANDY

In a minute...

Elaine disappears. Andy checks his watch. His eyelids are heavy. He puts his head down on the desk.

CUT TO:

INT. THE ACADEMY.

Andy's face presses against an ancient door. It creaks open. Before him a vast hall – everything is strange and shadowy, for this is Andy's DREAM.

As Andy peers into the gloom, light spears through arched windows to reveal...

Old people. Closest to him – four men, then one woman, behind another four men and one woman then another, and another – rank upon rank, a vast phalanx of old people. 6,028 Academy members – an ancient army in Ted Baker shirts. Amongst these just 61 are black, 120 are Latino. On the front row one East Asian man suddenly catches Andy's eye, and nods. Yes. As Andy stares the members step forward as one and push the door shut in Andy's face.

Andy looks up. A sign above the door reads 'The Academy'.

Andy wakes with a start.

> ANDY
>
> I've got to tell Sam...

INT. INVESTIGATOR'S OFFICE, NIGHT

The office is even messier. Andy is pacing. A board behind him is covered with statistics.

> ANDY
>
> ... and nearly four out of five Academy members are men: old men – only fourteen percent are under fifty. The average age is sixty-two.

> SAM
>
> Sixty-two, huh?

> ANDY
>
> Those figures are from 2012. By 2013 the average had gone up to sixty-three. The average Academy member looks like this.

Andy indicates a picture on the board of Ed Harris.

> SAM
>
> That's Ed Harris.

> ANDY
>
> It is.

Sam runs a hand through his hair.

> SAM
>
> What the hell are the Academy doing about this?

> ANDY
>
> They've announced a diversity initiative – invited almost seven hundred new members, over forty percent people of colour.

Andy indicates photos of Idris Elba, Daniel Dae Kim and Freida Pinto, all wearing very little.

> SAM
>
> Why are they wearing so little?

ANDY

Old movie trick. If you're trying to convey a lot of information, you make good-looking actors take their clothes off so the audience don't get bored.

SAM

Clever. So the Academy think that'll stave off an Oscars boycott? That's gotta change the demographic?

ANDY

Not really. Academy members serve for life, so change is glacial, even if all the invitees accept, the make-up of the Academy'll only change by a tiny margin. But Boone-Isaacs says she's reviewing the recruitment process to become a member.

SAM

What is the recruitment process?

ANDY

Let me show you a movie called 'How to join the Academy'.

Andy pulls up a flat screen.

ANDY (CONT'D)

Let's start with the credits.

Andy points the remote. The credits roll.

ANDY (CONT'D)

Writers, producers and directors need a minimum of two credits, actors; three, and an 'unusually high level of distinction' in their fields, but you can bypass all that if you've got two friends to sponsor you...

Andy plays a clip: Oscar nominee Stand By Me. Two young white boys smoke cigarettes in a tree-house. On the floor is a trap door. A knock at it.

GORDIE (FROM STAND BY ME)

That's not the secret knock!

VERN (FROM STAND BY ME)

Forget the secret knock let me in!

GORDIE/CHRIS

Vern!

The white boys let the third white kid in.

ANDY
But only...

Andy clicks his remote to cue up the next movie...

ANDY (CONT'D)
If the board approves.

Andy presses play. The Shawshank Redemption. Four old white guys and an old white woman sit in judgement as our hero, Oscar nominee Morgan Freeman, walks towards them. His footsteps echo.

ANDY (CONT'D)
But the surest way to become a Member of the Academy – the way you are automatically considered for membership – is to get nominated.

SAM
But there were no non-white nominees! The snake is biting its tail! How do you get nominated?

ANDY
I don't know.

SAM
Go see Hutchinson. Old friend of mine. He might be able to help us.

CUT TO:

AN UNDERGROUND CAR PARK, NIGHT.

Andy meets Hutchinson, 65. Andy checks they are alone.

ANDY
Hutchinson?

Hutchinson nods.

ANDY (CONT'D)
Not very talkative are you?

Hutchinson shrugs.

ANDY (CONT'D)
You know how to get nominated?

Hutchinson hands over a heavy brown envelope. Andy takes out pages and pages of data.

ANDY (CONT'D)

Throw me a bone here. I'm just trying to find out why the Oscars are so white.

Hutchinson stubs out a cigarette.

HUTCHINSON

In that case... Get in.

Hutchinson indicates his battered Prius. Andy and Hutchinson swing into it. Hutchinson engages the engine and speeds off.

HUTCHINSON (CONT'D)

It works like this.

CUT TO:

INT. LEONARDO DI CAPRIO'S MANSION

LEONARDO DI CAPRIO (Leo) drinks tea in his posing pouch.

HUTCHINSON V/O

Members vote on potential nominees for standard awards in up to 25 categories...

Leo's PA, brings Leo a letter with tastefully embossed writing.

HUTCHINSON

...yet members from each field may only put forward nominees in their respective field – actors vote for actors etc.

Out of the envelope falls... The ballot sheet. It says 'Please rank in order of preference 1,2,3,4,5'. Next to number one, Leo writes 'Leonardo di Caprio'.

HUTCHINSON V/O

The Academy instructs voters to "follow their hearts".

Leo writes 'Leonardo Di Caprio' in all four of the other slots.

CUT TO:

INT. CAR, NIGHT.

Andy waves the brown envelope.

ANDY

What if their hearts are full of unconscious bias?

Hutchinson screeches round a corner.

CUT TO:

MONTAGE: THE JOURNEY OF THE CARD.

The nomination card is put in another envelope. Into a handbag... a collection box... a mail bag... a mail van and up the stairs into offices marked 'Price Waterhouse Cooper'. Onto a desk. A manicured hand takes out the card. And places it on a pile marked 'Leonardo do Caprio'.

CUT TO:

EXT. LEONARDO DI CAPRIO'S MANSION, MORNING INTERCUT/ THE BALLOT STATION/THE CAR PARK

Leo, in swimming trunks, stretches in the sunshine.

> HUTCHINSON V/O
> Price Waterhouse Coopers are looking for the 'magic number', the number of votes that turns a name on the ballot into an official nominee. Let's say there are most first choice votes for Leonardo di Caprio.

In the ballot station, a hand holds up Leo's card/Leo stands on tiptoes at the edge of the pool. And dives into lane one.

Hutchinson's Prius screeches round a corner.

> HUTCHINSON
> ...the ballots that named him as a first choice are set aside...

On the ballot desk, a pile of cards for Matt Damon.

> HUTCHINSON V/O
> There are now four spots left.

In Leo's pool, in lane two, Matt Damon dives in.

> HUTCHINSON V/O
> The actor with the fewest first-place votes is automatically knocked out, and those ballots are redistributed based on the voters' second place choices...

In lane three, Michael Fassbender dives in. Michael sees Matt, crawling fast, and begins to race.

> HUTCHINSON V/O (CONT'D)
> And so on.

In lane four Bryan Cranston dives.

> HUTCHINSON V/O (CONT'D)
> Until we have our five nominees...

Eddie Redmayne dives into lane five. All race. Down into the water, the darkness of the pool, of the tarmac.

CUT TO:

INT. CAR PARK.

Hutchinson pulls into exactly the same parking spot he was in before.

> ANDY
> Isn't this where we started?

> HUTCHINSON
> Well, to be in the race...

CUT TO:

INT. INVESTIGATOR'S OFFICE, NIGHT.

Andy is reporting to Sam. Hutchinson's and Andy's voices merge together.

> HUTCHINSON/ANDY
> ... you got to be on the ballot.

> SAM
> So it's a catch 22 – without more diverse film-makers the Academy
> is unlikely to nominate more diverse film-makers?

> ANDY
> There is another possibility.

> SAM
> What's that?

Andy shrugs.

> ANDY
> Maybe there was no one to nominate this year...

> SAM
> What are you saying? You can't mean...

ANDY

Yes! It's just a hunch but maybe it's not just the Academy which is prejudiced but the whole film industry. Just look at this screenplay!

(MORE)

ANDY (CONT'D)

Why is my character called 'Andy' when in real life I'm called Kulraj? Why are you called Sam when you are based on Professor Kandola? Why is Elaine, my wife, seventeen years younger than me, beautiful and almost mute? We deal in stereotypes and call them archetypes. What did Will Smith say?

SAM

"The nominations reflect the Academy. The Academy reflects the industry, and then the industry reflects America."

ANDY

Let's hope that all the discussion around diversity might make the Academy more aware of their own prejudices in 2017...

SAM

I'll believe it when I see it.

CUT TO:

THE OSCAR CEREMONY 2017

Warren Beatty double-checks the envelope.

WARREN BEATTY

And the Academy Award for Best Picture...

FAYE DUNAWAY

La La Land.

CUT TO:

INT. INVESTIGATOR'S KITCHEN, EVENING.

Sam, Andy and Elaine are watching the Oscars. Andy sighs.

JORDAN HOROWITZ

I'm sorry! No! There a mistake. Moonlight! You guys won best picture!

Sam and Andy look at each other. Andy begins to grin.

THE END.

The Oscars

Franklin, D. Industry Exec on Fixing Hollywood's Race Problem: This "has to be a long-term commitment". The Hollywood Reporter. Retrieved 9 September 2017, from (2017) http://www.hollywoodreporter.com/news/oscarssowhite-industry-exec-fixing-hollywoods-857418.

Garza, F. The little we know about the 6,000 Academy members who vote on the Oscars tells us a lot. QUARTZ, pp. 1-4. Retrieved from (2016) http://qz.com/597343/the-little-we-know-about-the-6000-academy-members-who-vote-on-the-oscars-tells-us-a-lot/.

Gray, T. Academy nominates all white actors for second year in row. Variety. Retrieved 9 September 2017, from (2017) http://variety.com/2016/biz/awards/oscar-nominations-2016-diversity-white-1201674903/.

Horn, J. Unmasking Oscar: Academy voters are overwhelmingly white and male.
Los Angles Times, pp. 1-7. Retrieved from (2016) http://www.latimes.com/entertainment/la-et-unmasking-oscar-academy-project-20120219-story.html.

Hutchinson, S. How are Oscar nominees chosen. Mental Floss, pp. 1-6. Retrieved from (2016) http://mentalfloss.com/article/54560/how-are-oscar-nominees-chose.

Needham, A. Chris Rock at the 2016 Oscars: 'You're damn right Hollywood's racist'. The guardian. Retrieved 10 September 2017, from (2017) https://www.theguardian.com/film/2016/feb/29/chris-rock-at-the-oscars-youre-damn-right-hollywoods-racist.

Nolfi, J. Oscars make history with most black winners ever. Entertainment Weekly. Retrieved 9 September 2017, from (2017) http://ew.com/awards/2017/02/26/oscars-2017-black-acting-winners/.

Spera, S. Why this year's Oscars might diverge from past prejudice. The Variety. Retrieved 9 September 2017, from (2017) https://thevarsity.ca/2017/01/22/why-this-years-oscars-might-diverge-from-past-prejudice/.

Woo, E. 6 Facts that prove that the Oscars is more racist than you think. Venngage. Retrieved 9 September 2017, from (2017) https://venngage.com/blog/oscar-racism-interactive-infographic/.

Chapter 12

A call to action

In 1950, UNESCO[1] set out to show the world how racial harmony could be achieved and racial discrimination reduced, if not eliminated. The country the agency chose as its example was Brazil, a melting pot of races, colours, languages and cultures. Unfortunately, its in-depth investigation revealed not the secrets of a modern-day, egalitarian Eden but plentiful evidence of the same racial divisions and discrimination that can be found elsewhere.

UNESCO's experience serves as a good example to today's organisations. You may think that your organisation has left racial discrimination and racist behaviour far behind. The truth is, you are not looking closely enough. My first piece of advice to leaders is: PAY ATTENTION. We all like to see ourselves as fair, liberal, tolerant and open-minded. But despite our dearly held beliefs, we may not be the paragons we imagine. If you want an idea of how fair your organisation is take a look at the indicators on the Wanted poster on page 209 According to Arthur Schopenhauer, the nineteenth-century German philosopher, we repress the ideas and emotions we find painful, and instead focus on those which make us feel more comfortable.[2] We only become aware of these unconscious motivations and attitudes when we are able to reflect on our behaviour.

Schopenhauer's view is similar to the modern idea of *aversive racism*. Some of us may be so concerned about being racist – which would represent a stain on our self-image – that we will avoid any prolonged and meaningful contact with minorities. This defensive strategy, which may not be consciously articulated, preserves our self-esteem – but also leaves our biases unexamined and intact. Establishing meaningful contact with other groups is the most effective way of reducing prejudice. The key word here, of course, is *meaningful*. Contact which is pleasant but has no real purpose does nothing to reduce discrimination against minority groups. Such contact makes the person in the dominant group feel better about themselves, but doesn't require them to acknowledge and deal with their own biases.[3]

The Nature of Prejudice,[4] psychologist Gordon Allport's classic work of 1954, identified four features of intergroup contact which are necessary to increase understanding and reduce prejudice:

1. The people from both groups have equal status – there is no sense of hierarchy between people.

2. Both groups are working towards the same objectives.

3. The groups are not set against each other – they work together cooperatively rather than being seen as being in competition.

4. The exercise has the backing of a non-participating senior authority figure who recognises the value of what is being done.

Without these conditions, bias will tend to increase.

In this chapter I suggest sets of actions for various people within organisations, all of whom are critical in reducing bias. I have drawn upon a number of key sources for this chapter: the Kirwan Institute's invaluable series of reports into bias led by Cheryl Staats,[5,6,7,8] Rupert Brown's book on prejudice,[9] *The Psychology of Diversity* by James Jones, John Dovidio and Deborah Vietze,[10] and *Inclusion Nudges* by Tinna C. Nielsen and Lisa Kepinski.[11] What these publications show is that there is considerable agreement about the actions we can take to reduce bias in organisations – and much of it is not so difficult to do, if we can be bothered to do it.

When leaders talk about race, or they are encouraged to talk about it, the standard line – which is something of a cliché – is that we must not be afraid to have 'the conversation'. Race has been labelled a taboo subject. I believe that the reason race is not discussed is that different groups have very different perceptions about its significance in organisations. Minorities see race as having a continued negative impact on their working lives, but the white majority see it as far less significant. The tension arises not about race as a subject per se but because the white majority do not consider race discrimination to be that important. Also, research has shown that organisations see gender equality as more important than race equality.[12] The McGregor-Smith Review carried out in the UK looking at race equality, thankfully, took a different view: that it was not about talking but about taking action.[13]

I've grouped my advice into sets of tips for leaders, HR professionals and those involved with learning and development in an organisation. If you play a part in creating the conditions in which different groups of people work together, you will find practical guidance here. I finish with a set of rules crafted for the greatest group of all: the human family, of which we're all equal members.

Five rules for leaders

Rule 1: Your role is critical – don't ignore it

As Allport's condition for reducing prejudice reminds us, the support of authority figures is critical. Occasionally a CEO or other senior figure will make a statement to the effect that 'race discrimination is bad', as if the mere pronouncement of this platitude will automatically lead to the eradication of racist behaviour. Leaders are judged on their actions, not their words. If a racist incident occurs in an organisation and the perpetrators are not challenged, then people will draw their own conclusions about the leader's sincerity and the climate will not improve. Leaders' genuine commitment to ensuring all their staff are treated fairly is an essential element of leadership, not a 'nice to have'.

Rule 2: Accept there's a problem. Stop denying it

Most of us like to see ourselves as fair-minded, open and tolerant. But we all have racial biases of one kind or another, whether or not we are consciously aware of them. This applies to leaders too. Elevation to a leadership position does not automatically make anyone wiser, fairer or more clear-sighted. You may fervently deny that you or your organisation has a problem, but that's just what it is: denial.

A wonderfully effective way to remain in a state of denial is not to collect any data. There are some countries in the world where collecting data about race is illegal. In France, for example, data on ethnicity is not collected because it is felt that identifying and categorising people in this way will undermine the concept that everyone is French and equal in the eyes of the law. An idea born in the French Revolution, this rationale has a considerable emotional pull. Philosophically it is idealistic; psychologically it is naïve. But the act of collecting data does not create categories: it makes explicit the categories we have already invented. Not having any data means we can ignore discrimination, perpetuate a belief in our colour-blindness, and avoid having to confront uncomfortable truths.

In countries where race data can legally be collected, not all organisations choose to do so. This is often because they dislike having to discuss the subject, and so the emotional discomfort leads to an unwillingness to obtain data. Where organisations do obtain data, they often solicit it in ways which ensure the return rates are low. The poor participation of employees makes unwelcome results easier to reject.

The categories we use when collecting data can also cause problems. It is not unusual to find organisations collapsing data from a number of groups into one catch-all category such as 'BAME' or 'minorities'. The rationale for this approach is often that the sample size for some minorities is too small to allow any meaningful analysis, so the data is combined to create a larger sample size. But this defeats the purpose of the exercise. The fact that a sample is too small for some groups is actually an important part of the story that the organisation needs to understand. Combining categories also provides a greater sense of false security about the problem's scale.

However, even more conscientious data collection can lead to biased interpretations. When data is collected separately by ethnic groups, differences between them will inevitably appear. For example, it may transpire that some minorities are more likely to be recruited than others. One member of a 'Big Four' accountancy firm told me the data showed that 'we're recruiting too many Asian people'. Differences revealed by data collection are interpreted as competition between ethnic groups – casting minorities as outsiders fighting each other to infiltrate the organisation.

At a regular leadership meeting at one British university, a presentation was given about the lack of diversity in the organisation. There was some discomfort about being challenged in this way. Geoffrey Beattie, a professor of psychology, looked around the room 'to see what colour-blindness has brought us: an all-White cast that is bristling with indignation at the hint that something may not be quite right'.[14 (p30)] The simplest way you can measure the race make-up of your organisation is to look around you. Who is represented in your senior cadre? How many minorities do you, as a leader, meet, in a meaningful way, during the course of your day, week or month? When you look around you, do you see yourself looking back?

Rule 3: Make your presence felt; don't be invisible

Many senior leaders get involved in diversity efforts at a token level: speaking at a conference (and then disappearing immediately for another, more pressing engagement), endorsing policies, permitting activities such as minority network groups and looking favourably on a slew of themed 'heritage' weeks. (I once met a British politician at a community event whose speech was notable for its total lack of inspiration. Struggling to say anything genuinely complimentary to him, I said, 'Nice tie.' He responded, 'Thank you. I have a Finance Committee meeting later. I wouldn't have worn it just for this.')

Tokenistic gestures make people feel warm and righteous. But such actions are the bare minimum. Like signing an online petition, or wearing a T-shirt with a slogan, this is an action that can be carried out with minimal effort – and often without leaving your desk. The term for this kind of behaviour, 'virtue signalling', was only coined in 2015,[15] yet it seems instantly familiar.

Demonstrating real action requires more than a minimum effort. Leaders must be visible. If the organisation has set up networks and events, then turn up, ask questions and spend some time talking to people about their experiences and opinions. Perhaps the most important action leaders can take is to listen to employees they may not have much contact with in the course of a typical day. In my experience, the leader's personal presence and involvement will be noticed and appreciated.

Rule 4: Acknowledge that race impacts decisions. Don't believe you are somehow exempt

Race is an anxiety-ridden topic. It is difficult to discuss race without being concerned that you might say something out of place or use a word that causes offence to someone. But the prospect of error or discomfort is no reason for leaders to avoid discussing the topic. Leaders tackle difficult subjects all the time. That is what they are paid for.

Participating in race-related events and talking about their involvement is an easy way to start. Sharing experiences and the learning gained encourages others to get involved. Another way for leaders to enter the dialogue and find their voice is to use a coach – someone with whom they can have private conversations, who is knowledgeable about the subject and can help develop their confidence.

Rule 5: Create the climate for change: make your actions match your words

Leaders have the authority and status to create a climate in which equality and diversity are taken seriously. They set the priorities, and others follow. Many leaders have paid scant attention to race equality over the years and believe that society has moved beyond racial discrimination. Today's leaders have a critical role in correcting these omissions and challenging incorrect perceptions.

To demonstrate how fair they are, leaders of European and American organisations will often point to the multi-racial nature of their executive teams. Typically, however, such teams are multinational, with representatives from the USA, Europe and increasingly Asia (but not, in my experience, from Africa or South America). The people sitting around the executive boardroom table represent different regions of the world. Unfortunately, visible minorities from the country in which the company is based are hardly ever included, because, despite what people may say, they are not seen as representative of their own country – but white people are.[16] The people representing the headquarters nation – this could be the UK, USA, France, Germany, etc. – will invariably be white.

Bringing about real change requires leaders to set the agenda, monitor progress and remain focused. It also requires leaders to ensure that they take the lead in ensuring that people are selected, assessed, appraised, promoted and treated fairly. It is not just about ensuring that processes are fair, but ensuring that we are. Taking personal action and letting others know about it sets a positive example for others.

Five rules for HR

Rule 1: Review your key HR processes regularly – don't assume they are fair

The processes relating to gaining access to the organisation – recruitment and selection – and those relating to performance and progression are key to fairness. These processes include performance management systems, 360-degree feedback processes, pay, promotion and talent identification.

Put in the resources to examine how fair and effective your organisation's processes actually are. Fair procedures which evaluate people as objectively and accurately as possible are crucial to ensure that people feel they are working in a truly inclusive organisation. Although HR departments in both public and private sectors generally say they do this, my experience is different. Departments tend to focus their efforts on the technical details of a new policy, communicating the change and designing the rules. Far less effort goes into examining the fairness of the new policy.

Imagine that an organisation is introducing a new performance appraisal system. The HR team is asked to consider the process's fairness and potential adverse impact. But, after much deliberation, the team decides it doesn't need to do this. Fast-forward eighteen months, and the same team is beginning a complete review of the process, having found out that minorities are receiving lower performance ratings than majority staff. The damage – which was completely avoidable – has already been done. A small team is then employed to investigate this further, none of whom has any experience of the subject. They start to review the process itself, with a view to introducing changes. This takes us right back to where we started. Unfortunately, this is not a made-up example. Care, consideration and professionalism would have avoided the problem arising in the first place – and some minorities would not have suffered stalled careers due to their being perceived as less successful and capable than they actually are.

Rule 2: Ensure people are trained – don't believe a good process is sufficient

'A common mistake that people make when trying to design something completely fool-proof is to underestimate the ingenuity of complete fools.' So says Douglas Adams in his 1992 novel *Mostly Harmless*. And so it is with your processes. However well designed you believe your processes to be, you must train people to use them properly.

It isn't enough to provide passive online training. People must practise interacting with others and receive feedback. All training needs to incorporate sessions on bias and how it impacts decision-making. Incorporating this information with relevant case studies enables people to understand their own decision-making behaviour, and helps them develop skills to combat bias.

Rule 3: Make people accountable – don't let them think they can get away with racist behaviour

Increasing accountability is simple: ensuring people are asked to justify the decisions they take. This could involve examining decisions managers have made about selection, performance ratings, pay and promotion. Where concerns exist about diversity, or a lack of it, then explanations need to be provided.

HR controls these processes, but how often is this type of challenge made? Not often, in my experience. Yet in terms of outcomes and fairness in organisations, the impact of HR decisions is bigger than that of training.[17] When people know they are going to be held responsible, they:

- take longer to make their decisions

- are less likely to stereotype

- are more likely to follow a given process, including proper use of criteria

- are more likely to record their decisions and to analyse information more carefully.[18]

Rule 4: Take positive action – don't ignore the effect of past and present discrimination

The effects of current and past discrimination should not be underestimated or ignored. This means we need ways of attracting people from under-represented groups to join our organisations. We also need to find ways of enabling people who have been victims of discrimination to have their talents fully recognised. This will mean some form of positive or affirmative action. The ways in which positive, or affirmative action, programmes are introduced has an impact on their acceptance.

The emphasis needs to be on identifying, tapping and developing underused talent pools and empowering people to achieve their full potential. We must avoid taking these actions for paternalistic, benevolent or charitable reasons. Black History months or weeks generally fall into the 'benevolent' or 'paternalistic' category. Having meals from around the world served in staff restaurants is a great way of celebrating diversity, but does little to address the underlying patterns of inequality in the organisation.

The impact of affirmative action programmes and initiatives varies greatly. The spectrum extends from encouraging a greater diversity of people to apply for jobs to establishing quotas for the employment of types and numbers of people. At one end of the scale, emphasis is placed on the actions of minority members themselves, while at the other end the emphasis is on the decision-makers. However we look at this spectrum, successful affirmative action is a two-way street:

organisations must plan and act to attract and recruit candidates, but suitable candidates must also be sufficiently interested and motivated to complete the application process.

Different groups have different views about affirmative action, with women being more positive than men and black people being more positive than white people. There is also a political dimension, with liberals being more in favour of affirmative action than conservatives. Attitudes towards specific actions are strongly linked to perceptions of fairness. Generally speaking, types of affirmative action which place the responsibility for action on the under-represented group have greater acceptance than those which appear to interfere with the organisation's decision-making process.

More ambivalent attitudes are expressed about the provision of additional training or development for a specific group of people. On the one hand, people understand the impact of discrimination, but on the other hand they also feel that such initiatives give the under-represented groups an advantage. The more that affirmative action policies are seen as affecting decisions (such as promotion), the more likely it is that the beneficiaries of such policies are viewed as less competent and less qualified.[19] These effects can be mitigated by being open and transparent about how decisions are made and by demonstrating the experience and qualifications of the people appointed. The way affirmative action policies are discussed, and the type of policies that are adopted, both have an impact on their acceptance and the reception given to people who are perceived to be the beneficiaries.

A clear communication strategy is needed to increase the chance of affirmative action programmes being accepted within an organisation. Describing programmes in terms of addressing past injustices is viewed more positively than focusing on improving the representation of different groups. However, the acceptance of any programme also depends on the group at which it is targeted. In a survey of white Americans, half of the sample were asked this question:

> *Some people say that because of past discrimination, women should be given preference in hiring and promotion. Others say that preference in hiring is wrong as it is discriminating against men. What about your opinion – are you for or against professional hiring and promotion of women?*[20] (p179)

The other half of the sample received the question in the same format – but this time race was the topic, with preferential treatment being suggested for black people and white people being seen as being discriminated against. Analysis of the results showed that there was general opposition to any form of affirmative action. However, opposition to affirmative action on the grounds of race was stronger than opposition to gender-based action.[20] This suggests that, while it is no easy task to implement gender-related affirmative action in organisations, it is at least easier than implementing race-based action. Attitudes towards race are more of an obstacle to affirmative action than attitudes about affirmative action itself.

When the initiatives were not sufficiently well explained by leaders, middle managers can act as an obstacle by not providing their support, possibly because they see them as a block to their own career development.[17] Such programmes are important but need to be well thought through in order for the benefits to be maximised. When planning such initiatives, the emotional reaction of staff and any potential backlash need to be considered.

Rule 5: Create a culture of fairness – it is not just about the numbers

Achieving fairness in organisations is an aspiration towards which we will always be striving. It's about creating a climate and culture in which people recognise that fairness is important. Too often in the field of diversity, the focus is on the 'body count' rather than any real attempt to examine the reasons behind racial inequality.[17] The concept of fairness, or organisational justice, is important because it provides a touchstone for decisions.[21] Fairness is good for business because it means people are judged on their abilities – and it is the right moral choice. An organisation publicly committed to affirmative action may establish targets, goals or even quotas. The diversity of the candidates applying for employment almost becomes secondary to the decision-maker's process for selecting among the different candidates available.

There is an unfortunate, but clear, tendency for those responsible for diversity to adopt a 'Whose turn is it now?' approach in their work. For example, organisations may believe that they have 'done' gender, so now it's time to turn the spotlight elsewhere – a CEO of one multinational proudly proclaimed 'Gender: Mission Accomplished' to his somewhat astonished London workforce during the company's 2015 Diversity Week.

While broadening the scope of diversity issues is a good thing, what typically occurs is simply a shift of focus from one topic to another. This has a number of consequences. First, we find a recurring a pattern of attention, action, progress and decline. Second, focusing on specific demographic characteristics helps us make some progress but ignores the complexity of real life. A divide-and-rule approach can mean that minority women, for example, become invisible. Such an approach can also make target-setting infeasible.

Establishing gender targets has become the most visible way in which an organisation can demonstrate its commitment to diversity. And yet I believe this is one of the reasons why relatively little progress has been achieved on racial equality. Progress on gender has become the priority, with race and other areas more or less ignored. There is a reluctance to engage in positive action on race rather than on gender, which in itself indicates a subtle form of racism. Apart from Catalyst, a global non-profit whose vision is 'workplaces that work for women', organisations and individuals which champion gender diversity usually have little or nothing to say about racial equality. But if an organisation has set targets for gender, what logical argument can there be for not having targets for race?

There are many arguments for dispensing with targets altogether. First, targeting a single group means that other forms of discrimination are ignored. Second, there are the practical issues of having to deal with multiple targets. I was told by one Global Director of Diversity that appointing minority women was seen as scoring a 'double notch' – helping leaders meet their gender and minority targets more quickly, and thereby allowing them to select more white men. Third, if one minority group is less well represented than others, should there be specific targets for this group? How do we deal with intersectionality issues? Should there be separate targets for women of a particular ethnicity? These questions are not easily answered. Indeed, it may not be possible to answer them at all.

Fourth, having multiple targets means that some minorities will be penalised for being successful. Although targets for universities can be controversial, it is often forgotten that US universities first introduced quotas (elegantly presented as numerus clausus) to restrict the number of Jewish students.[22] In the USA Asians may also be subject to a similar, but less publicised, policy. One Princeton University study showed that, for university admissions, being Asian was 'comparable to the loss of 50 SAT points'.[23 (p1431)]

When the director of diversity of a professional services firm said, 'We employ too many Asians', she was implicitly suggesting that the lack of black people employed in the firm was due to preference being given to another minority. Racial diversity can devolve into a competition between different minority groups, organised and judged by the dominant group.

Fifth, when people are selected using positive or affirmative action policies, they are seen as being less competent than others. An organisation publicly committed to affirmative action may establish targets, goals or even quotas. The diversity of the candidates applying for employment almost becomes secondary to the decision-maker's process for selecting from the different candidates available.[19] The minorities and women selected are regarded as having required extra assistance to join the organisation, without which they would have been rejected.

The focus needs to be on creating a climate that fosters a sense of equality and justice for all people. Data should be used to highlight where specific problem points exist, but not to establish targets or quotas.

Five rules for learning and development (L&D) departments
Rule 1: Get motivated – it's not all about ability
There are some straightforward actions we can take to reduce both conscious and unconscious bias. However, we need first to recognise that we are biased. Second, we must be bothered enough to do something about the situation. It's a question of our motivation, not just our ability to change.

Increasing people's motivation to change is not easily done, but there are measures we can take to enable change. One way of increasing motivation is to make people aware of discrepancies between their own stated values and their behaviour.[24,25] For example, in one study some people were told that they had shown an anti-gay bias when shortlisting CVs. Others were not given this feedback. Those accused of bias experienced tension between their supposed action (anti-gay bias) and their personal values (treating people fairly). They were subsequently more likely than the control group to read an essay on how to reduce bias.

The same effect has been achieved by asking people first to create the goal of being egalitarian and then to think of a time when they did not behave in an egalitarian way. This makes people more willing to focus on their commitment and to consider factors which may be obstructing its achievement.[26]

We do not like to think of ourselves as hypocrites, so the tension generated in these situations encourages us to focus on the goal of being fair. When we become aware of not achieving a goal, or not behaving in line with a goal, we pause. This is called a behavioural inhibition system (BIS) and it helps us to:

- focus on what is happening around us

- identify what is causing the discrepancy

- take action to correct it.

When people receive negative feedback – for example, about their responses to photos of black people – they respond with greater care and attention in the future.[27]

Rule 2: Get people to focus on accuracy, and make them accountable
The goals we set affect how we make decisions about people. People involved in recruitment often focus on speed of outcome. The focus in talent development is often on promoting team members. By altering the goal, we can change the process and, potentially, the outcome.

When people are asked to be accurate in their assessments of people, they take more time to make their decisions, evaluate a more complete range of factors, look more closely at personal qualities, and are less likely to draw on stereotypes in reaching their conclusions.[28,29]

The reduced reliance on stereotypes is significant and leads to a reduction in self-fulfilling prophesies, a greater preparedness to attribute behaviour and results to someone's personality, and a greater willingness to consider evidence that is counter-stereotypical.[27]

Rule 3: Give people rules that support them – don't make them defensive

The idea that the white, male majority needs to be made more aware of its privileges is widely canvassed today. These privileges are both unearned and undeserved, thereby undermining the principle of merit which supposedly governs organisational decision-making. Although it might be tempting to run workshops designed to bring this message home to members of the majority group, the evidence suggests that this approach is more likely to provoke modern racism by creating a backlash effect.[30] Participants naturally see this approach as an attack on their identity and are prompted to defend themselves. In fact, events that focus on majority privilege are *more* likely to lead to people agreeing with statements like 'discrimination against blacks is no longer a problem'.

People make better decisions when they are given clear, simple and straightforward messages about how the process should be run. A discussion of bias needs to be incorporated in the briefing phase of the process. This guidance and support needs to be tailored for each specific purpose because bias operates in different ways for selection interviews than it does for, say, performance reviews. A key aspect of the message is that we are all biased – including minorities.

We can all learn from the example of legal researchers and justice departments, which are seeking to make the judicial system fairer by helping juries to evaluate evidence properly and to recognise the ways in which bias can interfere with decision-making. An evaluation of nearly 400,000 cases in the UK concluded that juries were operating fairly.[31] The key factors included a formal outlining of the jury's role and objectives; instructions to focus on evidence, not opinion; a willingness to challenge one another; and motivation to reach the right outcome. All of these components help to improve fairness. By way of contrast, however, judges' decisions overall were found to display bias in their sentencing decisions.[32]

Feedback mechanisms should be introduced to enable people to reflect on and learn from their experiences. I had the opportunity to talk to a number of partners of a law firm prior to their carrying out performance reviews. We started the session by reflecting on the previous year's ratings by gender, which showed that women were given lower ratings on average than men. We considered why this might be. A range of possibilities emerged, from the idea that women had performed less well than men to the possible gender bias of the partners. The discussion was open, reflective and developmental. No one was blamed. The performance reviews for the following year showed a much smaller gap between ratings given to men and women. This straightforward mechanism of feedback, discussion and reflection helped to create a climate for change. Making people feel defensive, or even making them feel bad about themselves, can be counterproductive and can lead to more, rather than less, bias.[33,34]

Rule 4: Send the right message about development and potential – don't treat potential as something that is fixed and permanent

This rule is designed to address perceptions and beliefs that minorities have about themselves and their performance.[35] People feel more threatened by stereotypes associated with their groups under certain conditions. First, if the task the person is engaged in is important to them. Second, if people are being assessed in some way and so they are under heightened scrutiny. Third, if they are made aware of their minority status. These factors clearly apply to talent identification and management processes, which could include, for example, a development centre in which participants may spend several days having their capabilities assessed and their suitability for senior leadership roles determined. The feeling of scrutiny may also be greater if individuals feel they are applying for roles that are not typically performed by minorities.

The threat can be reduced by making it clear that:

- Everyone has potential.

- Everyone has strengths as well as development needs.

- Everyone will receive constructive feedback designed to help build on their strengths and improve their areas for development.

These messages, given to everyone, help to reduce the additional threat that some people may be experiencing, while avoiding putting them under a spotlight and increasing the level of scrutiny even further.

Rule 5: Engage with your Employee Resource Groups; don't keep them isolated

There are mixed opinions about Employee Resource Groups (ERGs), or network groups. On the one hand, they provide support to out-groups. On the other, they increase the sense of separation between groups. ERGs are neither the solution nor the problem; they are a symptom. The problem is the out-groups, which are excluded from the informal networks of an organisation and so seek out people who are like them.

ERGs, in my experience, seem to inhabit a world of their own. Occasionally they may be asked to respond to a request from leaders, but apart from that they are autonomous, self-contained entities with little impact beyond the group itself. I have yet to see an L&D department feel it has any role to play in the development of the group. Perhaps now is the time to try. If ERGs were seen as an opportunity to develop, through informal as well as formal methods, the capabilities and – more critically – the confidence of its members, then they could be a more powerful influence in your organisation.

Five essential rules to reduce bias

Rule 1: Context matters

The context in which we operate has a significant influence on the fairness and objectivity of our decision-making. This means having:

- leaders committed to racial equality

- teams prepared to discuss the subject of racial equality

- a climate where it is okay to challenge one another on fairness

- an organisation that is prepared to learn from its mistakes.

The resulting environment is one in which it is not acceptable to be unfairly discriminatory.

Achieving real equality is about the culture of the organisation and not just about the numbers. By building a fairer organisation, which involves incorporating the actions in this chapter, we ensure better outcomes in all areas from selection to performance management and to leadership appointments. The changes as measured in raw numbers may not be as rapid as some might wish, but the gains will be more sustainable. We don't need platitudes from leaders about the importance of racial equality, followed by inaction. We don't want complacent HR teams reacting defensively to any criticism of their processes. And we can't accept continued failure to listen to the experience of minorities within organisations. We have it within our power to create and sustain the right context for race equality. It's up to us to make the choices that enable such a context to flourish – and which will nourish happier, fairer and more productive organisations which we can all be proud of.

Rule 2: Contact matters

It is easy for people to avoid meaningful contact with people from other communities. When we stay in our own boxes, we don't have to confront our own racial prejudices and experience the ensuing discomfort. And this behaviour doesn't just apply to the relationship between majorities and minorities – minorities need contact with other minorities.

Organisations are great places to bring people of different communities together. Whether it's inviting eminent leaders to speak or getting involved with community projects, creative organisations quickly find ways to start conversations and grow their experiences.

Rule 3: Create the right conditions

One way of characterising an organisation is to see it as a device for making decisions. The technical paraphernalia of the contemporary organisation and the complexity of its operations can obscure the realisation that, ultimately, all decisions are taken by human beings – fragile and imperfect creatures dealing with high cognitive loads in sometimes ambiguous circumstances. It follows that, the more conducive we can make the organisation to better decision-making, the more effective the organisation will be.

People are more likely to make biased decisions when they are under time pressure or overloaded (having to do several things at the same time). We make more biased decisions about people when we base them on our overall impressions – emotional responses such as whether or not we like them. We make poor decisions when we are hungry or tired.

Simply recognising the existence of these factors and their impact can make a huge difference in organisational fairness. We can reschedule decisions when time pressures arise. We can limit the number of simultaneous tasks a decision-maker undertakes. We can direct our attention to specific factors rather than overall impressions. And we can refuse to take decisions when our human capacity for rational thought is obstructed by fatigue. In these ways we can deny bias the space to operate unrecognised and unchallenged.

Rule 4: Consider others' viewpoints

Perspective-taking is making a deliberate attempt to understand another person's point of view. This practice requires us to see, think and feel what another person is experiencing in a given situation. It also means checking our understanding with the other person rather than assuming our initial perceptions are correct. We should strive to make this practice a basic element of our communication habits. Mindfulness and meditation are now being introduced to some workplaces as a way of improving employee well-being and satisfaction. Many organisations believe there will be productivity benefits as well. The growing acceptance of such approaches, which would once have seemed obscure and a tad 'touchy-feely', give me hope that traditions based on mutual respect and care can also help bring greater equality to our organisations. Loving-Kindness meditation, for example, is based on a Buddhist tradition of developing warm and friendly feelings towards others. The words 'loving' and 'kindness' are not exactly common in workplaces – and, if they were, no doubt HR would seek to discipline someone for their use. Perhaps, one day, we will learn to measure the worth of our organisations by the strength, plurality and resilience of their human bonds, rather than being distracted by the accidental differences in their people's appearance or origins.

Rule 5: Be self-aware

None of us is free from bias. Not you, not me. Recognising and accepting this fact is the most important step on the journey to real equality.

When we're tempted to join in the easy outrage that follows a particularly egregious example of racist behaviour, let's remember that we all have the potential to make similar mistakes. It's harder to see our own faults than those of others, but we're no 'better' than anyone else.

We must all rise to the challenge of understanding our reactions to other people. We are too smart and successful a species to carry on wasting our talents and excluding our fellow beings just because it's easy and familiar to think and respond in narrow, unimaginative ways. The work of racial equality is a head-spinning, heart-spanning conversation to which everyone is invited – and in which everyone can find their true selves.

1. Shecaira, S.S. Racism in Brazil: A historical perspective. *Rev. Int. droit pénal* **73**, 141 (2002).

2. Evans, J.S.B.T. & Frankish, K. *In Two Minds: Dual Processes and Beyond* (Oxford University Press, 2009).

3. Jackman, M.R. *The Velvet Glove: Paternalism and Conflict in Gender, Class and Race Relations* (University of California Press, 1994).

4. Allport, G.W. *The Nature of Prejudice* (Addison-Wesley, 1954).

5. Staats, C., Patton, C., Rogers, C. & Rudd, T. State of the science: Implicit bias review. Kirwan Inst. Study Race Ethn. (2013).

6. Staats, C. State of the science: Implicit bias review. *Kirwan Inst. Study Race Ethn.* (2014).

7. Staats, C., Capatosto, K., Wright, R.A. & Contractor, D. State of the science: Implicit bias review. *Kirwan Inst. Study Race Ethn.* (2015).

8. Staats, C., Capatosto, K. & Jackson, V.W. State of the science: Implicit bias review. *Kirwan Inst. Study Race Ethn.* (2016).

9. Brown, R. *Prejudice: Its Social Psychology* (Blackwell, 1995).

10. Jones, J.M., Dovidio, J.F. & Vietze, D.L. *The Psychology of Diversity: Beyond Prejudice and Racism* (Wiley-Blackwell, 2014).

11. Nielsen, T.C. & Kepinski, L. *Inclusion Nudges Guidebook: Practical Techniques for Changing Behaviour, Culture and Systems to Mitigate Unconscious Bias and Create Inclusive Organisations*, 2e (CreateSpace Independent Publishing Platform, 2016).

12. Yates, C. & Sachdev, P. Rewire: *A Radical Approach to Tackling Diversity and Difference* (Bloomsbury, 2015).

13. McGregor-Smith, R. *Race in the Workplace. Issues Faced by Businesses in Developing Black and Minority Ethnic (BME) Talent in the Workplace* (https://www.gov.uk/government/uploads/system/uploads/attachment_data/file/594336/race-in-workplace-mcgregor-smith-review.pdf) (2017).

14. Beattie, G. *Our Racist Heart? An Exploration of Unconscious Prejudice in Everyday Life* (Routledge, 2013).

15. Bartholomew, J. I invented 'virtue signalling'. Now it's taking over the world. *The Spectator*. Available at: www.spectator.co.uk/2015/10/i-invented-virtue-signalling-now-its-taking-over-the-world/ (accessed 5 November 2017).

16. Devos, T. & Banaji, M.R. American = White? *J. Pers. Soc. Psychol.* **88**, 447–466 (2005).

17. Nkomo, S. Moving from the letter of the law to the spirit of the law: The challenges of realising the intent of employment equity and affirmative action. *Transformation* **77**, 122–135 (2011).

18. Lerner, J.S. & Tetlock, P.E. Accounting for the effects of accountability. *Psychol. Bull.* **125**, 255–275 (1999).

19. Landy, F.J. & Conte, J.M. *Work in the 21st Century: An Introduction to Industrial and Organizational Psychology*, 5e (Wiley, 2015).

20. Banaji, M.R. & Greenwald, A.G. *Blindspot: Hidden Biases of Good People* (Delacorte Press, 2013).

21. Cropanzana, R., Bowen, D. & Gilliland, S. The management of organizational justice. *Acad. Manag. Perspect.* **21**, 34–49 (2007).

22. Greenblatt, S. Shakespeare's cure for xenophobia. *The New Yorker*. Available at: www.newyorker.com/magazine/2017/07/10/shakespeares-cure-for-xenophobia (accessed 5 November 2017).

23. Espenshade, T.J. et al. Admission preferences for minority students, athletes, and legacies at elite universities. *Social Science Quarterly*, **85**, 5, 1422–1446, (2004).

24. Monteith, M.J., Zuwerink, J., Adamson, M. & Brenner, L. Self-regulation of prejudiced responses: Implications for progress in prejudice-reduction efforts. *J. Pers. Soc. Psychol.* **65**, 469–485 (1993).

25. Monteith, M.J. & Voils, C.I. Exerting control over prejudiced responses. *Cognitive social psychology: The Princeton Symposium on the Legacy and Future of Social Cognition.* 375–388 (2001).

26. Moskowitz, G.B. Preconscious effects of temporary goals on attention. *J. Exp. Soc. Psychol.* **38**, 397–404 (2002).

27. Moskowitz, G.B. & Halvorson, H.G. *The Psychology of Goals*. (Guilford Press, 2009).

Fiske, S.T. & Neuberg, S.L.A continuum of impression formation, from category-based to individuating processes: Influences of information and motivation on attention and interpretation in *Advances in Experimental Social Psychology.* **23** (ed. M.P. Zanna) 1–74 (New York: Academic Press, 1990).

28. Tetlock, P.E. Accountability: The neglected social context of judgement and choice. *Res. Organ. Behav.* **7**, 297–332 (1985).

29. Branscombe, N.R., Schmitt, M.T. & Schiffhauer, K. Racial attitudes in response to thoughts of white privilege. Eur. *J. Soc. Psychol.* **37**, 203–215 (2007).

30. Lammy, D. The Lammy Review: An independent review into the treatment of, and outcomes for, Black, Asian and Minority Ethnic individuals in the Criminal Justice System. (https://www.gov.uk/government/publications/lammy-review-final-report).

31. Kandola, B. Juries, not judges, lead the way against racial bias in our justice system I Binna Kandola | Public Leaders Network | *The Guardian*. Available at: https://www.theguardian.com/public-leaders-network/2017/sep/15/racial-bias-criminal-justice-system-lammy-review-magistrates-courts-jury (accessed: 9th October 2017).

32. Fein, S. & Spencer, S.J. Prejudice as self-image maintenance: Affirming the self through derogating others. *J. Pers. Soc. Psychol.* **73**, 31–44 (1997).

33. Fiske, S.T. What we know now about bias and intergroup conflict, the problem of the century. *Curr. Dir. Psychol. Sci.* **11**, 123–128 (2002).

34. Good, C., Aronson, J. & Inzlicht, M. Improving adolescents' standardized test performance: An intervention to reduce the effects of stereotype threat. *J. Appl. Dev. Psychol.* **24**, 645–662 (2003).

WANTED

★★★★★★★★★★★★★★★★★★★★★★★

THE RBO GANG

A.K.A. THE RACE-BASED ORGANISATION

WARNING: THERE ARE LOTS OF THEM

An RBO has these features:

1. Diversity of employees at entry level

2. Few minorities in leadership roles – frosted-glass ceiling

3. A colour-blind diversity policy

4. Gender programmes include few minority women. No recognition given to the experience of minority women

5. CEO says he and his (all white) executive team are committed to diversity and that progress is based on merit

6. Asians in technical roles but few in sales roles

7. Belief that racism does not exist here – there's no data to prove that it does

8. It collects no data

9. The website has pictures of smiling, lighter-skinned minorities. But rarely on their own and never as being in charge

10. It wins diversity awards

If you are a minority do not attempt to tackle the RBO – the risks are very great

★ REWARD ★

A FAIRER, MORE PROFITABLE ORGANISATION

Glossary

Bias – 'a prejudice that leads to a tendency to favour one entity over another, often unfairly. Biases can be explicit or implicit.' [1] (p73)

Explicit attitudes and beliefs – 'ones that individuals profess publicly or express directly. These attitudes and beliefs are conscious and acknowledged by the individuals who hold them.' [1] (p74)

Implicit Bias – 'also known as unconscious bias or hidden bias, implicit biases are negative associations that people unknowingly hold. They are expressed automatically and without conscious awareness. Implicit biases have been shown to trump individuals' stated commitments to equality and fairness, thereby producing behaviour that diverges from the explicit attitudes that many people profess.' (1) (p75/76) Furthermore, 'everyone is susceptible.' [2] (p14)

In-group – 'a group with which one feels the sense of membership, solidarity or shared interest. In-group members may be established among numerous identities such as race, religion, sexual orientation, etc.' [1] (p76)

In-group bias – 'positive attitudes that people tend to feel towards members of their in-group. Feelings of safety and familiarity are often associated with in-group members. In-group members are inclined to forgive members of their in-group more quickly than they are members of out-groups.' [1] (p76)

Out-group – 'groups with which one does not belong or associate. Some people feel a sense of dislike or contempt towards members of out-groups.' [1] (p76)

Stereotype – 'a standardised and simplified belief about the attributes of the social group. Although not always accurate stereotypes are often widely held and can have both positive and negative impacts on individuals. The act of stereotyping involves creation (making the cognitive association) and application (using that association to make a judgement about a person or group).' [1] (p77)
(The Psychology of Diversity – Dovidio)

Prejudice – 'negatively biased attitudes towards, and generally unfavourable evaluations of, a group that are then described to individual members of the group. Stereotypes and prejudice often leads to preferential treatment for some groups and discrimination against others.' [3] (p391)

Modern prejudice – 'this can take many forms, but it does not involve openly expressed or direct negative attitudes. The manifestations of modern prejudice are inherent and can involve beliefs that minorities receive underserved favours and may object to policies such as positive or affirmative action.[4] It includes:

- avoiding other groups

- individuals not expressing any positive attitudes about a group

- exaggerating differences between the majority in-group and minority out-groups on dimensions such as values, language and religion'.

1. Staats C, Patton C, Rogers C, Rudd T. State of the science: Implicit bias review. Kirwan Inst study Race Ethn (2013). Available at: http://www.kirwaninstitute.osu.edu/ reports/2013/03_2013_SOTS-Implicit_Bias.pdf.

2. Staats C, Capatosto K, Jackson V.W. State of the science: Implicit bias review. Kirwan Inst study Race Ethn (2016). Available at: http://kirwaninstitute.osu.edu/wp-content/ uploads/2016/07/implicit-bias-2016.pdf.

3. Jones J.M., Dovidio J.F., Vietze D.L. *The Psychology of Diversity: Beyond Prejudice and Racism* (Wiley Blackwell, 2014).

4. Brown R. *Prejudice: Its Social Psychology* (Blackwell, 1995).

Index

Italic page numbers are used for figures. *Italic* font is used for titles of publications.

Reference List

Adesina, Z. & Marocico, O. Is it easier to get a job if you're Adam or Mohamed? BBC News. Available at: http://www.bbc.co.uk/news/uk-england-london-38751307 (accessed 21 September 2017).

Aldridge, D. Black women and the new world order: Toward a fit in the economic marketplace. In *Latinas and African American Women at Work: Race, Gender and Economic Inequality* (ed. I. Browne.) (Russell Sage Foundation, 1999).

Allport, G.W. *The Nature of Prejudice* (Addison-Wesley, 1954).

Amnesty International UK. Black and Asian women MPs abused more online. Available at: https://www.amnesty.org.uk/online-violence-women-mps (accessed 11 October 2017).

Antonio, A. L. et al. Effects of racial diversity on complex thinking in college students. *Psychol. Sci.* **15**, 507–510 (2004).

Appiah, K.A. *The Ethics of Identity* (Princeton University Press, 2007).

Arends-Toth, J. & Van de Vijver, F.J.R. Multiculturalism and acculturation: Views of Dutch and Turkish-Dutch. *Eur. J. Soc. Psychol.* 33, 249–266 (2003).

Arnold, J. & Randall, R. *Work Psychology: Understanding Human Behaviour in the Workplace* (Pearson Education, 2010).

Aronson, J. et al. When White men can't do math: Necessary and sufficient factors in stereotype threat. *J. Exp. Soc. Psychol.* **35**, 29–46 (1999).

Atewologun D, Sealy R, Vinnicombe S. Revealing Intersectional Dynamics in Organizations: Introducing "Intersectional Identity Work." Gender, Work Organ [Internet]. 2016 May 1 [cited 2017 Oct 6];23(3):223–47. Available from:http://doi.wiley.com/10.1111/gwao.12082.

Australian Human Rights Commission. Casual racism FAQs. Available at: https://www.humanrights.gov.au/our-work/race-discrimination/projects/casual-racism-faqs (accessed 11 October 2017).

Axt, J.R., Ebersole, C.R. & Nosek, B.A. The rules of implicit evaluation by race, religion and age. *Psychol. Sci.* 1–12 (2014).

Ayres, I. & Siegelman, P. Race and gender discrimination in bargaining for a new car. *Am. Econ. Rev.* **85**, 304–321 (1995).

Bagati D. Women of Color in Professional Services Series | 1 Women of Color in Professional Services Series. [cited 2017 Oct 7]; Available from: http://www.catalyst.org/system/files/Women_of_Color_in_U.S._Law_Firms.pdf.

Banaji, M.R. & Greenwald, A.G. *Blindspot: Hidden Biases of Good People* (Delacorte Press, 2013).

Baron, A.S. & Banaji, M.R. The development of implicit attitudes. *Psychol. Sci.* **17**, 53–58 (2006).

Barrett, L.F. & Swim, J.K. Appraisals of prejudice and discrimination in *Prejudice: The Target's Perspective* (eds J.K. Swim & C. Stangor) (Academic Press, 1998).

Bartholomew, J.I. invented 'virtue signalling'. Now it's taking over the world. *The Spectator*. Available at: www.spectator.co.uk/2015/10/i-invented-virtue-signalling-now-its-taking-over-the-world/ (accessed 5 November 2017).

Baxandall, R., Gordon, L. & Reverby, S. *America's Working Women: A Documentary History, 1600 to the Present* (Random House, 1976).

BBC pay: How much do its stars earn? BBC News. Available at: http://www.bbc.co.uk/news/entertainment-arts-40653861 (accessed: 23rd November 2017).

Beale, F. Double jeopardy: To be black and female in *The Black Woman* (ed. T. Cade) (New American Library, 1970).

Beattie, G. *Our Racist Heart? An Exploration of Unconscious Prejudice in Everyday Life* (Routledge, 2013).

Ben-Zeev, A., Dennehy, T.C., Goodrich, R.I., Kolarik, B.S. & Geisler, M.W. When an 'educated' black man becomes lighter in the mind's eye: Evidence for a skin tone memory bias. *SAGE Open* **4**, 1–9 (2014).

Berdahl, J.L. & Moore, C. Workplace harassment: Double jeopardy for minority women. *J. Appl. Psychol.* **91**, 426–436 (2006).

Berglund, K. The Keen Eye: Linnaeus: The Man Who Saw Everything in *The Linnaean Legacy: Three Centuries After His Birth* (eds. M.J. Morris & L. Berwick) (Wiley Blackwell, 2008).

Bergsieker, H.B., Shelton, J.N., Richeson, J.A. To be liked versus respected: divergent goals in interracial interactions. *J. Personal. Soc. Psychol.* **99**, 248–264 (2010).

Berman, J. Soon, not even 1 percent of Fortune 500 companies will have black CEOs. *Huffington Post.* Available at: www.huffingtonpost.com/2015/01/29/black-ceos-fortune-500_n_6572074.html (accessed 5 November 2017).

Bertrand, M. et al. Implicit discrimination. *Am. Econ. Rev.* 95, 94–98 (2005).

Bhuyan, A.Z. Powell rejects Islamophobia. OnFaith. Available at: www.onfaith.co/onfaith/2008/10/19/powell-rejects-islamophobia/103 (accessed 5 November 2017).

Bodkin-Andrews, G., O'Rourke, V., Grant, R., Denson, N. & Craven, R.G. Validating racism and cultural respect: Testing the psychometric properties and educational impact of perceived discrimination and multiculturation for Indigenous and non-Indigenous students. *Educ. Res. Eval.* **16**, 471–493 (2010).

Bogardus, E. S. A social distance scale. *Sociol. Soc. Res.* 17, 265–271 (1933).

Bohnet, I., School, H.K., Van Geen, A. & Bazerman, M.H. When Performance Trumps Gender Bias: Joint Versus Separate Evaluation Faculty Research Working Paper Series. *Manage. Sci.* 62, 1225–1234 (2016).

Bolino, M. C. & Turnley, W. H. Counternormative impression management, likeability, and performance ratings: The use of intimidation in an organizational setting. *J. Organ. Behav.* 24, 237–250 (2003).

Boliver V. How Fair Is Access To More Prestigious UK Universities. Br J Sociol. 2013;64(2):344–64.

Bonilla-Silva, E. *Racism Without Racists: Color-Blind Racism and the Persistence of Racial Inequality in America* (Rowman & Littlefield, 2010).

Bowles, Hannah Riley and Babcock, Linda and Lai, Lei, It Depends Who is Asking and Who You Ask: Social Incentives for Sex Differences in the Propensity to Initiate Negotiation (July 2005). KSG Working Paper No. RWP05-045. Available at SSRN: https://ssrn.com/abstract=779506 or http://dx.doi.org/10.2139/ssrn.779506

Brackett, J.K. Race and Rulership: Alessandro de' Medici, first Medici duke of Florence, 1529-1537 in *Black Africans in Renaissance Europe* (eds. T.F. Earle & K.J.P. Lowe) (Cambridge University Press, 2005).

Branscombe, N.R., Schmitt, M.T. & Schiffhauer, K. Racial attitudes in response to thoughts of white privilege. *Eur. J. Soc. Psychol.* **37**, 203–215 (2007).

Breach, A., Society, F. & Yaojun, L. Gender Pay Gap by Ethnicity in Britain – Briefing. (2017). https://www.fawcettsociety.org.uk/gender-pay-by-ethnicity-britain

Brescoll, V.L., Dawson, E. & Uhlmann, E.L. Hard-won and easily lost: The fragile status of leaders in gender-stereotype-incongruent occupations. *Psychol. Sci.* **21**, 1640–1642 (2010).

Brett, J.F., Atwater, L.E. & Waldman, D.A. Effective delivery of workplace discipline: do women have to be more participatory than men? *Gr. Organ. Manag.* 30, 487–513 (2005).

Brewster, Z.W. & Lynn, M. Black-white earnings gap among restaurant servers: A replication, extension and exploration of consumer racial discrimination in tipping. *Sociol. Inq.* 84, 545–569 (2014).

Brief, A.P. et al. Just doing business: Modern racism and obedience to authority as explanations for employment discrimination. *Organ. Behav. Hum. Decis. Process.* **81**, 72–97 (2000).

Brosch, T., Bar-David, E. & Phelps, E.A. Implicit race bias decreases the similarity of neural representations of Black and White faces. *Psychol. Sci.* **24**, 160–166 (2013).

Brown, R. *Prejudice: Its Social Psychology* (Blackwell, 1995).

Browne, I., Hewitt, C., Tigges, L. & Green, G. Why does job segregation lead to wage inequality among African Americans? Person, place, sector, or skills? *Soc. Sci. Res.* **30**, 473–495 (2001).

Burdsey D. Race, ethnicity, and football : persisting debates and emergent issues [Internet]. Burdsey D, editor. London: Routledge; 2011. 287 p. Available from: https://www.routledge.com/Race-Ethnicity-and-Football-Persisting-Debates-and-Emergent-Issues/Burdsey/p/book/9780415882057.

Burdsey D. They Think It's All Over...It Isn't Yet! The Persistence of Structural Racism and Racialised Exclusion in Twenty-First Century Football. In: Burdsey D, editor. Race, Ethnicity and Football: Persisting Debates and Emergent Issues. London: Routledge; 2011.

Burdsey, D. That joke isn't funny anymore: Racial microaggressions, color-blind ideology and the mitigation of racism in English men's first-class cricket. *Sociol. Sport J.* **28**, 261–283 (2011).

Byrne, D. & Griffitt, W. Interpersonal attraction. *Annu. Rev. Psychol.* **24**, 317–336 (1973).

Calvó-Armengol, A. & Jackson, M.O. Networks in labor markets: Wage and employment dynamics and inequality. *J. Econ. Theory* **132**, 27–46 (2007).

Carli, L.L. Gender and social influence. *J. Soc. Issues* **57**, 725–741 (2001).

Carlsson, M. & Rooth, D.-O. Evidence of ethnic discrimination in the Swedish labor market using experimental data. *Labour Econ.* **14**, 716–729 (2007).

Carton, A.M. & Rosette, A.S. Explaining bias against black leaders: Integrating theory on information processing and goal-based stereotyping. *Acad. Manag. Journal* **54**, 1141–1158 (2011).

Casares, A.M. Free and Freed Black Africans in Granada in the Time of the Spanish Renaissance in *Black Africans in Renaissance Europe* (eds. T.F. Earle & K.J.P. Lowe) (Cambridge University Press, 2005).

Cejka, M.A. & Eagly, A.H. Gender-stereotypic images of occupations correspond to the sex segregation of employment. *Personal. Soc. Psychol. Bull.* 25, 413–423 (1999).

Chronica do Descobrimento e Conquista da Guiné, by Gomes Eanes de Zurara, Paris, 1841; English version The Chronicle of the Discovery and Conquest of Guinea translated by Edgar Prestage, London, 1896-1899, volume 1, page 65-66.

Clark, K. Ethnic minority self-employment. *IZA World Labor* (2014). doi:10.15185/izawol.120.

Cokley, K., Dreher, G.F. & Stockdale, M.S. Toward the Inclusiveness and Career Success of African Americans in the Workplace in *The Psychology and Management of Workplace Diversity* (eds. M.S. Stockdale & F.J. Crosby) (Oxford: Blackwell, 2004).

Commission for Racial Equality. *Towards Fair Selection: A Survey of Test Practice and Thirteen Case Studies.* (1993).

Conference Board Of Canada. Racial Wage Gap – Society Provincial Rankings – How Canada Performs. Available at: http://www. conferenceboard.ca/hcp/provincial/society/racial-gap.aspx (accessed: 21st September 2017).

Cooper, L.A. et al. The associations of clinicians' implicit attitudes about race with medical visit communication and patient ratings of interpersonal care. *Am. J. Public Health* **102**, 979–987 (2012).

Correll, J., Park, B., Judd, C.M. & Wittenbrink, B. The police officer's dilemma: Using ethnicity to disambiguate potentially threatening individuals. *J. Pers. Soc. Psychol.* **83**, 1314–1329 (2002).

Craig, M.A. & Richeson, J.A. More diverse yet less tolerant? How the increasingly diverse racial landscape affects white Americans' racial attitudes. *Psychol. Soc. Psychol. Bull.* **40**, 750–761 (2014).

Crisp, R. *The Social Brain: How Diversity Made The Modern Mind* (Robinson, 2015).

Croizet, J. & Millet, M. Social Class and Test Performance: From Stereotype Threat to Symbolic Violence and Vice Versa. in *Stereotype Threat: Theory, Process, and Application* (eds. M. Inzlicht & T. Schmader) (Oxford University Press, 2011).

Cropanzana, R., Bowen, D. & Gilliland, S. The management of organizational justice. *Acad. Manag. Perspect.* **21**, 34–49 (2007).

Cuddy, A.J.C., Fiske, S.T. & Glick, P. The BIAS map: Behaviors from intergroup affect and stereotypes. *J. Pers. Soc. Psychol.* **92**, 631–648 (2007).

Cuddy, A.J.C. et al. Stereotype content model across cultures: Towards universal similarities and some differences. *Br. J. Soc. Psychol.* **48**, 1–33 (2009).

Cunningham, W.A. et al. Separable neural components in the processing of black and white faces. *Psychol. Sci.* **15**, 806–813 (2004).

Davidson, M. *The Black and ethnic minority woman manager: Cracking the concrete ceiling.* (Paul Chapman Pub. Ltd, 1997).

De Rue, D.S. & Ashford, S. Who will lead and who will follow? A social process of leadership identity construction in organizations. *Acad. Manag. Rev.* **35**, 627–647 (2010).

Dean, M.A., Bobko, P. & Roth, P.L. Ethnic and gender subgroup differences in assessment center ratings: A meta-analysis. *J. Appl. Psychol.* **93**, 685–691 (2008).

Del Carmen Triana, M., Porter, C.O.L.H., Degrassi, S.W. & Bergman, M. We're all in this together...except for you: The effects of workload, performance feedback and racial distance on helping behavior in teams. *J. Organ. Behav.* **34**, 1124–1144 (2013).

del Río Olga Alonso-Villar Coordinator, C., Rodríguez Míguez, E., Groups, E. & Alonso-Villar, O. The Evolution of Occupational Segregation in the: Gains and Losses of Gender- Race/ethnicity Groups The Evolution of Occupational Segregation in the: Gains and Losses of Gender. (1940).

Devine, P.G. Stereotypes and prejudice: Their automatic and controlled components. *J. Pers. Soc. Psychol.* **56**, 5–18 (1989).

Devos, T. & Banaji, M.R. American = White? *J. Pers. Soc. Psychol.* **88**, 447–466 (2005).

Di Marco, D., Hoel, H., Arenas, A. & Munduate, L. Workplace incivility as modern sexual prejudice. *J. Interpers. Violence* (2015). doi:10.1177/0886260515621083.

Doeringer, P.B. & Piore, M.J. Internal Labor Markets and Manpower Analysis. (Harvard University, Massachusetts Institute of Technology, 1971).

Donkin, R. *Blood, Sweat And Tears: The Evolution Of Work.* (Texere Publlishing, 2002).

Donovan, R.A. Tough or tender: (Dis) similarities in White college students' perceptions of Black and White women. *Psychol. Women Q.* **35**, 458–468 (2011).

Dovidio, J.F. & Gaertner, S.L. Aversive racism and selection decisions: 1989 and 1999. *Psychol. Sci.* **11**, 315–319 (2000).

Dovidio, J.F., Gaertner, S.L.E., Kawakami, K. & Hodson, G. Why can't we just get along? Interpersonal biases and interracial distrust. *Cult. Divers. Ethn. Minor. Psychol.* **8**, 88--102 (2002).

Dovidio, J.F., Gaertner, S.L., Nier, J.A., Kawakami, K. & Hodson, G. Contemporary racial bias: when good people do bad things in *The Social Psychology of Good and Evil* (ed. A.G. Miller) (Guilford Press, 2004).

Dovidio, J.F., Kawakami, K., Johnson, C., Johnson, B. & Howard, A. On the nature of prejudice: Automatic and controlled processes. *J. Exp. Soc. Psychol.* **33**, 510–540 (1997).

Duff, S. *ILead Toolkit Box Set: People, Task And Thought Leadership.* (Pearn Kandola Publishing, 2015).

Eberhardt, J.L., Dasgupta, N. & Banaszynski, T.I. Believing is seeing: The effects of racial labels and implicit beliefs on face perception. *Personal. Soc. Psychol. Bull.* **29**, 360–370 (2003).

Ebony Magazine. What makes you Black? 115–118 (1983).

Eddo-Lodge, R. *Why I'm No Longer Talking To White People About Race* (Bloomsbury Circus, 2017).

Ellis, A.P.J., West, B.J., Ryan, A.M. & DeShon, R.P. The use of impression management tactics in structured interviews: A function of question type? *J. Appl. Psychol.* **87**, 1200–1208 (2002).

Emery, C., Daniloski, K. & Hamby, A. The reciprocal effects of self-view as a leader and leadership emergence. *Small Gr. Res.* **42**, 199–224 (2011).

Espenshade, T.J. et al. Admission Preferences for Minority Students, Athletes, and Legacies at Elite Universities. Social Science Quarterly, **85**, 5, 1422-1446, (2004).

Essed, P. *Understanding Everyday Racism: An Interdisciplinary Theory* (Sage Publications, 1991).

European Test User Standards for Test Use in Work and Organisational settings. (The European Federation of Psychologists' Associations. http://www.eawop.org/uploads/datas/10/original/European-test-user-standards-v1-92.pdf?1297020028. (2005).

Evans, J.S.B.T. & Frankish, K. In Two Minds: Dual Processes and Beyond (Oxford University Press, 2009).

Evans, J.S.B.T. & Frankish, K. The duality of mind: An historical perspective in *In Two Minds: Dual Processes and Beyond* (eds. J.S.B.T. Evans & K. Frankish) (Oxford University Press, 2009).

Fein, S. & Spencer, S.J. Prejudice as self-image maintenance: Affirming the self through derogating others. *J. Pers. Soc. Psychol.* **73**, 31–44 (1997).

Festekjian, A., Tram, S., Murray, C.B., Sy, T. & Huynh, H.P. I see you the way you see me: The influence of race on interpersonal and intrapersonal leadership Perceptions. *J. Leadersh. Organ. Stud.* XX, 1–18 (2013).

Firat, R.B. Apathetic Racism Theory: A Neurosociological Study of How Moral Emotions Perpetuate Inequality (The University of Iowa, 2013).

Fiske, S.T. & Neuberg, S.L.A continuum of impression formation, from category-based to individuating processes: Influences of information and motivation on attention and interpretation. in *Advances in Experimental Social Psychology*, **23** (ed. M.P. Zanna) 1–74 (New York: Academic Press, 1990).

Fiske, S.T. What we know now about bias and intergroup conflict, the problem of the century. *Curr. Dir. Psychol. Sci.* **11**, 123–128 (2002).

Fiske, S.T. Stereotyping, prejudice and discrimination. In *Handbook of Social Psychology*, **2** (eds D.T. Gilbert, S.T. Fiske & G. Lindzey) (McGraw-Hill, 1998).

Fiske, S.T., Cuddy, A.J.C., Glick, P. & Xu, J.A model of (often mixed) stereotype content: Competence and warmth respectively follow from perceived status and competition. *J. Pers. Soc. Psychol.* **82**, 878–902 (2002).

Fleming, W.C. Myths and Stereotypes about Native Americans. *Phi Delta Kappan* 88, 213–217 (2006).

Fletcher, M.A. Tiger Woods says he's 'Cablinasian,' but the police only saw black. *The Undefeated* (2017). Available at: https://www.google.co.uk/amp/s/theundefeated.com/features/tiger-woods-dui-arrest-police-only-saw-black/amp/.

Foley, J. Multiculturalism and the Media. in *Multi-America: Essays on Cultural Wars and Cultural Peace* (ed. I. Reed) (Penguin Books, 1998).

Fra-Molinero, B. Juan Latino and His Racial Difference in *Black Africans in Renaissance Europe* (eds. T. F. Earle & K.J.P. Lowe) (Cambridge University Press, 2005).

Franklin, D. (2017). Industry Exec on Fixing Hollywood's Race Problem: This "Has to Be a Long-Term Commitment". The Hollywood Reporter. Retrieved 9 September 2017, from http://www.hollywoodreporter.com/news/oscarssowhite-industry-exec-fixing-hollywoods-857418.

Frazer, R.A. & Wiersma, U.J. Prejudice versus discrimination in the employment interview: We may hire equally, but our memories harbour prejudice. *Hum. Relations* **54**, 173–191 (2001).

Gaertner, S.L. & Dovidio, J.F. The subtlety of White racism, arousal and helping behavior. *J. Pers. Soc. Psychol.* **35**, 691–707 (1977).

Gaertner, S.L. & McLaughlin, J.P. Racial stereotypes: Associations and ascriptions of positive and negative characteristics. *Soc. Psychol. Q.* **46**, 23–30 (1983).

Galinsky, A.D., Hall, E.V. & Cuddy, A.J.C. Gendered races: Implications for interracial marriage, leadership selection, and athletic participation. *Psychol. Sci.* **24**, 498–506 (2013).

Garza, F. (2016). The little we know about the 6,000 Academy members who vote on the Oscars tells us a lot. QUARTZ, pp. 1–4. Retrieved from http://qz.com/597343/the-little-we-know-about-the-6000-academy-members-who-vote-on-the-oscars-tells-us-a-lot/.

Ghavami, N. & Peplau, L.A. An intersectional analysis of gender and ethnic stereotypes: Testing three hypotheses. *Psychol. Women Q.* **37**, 113–127 (2012).

Glick, P., Diebold, J., Bailey-Werner, B. & Zhu, L. The two faces of Adam: Ambivalent sexism and polarized attitudes toward women. *Personal. Soc. Psychol. Bull.* **23**, 1323–1334 (1997).

Goff, P.A., Thomas, M.A. & Jackson, M.C. 'Ain't I a woman?': Towards an intersectional approach to person perception and group-based harms. *Sex Roles* **59**, 392–403 (2008).

Goff, P.A., Eberhardt, J.L., Williams, M.J. & Jackson, M.C. Not yet human: Implicit knowledge, historical dehumanization and contemporary consequences. *J. Personal. Soc. Psychol.* **94**, 292–306 (2008).

Good, C., Aronson, J. & Inzlicht, M. Improving adolescents' standardized test performance: An intervention to reduce the effects of stereotype threat. *J. Appl. Dev. Psychol.* **24**, 645–662 (2003).

GOV.UK Ethnicity facts and figures. Available at: https://www.ethnicity-facts-figures.service.gov.uk/. (Accessed: 10th October 2017).

Graham, S. & Lowery, B.S. Priming unconscious racial stereotypes about adolescent offenders. *Law Hum. Behav.* **28**, 483–504 (2004).

Gray, T. (2017). Academy Nominates All White Actors for Second Year in Row. Variety. Retrieved 9 September 2017, from http://variety.com/2016/biz/awards/oscar-nominations-2016-diversity-white-1201674903/.

Greeley, A.M. & Sheatsley, P.B. Attitudes Toward Desegregation (National Opinion Research Center, Chicago, Ill. 1971).

Green, J. Deloitte thinks diversity groups are passé. Bloomberg. Available at: www.bloomberg.com/news/articles/2017-07-19/deloitte-thinks-diversity-groups-are-pass (accessed 5 November 2017).

Greenblatt, S. Shakespeare's cure for xenophobia. The New Yorker. Available at: www.newyorker.com/magazine/2017/07/10/shakespeares-cure-for-xenophobia (accessed 5 November 2017).

Greenwald, A.G., McGhee, D.E. & Schwartz, J.L. Measuring individual differences in implicit cognition: the implicit association test. *J. Pers. Soc. Psychol.* **74**, 1464–1480 (1998).

Grint, K. *The Sociology of Work* (Polity Press, 2005).

Grote, R. The Status and Rights of Indigenous Peoples in Latin America., Max-Planck-Institut für ausländisches öffentliches Recht und Völkerrecht (1999).

Gündemir, S., Homan, A.C., de Dreu, C.K.W. & van Vugt, M. Think leader, think white? Capturing and weakening an implicit pro-white leadership bias. *PLoS One* **9**, e83915 (2014).

Hehman, E. et al. Group status drives majority and minority integration preferences. *Psychol. Sci.* **23**, 46–52 (2012).

Heilman, M.E. & Eagly, A.H. Gender stereotypes are alive, well, and busy producing workplace discrimination. *Ind. Organ. Psychol. Perspect. Sci. Pract.* **1**, 393–398 (2008).

Heilman, M.E. Sex bias in work settings: The Lack of Fit model. *Res. Organ. Behav.* **5**, 269–298 (1983).

Heilman, M.E., Wallen, A.S., Fuchs, D. & Tamkins, M.M. Penalties for success: Reactions to women who succeed at male gender-typed tasks. *J. Appl. Psychol.* **89**, 416–427 (2004).

Herlihy, B. Watch out, IQ myth: Here comes another debunker. *Phi Delta Kappan Vol.* **59**, p298 (1977).

Herrnstein, R.J. & Murray, C. *The Bell Curve: Intelligence and Class Structure in American Life*. (Free Press, 1994).

Hirsch, A. Let's not lose sight of the BBC's shameful ethnic pay gap | Media | The Guardian. Available at: https://www.theguardian.com/media/2017/aug/06/lets-not-lose-sight-of-the-bbcs-shameful-ethnic-pay-gap. (Accessed: 21st September 2017).

Hirschfeld, L.A. On a folk theory of society: Children, evolution and mental representations of social groups. *Personal. Soc. Psychol. Rev.* **5**, 107–117 (2001).

Homan, A.C., van Knippenberg, D., Van Kleef, G.A. & De Dreu, C.K.W. Bridging faultlines by valuing diversity: Diversity beliefs, information elaboration and performance in diverse work groups. *J. Appl. Psychol.* **92**, 1189–1199 (2007).

Horn, J. (2016). Unmasking Oscar: Academy voters are overwhelmingly white and male. *Los Angles Times*, pp. 1-7. Retrieved from http://www.latimes.com/entertainment/la-et-unmasking-oscar-academy-project-20120219-story.html.

House of Commons Culture Media and Sport Committee. Racism in Football: Second Report of Session 2012–13. London: The Stationery Office Limited; 2012.

Hugenberg, K. & Bodenhausen, G.V. Facing prejudice: Implicit prejudice and the perception of facial threat. *Psychol. Sci.* **14**, 640–643 (2003).

Hutchinson, S. (2016). How are Oscar Nominees Chosen. Mental Floss, pp. 1–6. Retrieved from http://mentalfloss.com/article/54560/how-are-oscar-nominees-chose.

Hutnyk, J. The dialectic of here and there: Anthropology 'at home' and British Asian communism. *Soc. Identities* **11**, 345–361 (2005).

Ibarra, H. Race, opportunity, and diversity of social circles in managerial networks. *Acad. Manag. Journal* **18**, 673–703 (1995).

Ibarra, H., Kilduff, M. & Tsai, W. Zooming in and out: connecting to individuals and collectivities at the frontiers of organizational network research. *Organ. Sci.* **16**, 359–371 (2005).

Immigrants are bringing entrepreneurial flair to Germany. Available at: https://www.economist.com/news/europe/21716053-while-native-germans-are-growing-less-eager-start-businesses-new-arrivals-are-ever-more (accessed: 21st September 2017).

Insecure work and Ethnicity Report. (TUC. Available at: https://www.tuc.org.uk/research-analysis/reports/insecure-work-and-ethnicity. 2 June 2017).

Inzlicht, M. & Schmader, T. *Stereotype Threat: Theory, Process and Application* (Oxford University Press, 2012).

Jackman, M.R. *The Velvet Glove: Paternalism and Conflict in Gender, Class and Race Relations* (University of California Press, 1994).

Jackson, P. *Maps of Meaning: An Introduction to Cultural Geography*. (Routledge, 1989).

Jefferson, T. *Notes on the State of Virginia*. (J. W. Randolph, 1853).

Johnson, K.L., Freeman, J.B. & Pauker, K. Race is gendered: How covarying phenotypes and stereotypes bias sex categorization. *J. Pers. Soc. Psychol.* **102**, 116–131 (2012).

Johnson, R.L., Roter, D., Powe, N.R. & Cooper, L.A. Patient race/ethnicity and quality of patient–physician communication during medical visits. *Am. J. Public Health* **94**, 2084–2090 (2004).

Jones, J.M., Dovidio, J.F. & Vietze, D.L. *The Psychology of Diversity: Beyond Prejudice and Racism*. (Wiley Blackwell, 2014).

Jones, T. *Britain's Ethnic Minorities*. (London: Policy Studies Institute, 1993).

Jost, J.T., Banaji, M.R. & Nosek, B.A decade of system justification theory: Accumulated evidence of conscious and unconscious bolstering of the status quo. *Polit. Psychol.* **25**, 881–919 (2004).

Kamenou, N. & Fearfull, A. Ethnic minority women: A lost voice in HRM. *Hum. Resour. Manag. J.* **16**, 154–172 (2006).

Kandola, B. & Kandola, J. *The Invention of Difference: The Story of Gender Bias at Work* (Pearn Kandola Publishing, 2013).

Kandola, B. Juries, not judges, lead the way against racial bias in our justice system I Binna Kandola | Public Leaders Network | The Guardian. Available at: https://www.theguardian.com/public-leaders-network/2017/sep/15/racial-bias-criminal-justice-system-lammy-review-magistrates-courts-jury. (Accessed: 9th October 2017).

Kandola, B., Wood, R., Dholakia, B. & Keane, C. *The Graduate Recruitment Manual*. (Gower, 2001).

Kang, J. Communications law: Bits of bias. In *Implicit Racial Bias across the Law* (eds J.D. Levinson & R.J. Smith), pp.132–145 (Cambridge University Press, 2012).

Katz, D. & Braly, K. Racial stereotypes of one hundred college students. *J. Abnorm. Soc. Psychol.* **28**, 280–290 (1933).

Katz, I. & Hass, R. Racial ambivalence and American value conflict: Correlational and priming studies of dual cognitive structures. *J. Pers. Soc. Psychol.* **55**, 893–905 (1988).

Katz, I., Glass, D.C., Lucido, D. & Farber, J. Harm doing and victim's racial or orthopedic stigma as determinants of helping behavior. *J. Pers.* **47**, 340–364 (1979).

Kawakami, K., Dunn, E., Karmali, F. & Dovidio, J.F. Mispredicting affective and behavioral responses to racism. Science. 323, 276–278 (2009).

Kyriakidou O, Kyriacou O, Özbilgin M, Dedoulis E. Editorial: Equality, diversity and inclusion in accounting. Crit Perspect Account. 2016 Mar [cited 2017 Nov 22];35:1–12. Available from: http://linkinghub.elsevier.com/retrieve/pii/S104523541500129X.

Lammy, D. The Lammy Review: An independent review into the treatment of, and outcomes for, Black, Asian and Minority Ethnic individuals in the Criminal Justice System. (https://www.gov.uk/government/publications/lammy-review-final-report).

Landy, F.J. & Conte, J.M. *Work in the 21st Century: An Introduction to Industrial and Organizational Psychology.* (Hoboken, NJ: Wiley, 2016).

Landy, F.J. & Conte, J.M. *Work in the 21st Century: An Introduction to Industrial and Organizational Psychology*, 5e (Wiley, 2015).

Latane, B. & Darley, J.M. Group inhibition of bystander intervention in emergencies. *J. Personal. Soc. Psychol.* **10**, 215–221 (1968).

Lent, R.W. & Brown, S.D. Integrating person and situation perspectives on work satisfaction: a social cognitive view. *J. Vocat. Behav.* **69**, 236–247 (2006).

Lerner, J.S. & Tetlock, P.E. Accounting for the effects of accountability. *Psychol. Bull.* **125**, 255–275 (1999).

Leslie, S.-J., Cimpian, A., Meyer, M. & Freeland, E. Expectations of brilliance underlie gender distributions across academic disciplines. Science. 16 Jan 2015: Vol.347, Issue 6219, pp. 262-265. DOI: 10.1126/science.1261375. http://science.sciencemag.org/content/347/6219/262.

Lewis AM. "Counting Black And White Beans": Why We Need A Critical Race Theory Of Accounting. Eur J Contemp Econ Manag. 2015;2(2):1–13.

Lewis, H. The uses and abuses of intersectionality. *New Statesman*, 20 February (2014).

Lewis, M. *The Blind Side: Evolution of a Game* (W.W. Norton & Company Inc., 2007).

Lin, M.H., Kwan, V.S.Y., Cheung, A. & Fiske, S.T. Stereotype content model explains prejudice for an envied outgroup: Scale of anti-Asian American stereotypes. *Personal. Soc. Psychol. Bull.* **31**, 34–47 (2005).

Livingston, R.W., Rosette, A.S. & Washington, E.F. Can an agentic Black woman get ahead? The impact of race and interpersonal dominance on perceptions of female leaders. *Psychol. Sci.* **23**, 354–358 (2012).

Lizza, R. Let's be friends. *The New Yorker*, 10 September 2012. Available at: https://www.newyorker.com/magazine/2012/09/10/lets-be-friends (accessed 5 November 2017).

Lord, R.G. & Maher, K.J. Perceptions of leadership and their implications in organizations. Applied Social. Psychology & Organisational Settings. 129–154 (Lawerence Erbaum Associates, Hillsdale NJ 1990).

Lord, R.G., Brown, D.J., Harvey, J.L. & Hall, R.J. Contextual Constraints On Prototype Generation And Their Multilevel Consequences For Leadership Perceptions. *Leadersh. Q.* **12**, 311–338 (2001).

Lord, R.G., Foti, R.J. & De Vader, C.L. A test of leadership categorization theory: Internal structure, information processing, and leadership perceptions. *Organ. Behav. Hum. Perform.* **34**, 343–378 (1984).

Lovaglia, M.J. et al. Status processes and mental ability test scores. *Am. J. Sociol.* **104**, 195–228 (1998).

Lowe, J. Pro-EU Campaigner: 'We Made Brexit Voters Feel Like "Closet Racists"' Available at: http://www.newsweek.com/brexit-racists-trevor-phillips-595042. (Accessed: 10th October 2017).

Lowe, K. Introduction: The Black African Prescence Iin Renaissance Europe. In *Black Africans in Renaissance Europe* (eds T. Earle & K. Lowe) (Cambridge University Press, 2005).

Lowe, K. The stereotyping of Black Africans in Renaissance Europe in *Black Africans in Renaissance Europe* (eds. T. Earle & K. Lowe) (Cambridge University Press, 2010).

Luthans, F. *Organizational Behavior: An Evidence-Based Approach*, 12e (McGraw-Hill, 2011).

MacAskill, E. Clinton aides claim Obama photo wasn't intended as a smear. *The Guardian*. Available at: www.theguardian.com/world/2008/feb/25/barackobama.hillaryclinton (accessed 5 November 2017).

Mason, D. Changing ethnic disadvantage: An overview. In *Explaining Ethnic Differences: Changing Patterns of Disadvantage in Britain* (ed. D. Mason) (Policy Press, 2003).

Mason, D. Changing patterns of ethnic disadvantage in employment. In *Explaining Ethnic Differences: Changing Patterns of Disadvantage in Britain* (ed. D. Mason) (Policy Press, 2003).

McConnell, A.R. & Leibold, J.M. Relations among the Implicit Association Test, discriminatory behavior and explicit measures of racial attitudes. *J. Exp. Soc.* Psychol. **37**, 435–442 (2001).

McGregor Smith, R. *Race in the Workplace. Issues Faced by Businesses in Developing Black and Minority Ethnic (BME) Talent in the Workplace. The time for talking is over. Now is the time to act. Race in the workplace.* https://www.gov.uk/government/uploads/system/uploads/attachment_data/file/594336/race-in-workplace-mcgregor-smith-review.pdf (2017).

Meertens, R.W. et al. Is subtle prejudice really prejudice? *Public Opimon* Q. **61**, 54–71 (1997).

Michaels, E., Handfield-Jones, H. & Axelrod, B. *The War For Talent* (Harvard University Press, 2001).

Mirza, H.S. 'All the women are white, all the blacks are men – but some of us are brave': Mapping the consequences of invisibility for black and minority ethnic women in Britain in *Explaining Ethnic Differences: Changing Patterns of Disadvantage in Britain* (ed. D. Mason) (Policy Press, 2003).

Modood, T. Ethnic Differentials in Educational Performance. in *Explaining Ethnic Differences: Changing Patterns of Disadvantage in Britain* (ed. Mason, D.) (Policy Press, 2003).

Monteith, M.J. & Voils, C.I. Exerting control over prejudiced responses. *Cognitive social psychology: The Princeton Symposium on the Legacy and Future of Social Cognition.* 375–388 (2001).

Monteith, M.J., Zuwerink, J., Adamson, M. & Brenner, L. Self-regulation of prejudiced responses: Implications for progress in prejudice-reduction efforts. *J. Pers. Soc. Psychol.* **65**, 469–485 (1993).

Moskowitz, G.B. & Halvorson, H.G. *The Psychology of Goals.* (Guilford Press, 2009).

Moskowitz, G.B. Preconscious effects of temporary goals on attention. *J. Exp. Soc. Psychol.* **38**, 397–404 (2002).

Moyes G.D., Williams P.A., Quigley B.Z. The Relation between Perceived Treatment Discrimination and Job Satisfaction among African American Accounting Professionals. Account Horizons. 2000 Mar 9 [cited 2017 Nov 21];14(1):21–48. Available from: http://aaajournals.org/doi/10.2308/acch.2000.14.1.21.

Myrdal, G. & Bok, S. *An American Dilemma: The Negro Problem and Modern Democracy* (Transaction Publishers, 1996).

Neal, L.V.I., McCray, A.D., Webb-Johnson, G. & Bridgest, S.T. The effects of African American movement styles on teachers' perceptions and reactions. *J. Spec. Educ.* **37**, 49–57 (2003).

Needham, A. (2017). Chris Rock at the 2016 Oscars: 'You're damn right Hollywood's racist'. theguardian. Retrieved 10 September 2017, from https://www.theguardian.com/film/2016/feb/29/chris-rock-at-the-oscars-youre-damn-right-hollywoods-racist.

Newman, D.A. & Lyon, J.S. Recruitment efforts to reduce adverse impact: Targeted recruiting for personality, cognitive ability and diversity. *J. Appl. Psychol.* **94**, 298–317 (2009).

Nielsen, T.C. & Kepinski, L. *Inclusion Nudges Guidebook: Practical Techniques for Changing Behaviour, Culture and Systems to Mitigate Unconscious Bias and Create Inclusive Organisations,* 2e (CreateSpace Independent Publishing Platform, 2016).

Nigatu, H. 21 Racial microaggressions you hear on a daily basis. Buzzfeed, 9 December 2013. Available at: https://www.buzzfeed.com/hnigatu/racial-microaggressions-you-hear-on-a-daily-basis?utm_term=.blw71mLWx4#.mjxDPjpa1W (accessed 5 November 2017).

Ali N. I'm a Women's Equality Party candidate – here's why I'm standing against a female Labour MP. Available at: http://www.newstatesman.com/politics/june2017/2017/05/im-womens-equality-party-candidate-heres-why-im-standing-against-female-0 (accessed 21 September 2017).

Nisen, M. & Yanofsky, D. Rich countries and the minorities they discriminate against, mapped — Quartz. Available at: https://qz.com/304296/rich-countries-and-the-minorities-they-discriminate-against-mapped/. (Accessed: 10th October 2017).

Nkomo, S. Moving From The Letter Of The Law To The Spirit Of The Law: The Challenges Of Realising The Intent Of Employment Equity And Affirmative Action. *Transformation* **77**, 122–135 (2011).

Nolfi, J. (2017). Oscars make history with most black winners ever. Entertainment Weekly. Retrieved 9 September 2017, from http://ew.com/awards/2017/02/26/oscars-2017-black-acting-winners/.

Noon, M., Blyton, P. & Morrell, K. *The Realities of Work: Experiencing Work and Employment in Contemporary Society* (Palgrave Macmillan, 2007).

Nosek, B.A., Banaji, M. & Greenwald, A.G. Harvesting implicit group attitudes and beliefs from a demonstration website. *Gr. Dyn. Theory, Res. Pract.* **6**, 101–115 (2002).

OECD. Labour market integration of immigrants and their children: Developing, activating and using skills. in *International Migration Outlook 2014* (OECD Publishing, Paris, 2014).

Omi, M. & Winant, H. *Racial Formation in the United States: From the 1960s to the 1990s* (Routledge, 1994).

Ones, D.S. & Anderson, N. Gender and ethnic group differences on personality scales in selection: Some British data. *J. Occup. Organ. Psychol.* **75**, 255–276 (2002).

Ones, D.S. & Viswesvaran, C. Job-specific applicant pools and national norms for personality scales: Implications for range-restriction corrections in validation research. *J. Appl. Psychol.* **88**, 570–577 (2003).

Ono, K. & Pham, V. *Asian Americans and the media.* in (Polity Press, 2009).

Onuora, E. Pitch Black: The Story of Black British Footballers. Biteback Publishing; 2015

Onyeka. *Blackamoores: Africans in Tudor England, Their Presence, Status and Origins* (Narrative Eye Ltd, 2013).

Outtz, J. L. & Newman, D. A. A Theory of Adverse Impact. in *Adverse Impact: Implications for Organizational Staffing and High Stakes Selection* (ed. Outtz, J. L.) 53–94 (New York: Routledge, 2010).

Pager, D. The mark of a criminal record. *Am. J. Sociol.* **103**, 937–975 (2003).

Pager, D. The use of field experiments for studies of employment discrimination: Contributions, critiques and directions for the future. *Ann. Am. Acad. Pol. Soc. Sci.* **609**, 104–133 (2007).

Patten, E. Racial, gender wage gaps persist in U.S. despite some progress | Pew Research Center. Available at: http://www.pewresearch.org/fact-tank/2016/07/01/racial-gender-wage-gaps-persist-in-u-s-despite-some-progress/. (Accessed: 21st September 2017).

Payne, B.K. Weapon bias: Split-second decisions and unintended stereotyping. *Curr. Dir. Psychol. Sci.* **15**, 287–291 (2006).

Perkins, L.A., Thomas, K.M. & Taylor, G.A. Advertising and recruitment: Marketing to minorities. *Psychol. Mark.* **17**, 235–255 (2000).

Pettigrew, T.F. & Meertens, R.W. Subtle and blatant prejudice in western Europe. *Eur. J. Soc. Psychol.* **25**, 57–75 (1995).

Pew Research Centre. Public backs affirmative action, but not minority preferences. Available at: http://www.pewresearch.org/2009/06/02/public-backs-affirmative-action-but-not-minority-preferences/ (Accessed 10th October 2017).

Phelps, E.A. et al. Performance on indirect measures of race evaluation predicts amygdala activation. *J. Cogn. Neurosci.* **12**, 729–738 (2000).

Phillips, K.W., Kim-Jun, S.Y. & Shim, S.-H. The value of diversity in organizations: A social psychological perspective. *Organ. Manag. Ser.* 253–271 (2011).

Powell, G.N. & Butterfield, D.A. Exploring the influence of decision makers' race and gender on actual promotions to top management. *Pers. Psychol.* **55**, 397–428 (2002).

Prewitt, K. *What Is Your Race? The Census and Our Flawed Efforts to Classify Americans* (Princeton University Press, 2013).

Proudford, K.L. & Smith, K.K. Group membership salience and the movement of conflict: Reconceptualizing the interaction among race, gender and hierarchy. *Gr. Organ. Manag.* **28**, 18–44 (2003).

PwC publishes its BAME pay gap. Available at: https://www.pwc.co.uk/press-room/press-releases/PwC-publishes-BAME-pay-gap.html. (Accessed: 5th October 2017).

Rachlinski, J.J., Johnson, S.L., Wistrich, A.J. & Guthrie, C. Does unconscious racial bias affect trial judges? *Notre Dame Law Rev.* **84**, 1195–1246 (2009).

Rawlinson, K. White men 'endangered species' in UK boardrooms, says Tesco chairman | Business | The Guardian. Available at: https://www.theguardian.com/business/2017/mar/10/white-men-endangered-species-in-uk-boardrooms-says-tesco-chairman. (Accessed: 22nd November 2017).

Reeves, A. N. Written in black & white: Exploring confirmation bias in racialized perceptions of writing skills. *Yellow Pap. Ser. Nextions* (2014).

Regis C. My Story: The Autobiography Of The First Black Icon Of British Football. London: Andre Deutsch; 2010. 257 p.

Remedios, J.D., Chasteen, A.L. & Paek, J.D. Not all prejudices are experienced equally: Comparing experiences of racism and sexism in female minorities. *Gr. Process. Intergr. Relations* **15**, 273–287 (2012).

Richardson, E., Phillips, K.W., Rudman, L.A. & Glick, P. Double jeopardy or greater latitude: Do Black women escape backlash for dominance displays? (submitted publ. 2011) Ridgeway, C. L. Gender, Status and Leadership. Journal of Social Issues, **57**, 627-655.

Rivera, L.A. Hiring as cultural matching: The case of elite professional service firms. *Am. Sociol. Rev.* **77**, 999–1022 (2012).

Robbins, S.P., Judge, T.A. & Campbell, T.T. *Organizational Behaviour.* (Pearson Education Limited, 2010).

Roberson, L. & Kulik, C.T. Stereotype threat at work. *Acad. Manag. Perspect.* **21**, 24–40 (2007).

Ronquillo, J. et al. The effects of skin tone on race-related amygdala activity: An fMRI investigation. *Soc. Cogn. Affect. Neurosci.* **2**, 39–44 (2007).

Rosette, A.S., Koval, C.Z., Ma, A. & Livingston, R. Race matters for women leaders: Intersectional effects on agentic deficiencies and penalties. *Leadersh. Q.* **27**, 429–445 (2016).

Rosette, A.S., Leonardelli, G.J. & Phillips, K.W. The White standard: Racial bias in leader categorization. *J. Appl. Psychol.* **93**, 758–77 (2008).

Rudman, L.A. & Glick, P. Prescriptive gender stereotypes and backlash toward agentic women. *J. Soc. Issues* **57**, 743–762 (2001).

Rudman, L.A., Johnson, K., Julian, S., Phillips, E. & Zehren, K. Self-promotion as a risk factor for women: The costs and benefits of counterstereotypical impression management. *J. Pers. Soc. Psychol.* **74**, 629–645 (1998).

Ryan, A.M., Sacco, J., McFarland, L. & Kriska, S. Applicant self-selection: Correlates of withdrawal from a multiple hurdle process. *J. Appl. Psychol.* **85**, 163–179 (2000).

Sacco, J.M., Scheu, C.R., Ryan, A.M. & Schmitt, N. An investigation of race and sex similarity effects in interviews: A multilevel approach to relational demography. *J. Appl. Psychol.* **88**, 852–65 (2003).

Sackett, P.R., Borneman, M.J. & Connelly, B.S. High stakes testing in higher education and employment: Appraising the evidence for validity and fairness. *Am. Psychol.* **63**, 215–227 (2008).

Sackett, P.R. & Ryan, A.M. Concerns about generalizing stereotype threat research findings to operational high-stakes testing in *Stereotype Threat: Theory, Process, and Application* (eds. M. Inzlicht & T. Schmader), pp .259–263 (Oxford University Press, 2011).

Saggar, S., Norrie, R., Bannister, M, Goodhart, D. *Bittersweet Success? Glass ceilings for Britain's ethnic minorities at the top of business and the professions* https://policyexchange.org.uk/wp-content/uploads/2016/11/PEXJ5011_Bittersweet_Success_1116_WEB.pdf (2016).

Salès-Wuillemin, E. et al. Linguistic intergroup bias at school: An exploratory study of black and white children in France and their implicit attitudes toward one another. *Int. J. Intercult. Relations* **42**, 93–103 (2014).

Schein, V. E. A global look at psychological barriers to women's progress in management. *J. Soc. Issues* **57**, 675–688 (2001).

Schmidt, F.L. & Hunter, J.E. The validity and utility of selection methods in personnel psychology: Practical and theoretical implications of 85 years of research findings. *Psychol. Bull.* **124**, 262–274 (1998).

Schmit, M.J. & Ryan, A.M. Applicant withdrawal: The role of test-taking attitudes and racial differences. *Pers. Psychol.* **50**, 855–876 (1997).

Schug, J., Alt, N.P. & Klauer, K.C. Gendered race prototypes: Evidence for the non-prototypicality of Asian men and Black women. *J. Exp. Soc. Psychol.* **56**, 121–125 (2015).

Sen, M. How judicial qualification ratings may disadvantage minority and female candidates. *J. Law Court.* **2**, 33–65 (2015).

Settles, I.H. Use of an intersectional framework to understand black women's racial and gender identities. *Sex Roles* **54**, 589–601 (2006).

Shavit, Y. *History in Black: African-Americans in Search of an Ancient Past* (Routledge, 2013).

Shecaira, S.S. Racism in Brazil: A historical perspective. *Rev. Int. droit pénal* **73**, 141 (2002).

Sherif. Classics in the History of Psychology. (1954/1961) Chapter 7. Available at: http://psychclassics.yorku.ca/Sherif/chap7.htm?wptouch_preview_theme=enabled. (Accessed: 20th September 2017).

Shoda, T.M., McConnell, A.R. & Rydell, R.J. Having explicit-implicit evaluation discrepancies triggers race-based motivated reasoning. *Soc. Cogn.* **32**, 190–202 (2014).

Shondrick, S.J., Dinh, J.F. & Lord, R.G. Developments in implicit leadership theory and cognitive science: Application to improving measurement and understanding alternatives to hierarchical leadership. *Leadersh. Q.* **21**, 959–978 (2010).

Sidanius, J. & Pratto, F. *Social Dominance: An Intergroup Theory of Social Hierarchy and Oppression* (Cambridge University Press, 1999).

Sidanius, J. & Veniegas, R.C. Gender and race discrimination: The interactive nature of disadvantage in *'The Claremont Symposium on Applied Social Psychology' Reducing prejudice and discrimination* (ed. S. Oskamp), pp. 47–69 (Lawrence Erlbaum Associates, 2000).

Sigall, H. & Page, R. Current stereotypes: A little fading, a little faking. *J. Pers. Soc. Psychol.* **18**, 247–255 (1971).

Skuncke, M.-C. Linnaeus: An 18th Century Background in *The Linnaean Legacy: Three Centuries After His Birth* (eds. M.J. Morris & L. Berwick) (Wiley Blackwell, 2008).

Smedley, A. & Smedley, B.D. Race as biology is fiction, racism as a social problem is real: Anthropological and historical perspectives on the social construction of race. *Am. Psychol.* **60**, 16–26 (2005).

Smith, J.A., Mcpherson, M. & Smith-Lovin, L. Social distance in the United States: Sex, race, religion, age, and education homophily among confidants, 1985 to 2004. *Publ. Am. Sociol. Rev.* **793**, 432–456 (2014).

Snowden, F.M. *Before Color Prejudice: The Ancient View of Blacks.* (Harvard University Press, 1983).

Spalter-Roth, R. & Deitch, C. 'I don't feel right-sized; I feel out-of-work sized': Gender, race, ethnicity and the unequal costs of displacement. *Work and Occupations* **26**, 446–482 (1999).

Spera, S. (2017). Why this year's Oscars might diverge from past prejudice. The Variety. Retrieved 9 September 2017, from https://thevarsity.ca/2017/01/22/why-this-years-oscars-might-diverge-from-past-prejudice/.

Sports People's Think Tank. Ethnic minorities and coaching in elite level football in England: A call to action [Internet]. 2014. Available from: http://www.farenet.org/wp-content/uploads/2014/11/We-speak-with-one-voice.pdf.

Staats, C. State of the science: Implicit bias review. *Kirwan Inst. Study Race Ethn.* (2014).

Staats, C., Capatosto, K. & Jackson, V.W. State of the science: Implicit bias review. *Kirwan Inst. Study Race Ethn.* (2016).

Staats, C., Capatosto, K., Wright, R.A. & Contractor, D. State of the science: Implicit bias review. *Kirwan Inst. Study Race Ethn.* (2015).

Staats, C., Patton, C., Rogers, C. & Rudd, T. State of the science: Implicit bias review. *Kirwan Inst. Study Race Ethn.* **4**; pp 17-26 (2013).

Steele, C. M. A threat in the air: How stereotypes shape intellectual identity and performance. *Am. Psychol.* **52**, 613–629 (1997).

Steele, C.M. & Aronson, J. Stereotype threat and the intellectual test performance of African Americans. *J. Pers. Soc. Psychol.* **69**, 797–811 (1995).

Steele, C.M. A threat in the air: How stereotypes shape intellectual identity and performance. *Am. Psychol.* **52**, 613–629 (1997).

Sue, D.W. *Microaggressions in Everyday Life: Race, Gender and Sexual Orientation.* (Wiley, 2010).

Sy, T. et al. Leadership perceptions as a function of race-occupation fit: the case of Asian Americans. *J. Appl. Psychol.* **95**, 902–919 (2010).

Tajfel, H. & Turner, J.C. The social identity theory of intergroup behavior. *Psychology of Intergroup Relations* 7–24 (1986).

Tenenbaum, H.R. & Ruck, M.D. Are teachers' expectations different for racial minority than for European American students? A meta-analysis. *J. Educ. Psychol.* **99**, 253–273 (2007).

Tetlock, P.E. Accountability: the neglected social context of judgement and choice. *Res. Organ. Behav.* **7**, 297–332 (1985).

Thai, X. & Barrett, T. Biden's description of Obama draws scrutiny. CNN.com. Available at: http://edition.cnn.com/2007/POLITICS/01/31/biden.obama/ (accessed 5 November 2017).

Thomas, E.L., Dovidio, J.F. & West, T.V. Lost in the categorical shuffle: Evidence for the social non-prototypicality of Black women. *Cult. Divers. Ethn. Minor. Psychol.* **20**, 370–376 (2014).

Triandis, H.C. The future of workforce diversity in international organisations: A commentary. *Applied Psychology* **52**, 486–495 (2003).

Trotman Reid, P. & Clayton, S. Racism and sexism at work. *Soc. Justice Res.* **5**, 249–268 (1992).

Tylor, E.B. *Primitive Culture.* (Harper & Row (Original work published 1871), 1958).

van den Bergh, L., Denessen, E., Hornstra, L., Voeten, M. & Holland, R. W. The implicit prejudiced attitudes of teachers: Relations to teacher expectations and the ethnic achievement gap. *Am. Educ. Res. J.* **47**, 497–527 (2010).

van Dick, R., van Knippenberg, D., Hagele, S., Guillaume, Y.R.F. & Brodbeck, F.C. Group diversity and group identification: The moderating role of diversity beliefs. *Hum. Relations* **61**, 1463–1492 (2008).

Van Knippenberg, B., Van Knippenberg, D., De Cremer, D. & Hogg, M.A. Research in leadership, self, and identity: A sample of the present and a glimpse of the future. doi:10.1016/j.leaqua.2005.06.006.

van Knippenberg, D. & Schippers, M.C. Work group diversity. *Annu. Rev. Psychol.* **58**, 515–541 (2007).

Vanman, E.J., Paul, B.Y., Ito, T.A. & Miller, N. The modern face of prejudice and structural features that moderate the effect of cooperation on affect. *J. Pers. Soc. Psychol.* **73**, 941–959 (1997).

Vasili P. Colouring Over The White Line: The History Of Black Footballers In Britain. Edinburgh: Mainstream Publishing; 2000. 208 p.

Visram, R. *Asians in Britain: 400 Years of History*. (Pluto Press, 2002).

Walvin, J. *Passage to Britain: immigration in British History and Politics*. (Penguin in association with Belitha Press, 1984).

Waters, M.C. & Kasinitz, P. Discrimination, race relations and the second generation. *Soc. Res.* (New. York). **77**, 101–132 (2010).

Westphal, J. D. & Stern, I. Flattery will get you everywhere (especially if you are a male caucasian): How ingratiation, boardroom behavior, demographic minority status affect additional board appointments at U.S. companies. *Acad. Manag. J.* **50**, 267–288 (2007).

Wilde, J. *The Social Psychology Of Organizations: Diagnosing Toxicity And Intervening In The Workplace*. (Routledge, 2016).

Williams J. "Dark Town" and a "Game for Britishers": Some Notes on History, Football and Race in Liverpool. In: Burdsey D, editor. Race, Ethnicity and Football: Persisting Debates and Emergent Issues. London: Routledge; 2011.

Williams J. Reds: Liverpool Football Club: The Biography. Edinburgh: Mainstream Publishing; 2010.

Williams, J.C. Double jeopardy? An empirical study with implications for the debates over implicit bias and intersectionality. *Harvard J. Law Gend.* **37**, 185–242 (2014).

Williams, J.C., Phillips, K.W. & Hall, E.V. Tools for change: Boosting the retention of women in the STEM pipeline. *J. Res. Gend. Stud.* **6**, 11–75 (2016).

Williams, R. L. The BITCH-100: A Culture-Specific Test. (Washington University, St Louis. Mo 1972).

Willis, J. & Todorov, A. First impressions: Making up your mind after a 100ms exposure to a face. *Psychol. Sci.* **17**, 592–598 (2006).

Wolf, K.B. 'The Moors' of West Africa and the beginnings of the Portuguese slave trade. *J. Mediev. Renaiss. Stud.* **24**, 449–469 (1994).

Woo, E. (2017). *6 Facts That Prove That The Oscars is More Racist Than You Think. Venngage*. Retrieved 9 September 2017, from https://venngage.com/blog/oscar-racism-interactive-infographic/.

Wyatt, M. & Silvester, J. Reflections on the labyrinth: Investigating black and minority ethnic leaders' career experiences. *Hum. Relations* **68**, 1243–1269 (2015).

Xiao, W. S. et al. Individuation training with other-race faces reduces preschoolers' implicit racial bias: A link between perceptual and social representation of faces in children. *Dev. Sci.* **18**, 655–663 (2015).

Yates, C. & Sachdev, P. *Rewire: A Radical Approach to Tackling Diversity and Difference* (Bloomsbury, 2015).

Yavorsky, Jill, E., Cohen, Philip, N. & Qian, Y. Man up, man down: Race-Ethnicity and the hierarchy of men in female-dominated work. *Sociol. Q.* **20**, 733–758 (2016).

Zarate, M.A. *Cultural normality and social perception. Unpublished doctoral dissertation* (Purdue University, West Lafayette, IN, 1990).

Zwysen, W. & Longhi, S. Labour market disadvantage of ethnic minority British graduates: University choice, parental background or neighbourhood? Non-technical summary. (2016). https://www.iser.essex.ac.uk/research/publications/working-papers/iser/2016-02.pdf.